American ENGLISH FILE

Christina Latham-Koenig
Clive Oxenden

Paul Seligson and Clive Oxenden are the original co-authors of
English File 1 and *English File 2*

Contents

			Grammar	Vocabulary	Pronunciation
	1				
4	A	Mood food	*simple* present and continuous, action and nonaction verbs	food and cooking	vowel sounds
8	B	Family life	future forms: present continuous, *going to*, *will* / *won't* Ⓖ *each other*	family, adjectives of personality	sentence stress, word stress, adjective endings
12		▶ PRACTICAL ENGLISH Episode 1 *Meeting the parents*			
	2				
14	A	Spend or save?	present perfect and simple past	money	the letter *o*
18	B	Changing lives	present perfect + *for* / *since*, present perfect continuous	strong adjectives: *exhausted*, *amazed*, etc.	sentence stress, stress on strong adjectives
22		REVIEW & CHECK 1&2 ▶ On the street; Short movies *Goodwill Industries*			
	3				
24	A	Race across Miami	comparatives and superlatives	transportation	/ʃ/, /dʒ/, and /tʃ/, linking
28	B	Stereotypes – or are they?	articles: *a* / *an*, *the*, no article	collocation: verbs / adjectives + prepositions	/ə/, sentence stress, /ðə/ or /ði/?
32		▶ PRACTICAL ENGLISH Episode 2 *A difficult celebrity*			
	4				
34	A	Failure and success	*can*, *could*, *be able to* Ⓖ reflexive pronouns	*-ed* / *-ing* adjectives	sentence stress
38	B	Modern manners?	modals of obligation: *must*, *have to*, *should* Ⓖ *should have*	phone language	silent consonants, linking
42		REVIEW & CHECK 3&4 ▶ On the street; Short movies *Citi bikes*			
	5				
44	A	Sports superstitions	past tenses: simple, continuous, perfect	sports	/ɔr/ and /ər/
48	B	Love at Exit 19	*usually* and *used to*	relationships	linking, the letter *s*
52		▶ PRACTICAL ENGLISH Episode 3 *Old friends*			

104	Communication	132	**Grammar Bank**	165	**Irregular verbs**
113	Writing	152	**Vocabulary Bank**	166	**Sound Bank**
122	Listening				

G simple present and continuous, action and nonaction verbs
V food and cooking
P vowel sounds

1A Mood food

Do you drink a lot of coffee?

Yes, but I'm trying to cut down right now.

1 VOCABULARY food and cooking

a Take the quiz in pairs.

FOOD QUIZ

Can you think of...?
ONE red fruit, ONE yellow fruit, ONE green fruit
TWO kinds of food that some people are allergic to
THREE kinds of food that come from milk
FOUR vegetables that you can put in a salad
FIVE containers that you can buy food in
SIX things that people sometimes have for breakfast

b ▶ p.152 **Vocabulary Bank** *Food and cooking.*

c (1 4))) Listen to these common adjectives to describe food. Do you know what they mean? Then say one kind of food that we often use with each adjective.

canned   fresh   frozen   low-fat   raw   spicy   take-out

2 PRONUNCIATION vowel sounds

a Look at the eight sound pictures. What are the words and sounds?

1 (fish)	squid chicken spicy grilled	5 (clock)	sausage roast chocolate box
2 (sheep)	beef steamed beans breakfast	6 (horse)	pork fork boiled pour
3 (cat)	grapes salmon lamb cabbage	7 (bull)	cook sugar pudding food
4 (car)	margarine carton jar warm	8 (boot)	spoon zucchini fruit duck

b Look at the words in each list. Cross out the word that *doesn't* have the sound in the sound picture.

c (1 5))) Listen and check.

d ▶ p.166 **Sound Bank.** Look at the typical spellings of the sounds in **a**.

3 LISTENING & SPEAKING

FOOD & EATING

1 Is there any food or drink that you couldn't live without? How often do you eat / drink it?
2 Do you ever have
   a ready-made food?
   b take-out food? What kind?
3 What's your favorite
   a fruit?
   b vegetable?
   Are there any that you really don't like?
4 When you eat out do you usually order meat, fish, or vegetarian?
5 What food do you usually eat
   a when you're feeling a little down?
   b before playing sports or exercising?
   c before you have an exam or some important work to do?

a (1 6))) Listen to five people talking. Each person is answering one of the questions in *Food & Eating* above. Match each speaker with a question.

[4] Speaker A   [ ] Speaker D
[ ] Speaker B   [ ] Speaker E
[ ] Speaker C

b Listen again and make notes about their answers. Compare with a partner.

c Ask and answer the questions with a partner. What do you have in common?

4 READING

a Are the foods in the list **carbohydrates** or **proteins**? With a partner, think of four more kinds of food for each category.

cake   chicken   pasta   salmon

b With a partner, answer the questions below with either **carbohydrates** or **proteins**.

What kind of food do you think it is better to eat…?
- for lunch if you have an important exam or meeting
- for breakfast
- for your evening meal
- if you are feeling stressed

c Look at the title of the article. What do you think it means? Read the article once to find out, and to check your answers to **b**.

d Read the article again. Then with a partner, say in your own words why the following people are mentioned. Give as much information as you can.

1. Dr. Paul Clayton
2. people on diets
3. schoolchildren
4. Paul and Terry
5. Swiss researchers

e Find adjectives in the article for the verbs and nouns in the list. What's the difference between the two adjectives made from *stress*?

stress (noun) (x2)   relax (verb)   wake (verb)
sleep (verb)   power (noun)   benefit (noun)

f Ask and answer the questions with a partner.

1. What time of day do you usually eat protein and carbohydrates? How do they make you feel?
2. How often do you eat chocolate? Does it make you feel happier?
3. After reading the article, is there anything you would change about your eating habits?

Mood food

We live in a stressful world, and daily life can sometimes make us feel tired, stressed, or depressed. Some people go to the doctor for help, others try alternative therapies, but the place to find a cure could be somewhere completely different: in the kitchen.

Dr. Paul Clayton, a food expert from Middlesex University, says "The brain is affected by what you eat and drink, just like every other part of your body. Certain types of food contain substances that affect how you think and feel."

For example, food that is high in carbohydrates can make us feel more relaxed. It also makes us feel happy. Research has shown that people on diets often begin to feel a little depressed after two weeks because they are eating fewer carbohydrates.

On the other hand, food that is rich in protein makes us feel awake and focused. Research has shown that schoolchildren who eat a high-protein breakfast often do better at school than children whose breakfast is lower in protein. Also, eating the right kind of meal at lunchtime can make a difference if you have an exam in the afternoon or a business meeting where you need to make some quick decisions. In an experiment for a TV show, two chess players, both former champions, had different meals before playing each other. Paul had a plate of prosciutto and salad (full of protein from the red meat), and his opponent Terry had pasta with a creamy sauce (full of carbohydrates). In the chess match Terry felt sleepy and took much longer than Paul to make decisions about what moves to make. The experiment was repeated several times with the same result.

Another powerful mood food could become a replacement for some medications doctors prescribe for stress. In a study, Swiss researchers discovered that eating one dark chocolate candy bar (about 1.4 ounces) had beneficial effects on highly stressed people. Not only did eating the dark chocolate help reduce stress, it was also shown to improve mood and reduce high blood pressure.

Why does chocolate make people less stressed? First, it causes the body to reduce the level of the stress hormone cortisol. Second, it reduces the "fight or flight" hormone—a hormone that makes people want to start a fight or run away when they are very stressed. In addition, it contains other compounds that lower blood pressure and improve your mood. These three things, along with its delicious taste, make chocolate a powerful mood changer.

Mood food – what the experts say

- Blueberries and cocoa can raise concentration levels for up to five hours.
- Food that is high in protein helps your brain to work more efficiently.
- For relaxation and to sleep better, eat carbohydrates.
- Dark green vegetables (e.g., cabbage and spinach) and oily fish (e.g., salmon) eaten regularly can help to fight depression.

5 LISTENING & SPEAKING

a Ask and answer the questions with a partner.

RESTAURANTS

1 How often do you eat out?
2 What's your favorite…?
  a kind of food (Chinese, Italian, etc.)
  b restaurant dish
3 How important are these things to you in a restaurant? Number them 1–4 (1 = the most important).
  ☐ the food
  ☐ the service
  ☐ the atmosphere
  ☐ the price
4 Have you ever tried English food? What did you think of it?

b ◁)) 1 7 Read the text about Steve Anderson. Then listen to **Part 1** of an interview with him, and number the photos in the order he mentions them.

c Listen again. Why does he mention each thing?

d ◁)) 1 8 Now listen to **Part 2** and answer the questions.
1 What does he say is the best and worst thing about running a restaurant?
2 What's the main difference between British and Spanish customers?
3 What kinds of customers does he find difficult?
4 How does he think eating habits in Spain are changing?

e What about you? Answer the questions with a partner.
1 What was your favorite food when you were a child?
2 Is there anything that you like / don't like cooking?
3 In your country, when people eat out would they usually tell the chef what they really think about the food?
4 Do you know anyone who is a "difficult customer" in restaurants?

A

STEVE ANDERSON has always had a passion for food. He was first taught to cook by his mother, who is half Burmese. After studying physics in college, he got a summer job helping with a cooking course in Italy, where he met several famous chefs. One of them, Alastair Little, later hired him as a trainee chef. Two years later, he moved to Valencia in Spain and opened a restaurant, *Seu Xerea*, now one of the most popular restaurants in town.

6 GRAMMAR

simple present and continuous, action and nonaction verbs

a **1 9)))** Listen again to some of the things Steve said. Circle the form of the verb he uses.

1 This week for example, *I cook / I'm cooking* nearly every day. We *usually close / are usually closing* on Sundays and Mondays, but this Monday is a public holiday.
2 The British always *say / are saying* that everything is lovely.
3 Actually, I think *I prefer / I am preferring* that honesty, because it helps us to know what people like.
4 Unfortunately, I think *they get / they're getting* worse. People *eat / are eating* more unhealthily.

b With a partner, say why you think he has chosen each form.

c ▶ **p.132 Grammar Bank 1A.** Learn more about the simple present and the present continuous, and practice them.

d Make questions to ask your partner with the simple present or continuous. Ask for more information.

On a typical day
– What / usually have for breakfast?
– / drink soda? How many glasses / drink a day?
– Where / usually have lunch?
– What / usually have for lunch during the week?
– / ever cook? What / make?
– / prefer eating at home or eating out?

Right now / nowadays
– / need to buy any food today?
– / want anything to eat right now? What?
– / take vitamins or food supplements right now?
– / try to cut down on anything right now?
– / the diet in your country / get better or worse?

7 SPEAKING

WHAT DO YOU THINK?

1 Men are better cooks than women.
2 Both boys and girls should learn to cook at school.
3 Cheap restaurants usually serve bad food.
4 On a night out with friends, where and what you eat isn't important.
5 Not all fast food is unhealthy.
6 Every country thinks that their cuisine is the best in the world.

a **1 13)))** Listen to two people discussing sentence 1. Who do you agree with more, the man or the woman? Why?

b **1 14)))** Listen to the phrases in the **Useful language** box. Copy the intonation.

> 🔍 **Useful language: Giving your opinion (1)**
> I agree.   I'm not sure.   For example,...
> I don't agree.   (I think) it depends.   In my opinion...

c In small groups, say what you think about sentences 2–6. Try to use the **Useful language** phrases.

G future forms: present continuous, *going to*, *will / won't*
V family, adjectives of personality
P sentence stress, word stress, adjective endings

Are you seeing your grandparents this weekend?
No, I'm going to stay home. I'll probably see them next weekend.

1B Family life

1 VOCABULARY & SPEAKING
family

a Look at some photos showing family members. What's happening in each one? What do you think the relationship is between the people?

b With a partner, explain the difference between each pair.
1. a father and a parent
2. a mother and a stepmother
3. a brother and a brother-in-law
4. a grandfather and a great-grandfather
5. a nephew and a niece
6. a child and an only child
7. your immediate family and your extended family

c Read *Changing—for the better* and try to guess what the missing percentages are. Choose from the list.

| 11% | 43% | 60% | 67% | 75% |

d 🔊 1 15 Listen and check. Do any of the statistics surprise you? Which ones do you think would be very different if the survey was taken in your country?

e Work in small groups. Say what you think and give reasons.

> **Do you think that…?**
> - families should have a meal together every day
> - children should leave home as soon as they can afford to
> - parents and their teenaged children should spend a lot of time together
> - parents should be friends with their children on social networking sites, e.g., Twitter
> - elderly parents should live with their children when they are too old to live alone

> 🔍 **Useful language:**
> **Giving your opinion (2)**
> We often use *should* + verb to say what we think is the right thing or a good thing (to do), e.g.,
> *I think families **should have** dinner together every day because…*
> *I don't think parents **should be** friends with their children on Twitter because…*

Changing – for the better?

Family life is changing in the US, but not in the way we might think. The results of several different US surveys expected to find that family relationships were suffering because of the decline in traditional family structures.

However, some of the results were very surprising…

32% of young adults under 25 and **10%** of adults 30-34 still live at home with their parents.

¹43% of families eat together every day.

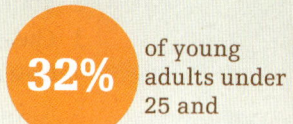 say they have the TV on during dinner.

 think a new baby in the family brings more happiness.

8

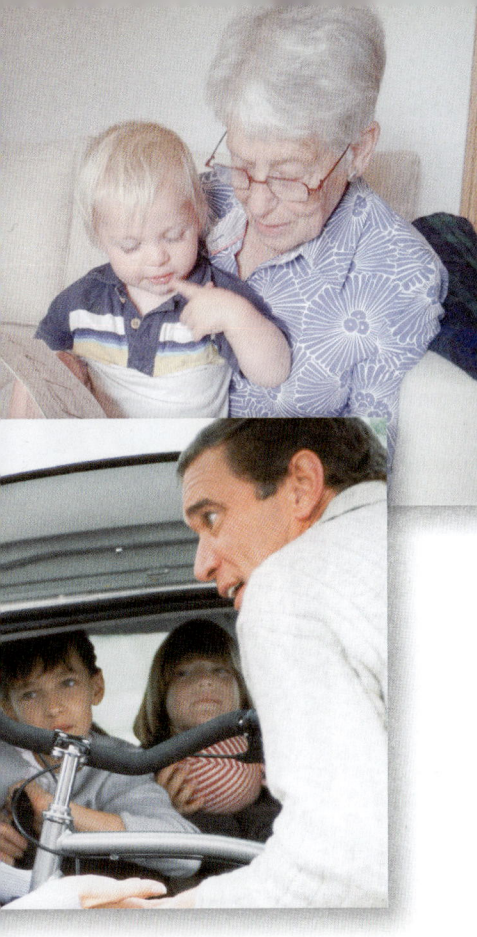

49% of adults are happy and enjoy their lives without a lot of stress.

2 ____ of adults are not happy and have a lot of stress or worry in their lives.

3 ____ of teens feel close to their family.

4 ____ of teens want to spend more time with their parents.

5 ____ of parents stay connected with their children on social networks.

40% of parents worry about what their kids post on social networks.

17% of elderly women live with a relative such as a daughter, daughter-in-law, or grandchild.

2 GRAMMAR future forms

a ► 1 16))) Listen to three dialogues between different family members. Who is talking to who (e.g., brother to sister)? What are they talking about?

b Listen again and match two sentences with each dialogue (1–3).
- A ☐ I'll make you a cup of tea.
- B ☐ You'll drive too fast.
- C ☐ I'm not going to go to college yet.
- D ☐ I'm staying overnight there.
- E ☐ I'll drive really slowly.
- F ☐ It's going to be cold tonight.

c With a partner, decide which sentence (A–F) is…
- ☐ a plan or intention
- ☐ a prediction
- ☐ an offer
- ☐ an arrangement
- ☐ a promise

d ▶ p.133 **Grammar Bank 1B**. Learn more about future forms, and practice them.

3 PRONUNCIATION sentence stress

> 🔍 **Sentence stress**
> An important aspect of speaking English is stressing the words in a sentence that carry the information, and not stressing the other ones. This will help you to communicate better and to speak with good rhythm.

a ► 1 21))) Listen to the rhythm in these three dialogues.

1 A Are you **coming home** for **dinner tonight**?
B **No**. I'm **going out** with my **friends**.
2 A **What** are you **going** to **do** in the **summer**?
B We're **going** to **rent** a **house** with my **sister** and her **husband**.
3 A Do you **think** they'll **have children soon**?
B I **don't think** so. **Not** for a **few years anyway**.

b Practice them with a partner. Copy the rhythm.

c Ask and answer the questions below. Give as much information as possible.

ARE YOU…?
- having dinner with your family tonight
- or is anyone in your family getting married soon
- doing something with a family member this week
- visiting a relative this weekend

ARE YOU GOING TO…?
- have a new nephew or niece soon
- have a big family get-together soon
- go on vacation with your family this year
- buy a present for a member of your family this month

DO YOU THINK…?
- the number of people getting divorced will go up or down in the future
- the birthrate will go up or down in your country
- anyone in your family will live to be 90 or more
- you will move away from (or back to) the area where your family lives

4 ► 1 22))) SONG *Our House* 🎵

5 READING

a Which do you think has more advantages, being an only child, or having brothers and sisters? Why?

b Work in pairs. **A** read *The Younger Brother*, **B** read *The Only Child*.

c Tell your partner about 1 and 2 below. Whose childhood sounds happier?
1 other family members who are mentioned
2 how the writer's experience as a child affects him / her now

d Look at the highlighted words in the two texts. Try to figure out their meaning from the context. Then match them with definitions 1–12.

1 _____ *adj* ill
2 _____ it's no surprise that
3 _____ *noun* competition between two people
4 _____ *noun* the time when you were a child
5 _____ *noun* a meeting of people, e.g., family
6 _____ *noun* people who are fully grown
7 _____ *adj* knowing about or being conscious of something
8 _____ *noun* a school where children can live during the year
9 _____ *verb* think that somebody or something is important
10 _____ *verb* divided something between two or more people
11 _____ *verb* try to hurt somebody else
12 _____ *noun* a group of friends

> **G each other**
> When brothers and sisters get older they value **each other** more.
> Use *each other* to talk about an action between two people or groups of people, e.g., *I don't get along very well with my father. We don't understand **each other**.*

e Talk to a partner. Do you have brothers and sisters, or are you an only child? Do you feel positive or negative about it?

Younger brother or only child?
HOW WAS IT FOR YOU?

THE YOUNGER BROTHER
NOVELIST TIM LOTT

Rivalry between brothers is normal, but there was a special reason for the tension between us. I was very ill when I was born, and spent three months in the hospital with my mother. My brother did not see her at all during that time because he went to stay with an aunt. When our mother returned home, it was with a sick newborn baby who took all the attention. No wonder he hated me (although if you ask Jeff, he will say that he didn't – we remember things differently).

My brother and I were completely different. We shared the same bedroom, but he was neat, and I was really messy. He was responsible; I was rebellious. He was sensible; I was emotional. I don't have any positive memories of our childhood together, though there must have been good moments. Jeff says we used to play "Cowboys and Indians," but I only remember him trying to suffocate me under the bedcovers.

My relationship with Jeff has influenced my attitude toward my own four daughters. If the girls fight, I always think that the younger child is innocent. But the good news about brothers and sisters is that when they get older, they value each other more. Jeff is now one of my best friends, and I like and admire him greatly. For better or for worse, we share a whole history. It is the longest relationship in my life.
Adapted from The Times

THE ONLY CHILD
JOURNALIST SARAH LEE

I went to boarding school when I was seven, and the hardest thing I found was making friends. Because I was an only child, I just didn't know how to do it. The thing is that when you're an only child, you spend a lot of your time with adults, and you're often the only child in a gathering of adults. Your parents go on living more or less the way they have always lived, only now you are there, too.

I found being an only child interesting because it gave me a view of the world of adults that children in a big family might not get. And I know it has, at least partly, made me the kind of person I am – I never like being one of a group, for example. If I have to be in a group, I will always try to go off and do something on my own, or be with just one other person – I'm not comfortable with being one of a gang.

My parents are divorced now and my mother lives in the US and my father in the UK. I feel very responsible for them – I feel responsible for their happiness. I'm the closest relative in the world to each of them, and I am very aware of that.

Adapted from The Guardian

6 VOCABULARY
adjectives of personality

a Without looking back at *The Younger Brother* text, can you remember who was *neat, responsible, and sensible* and who was *messy, rebellious, and emotional*? Do you know what the adjectives mean? Would you use any of them to describe yourself?

b ▶ **p.153 Vocabulary Bank** *Personality*.

c Write down the first three adjectives of personality that come into your head. Don't show them to your partner. Now go to ▶ **Communication** *Personality p.108*.

7 PRONUNCIATION
word stress, adjective endings

a ⓘ 1 26 ⟩⟩ <u>U</u>nderline the stressed syllable in these multisyllable adjectives. Listen and check.

1 jea|lous an|xious am|bi|tious ge|ne|rous re|bell|ious
2 so|cia|ble re|li|a|ble
3 re|spon|si|ble sen|si|ble
4 com|pe|ti|tive tal|ka|tive a|ggre|ssive sen|si|tive
5 un|friend|ly in|se|cure im|pa|tient i|mma|ture

b Listen again and answer the questions.
1 Is **-ous** pronounced /aʊs/ or /əs/?
2 Is **-able** pronounced /əbl/ or /eɪbl/?
3 Is **-ible** pronounced /əbl/ or /ɪbl/?
4 Is **-ive** pronounced /əv/ or /ɪv/?
5 Are **-ous** / **-able** / **-ible** / **-ive** stressed?
6 Are **un-** / **in-** / **im-** stressed?

8 LISTENING & SPEAKING

a What's your position in the family? Are you the oldest child, a middle child, the youngest child, or an only child?

b ⓘ 1 27 ⟩⟩ Look at the cover of Linda Blair's book. Now listen to a journalist talking about it on a radio program. Complete the chart by writing four more adjectives of personality in each column.

Oldest children	Middle children	Youngest children	Only children
sensible	relaxed	outgoing	self-confident

c Compare with a partner. Then listen to the four sections one by one. Check your answers. What reasons or examples does the journalist give?

d Look at the completed chart above. In pairs, say…

…if you think it is true for **you** – and if not, why not?

…if you think it is true for **other people** you know (your brothers and sisters, friends, etc.)

9 WRITING

▶ **p.113 Writing** *A description of a person*. Write a description of a friend you know well.

Practical English Meeting the parents

EPISODE 1

1 📹 INTRODUCTION

a Look at the photos. Describe Jenny and Rob.

b 📢 1 28)) Watch or listen to Jenny and Rob talking. Fill in the blanks.

Jenny Zielinski and Rob Walker work for a ¹_____ called *New York24seven*. She's American, and he's ²_____. Rob came to New York a few ³_____ ago. He had met Jenny when she went to ⁴_____ on a work trip. They got along very well, and he was offered a job for a month in ⁵_____. Later he was offered a ⁶_____ job. Jenny helped Rob ⁷_____ an apartment, and they are enjoying life in the US, although Rob misses his friends and ⁸_____.

> 🔍 **American and British English**
> *apartment* = American English
> *flat* = British English

2 📹 REACTING TO WHAT PEOPLE SAY

a 🔊 1 29)) Watch or listen to Jenny introducing Rob to her parents. What bad news does Rob have for Jenny? What good news does Jenny have for her parents?

> 🔍 **American and British English**
> *mom* = American English
> *mum* = British English

b Watch or listen again and mark the sentences **T** (true) or **F** (false). Correct the **F** sentences.
1 Rob left the chocolates at the office.
2 Rob's desk is usually very neat.
3 It's the second time that Rob has met Jenny's parents.
4 Sally has prepared a big dinner.
5 Jenny's new job is managing director.
6 Jenny is going to be Rob's manager.

12

c **1 30))** Look at some extracts from the conversation. Can you remember any of the missing words? Watch or listen and check.

1	Jenny	Don't forget the chocolates.
	Rob	OK. Oh, _____!
	Jenny	I don't _____ it. Don't tell me you forgot them?
	Rob	I think they're still on my desk.
	Jenny	_____ kidding.
2	Jenny	Mom, I'm really sorry – we bought you some chocolates, but we left them at the office.
	Sally	What a _____. _____ mind.
3	Jenny	But I also have some good news.
	Sally	_____? What's that?
4	Sally	So you've got a promotion? _____ fantastic!
	Harry	That's great _____!
5	Sally	Let's go and have dinner.
	Jenny	What a _____ idea!

d **1 31))** Watch or listen and repeat the phrases in the chart below. Copy the rhythm and intonation.

REACTING TO WHAT PEOPLE SAY

What you say when you hear...	
something surprising	You're kidding. I don't believe it.
something interesting	Really?
some good news	How fantastic! That's great news! What a great idea!
some bad news	Oh, no! What a pity. Never mind.

> **How + adjective, What + noun**
> We often use *How* + adjective or *What* + noun to respond to what people say.
> *How interesting! How awful! How amazing!*
> *What a pity! What a good idea! What terrible news!*

e Practice the dialogues in **c** with a partner.

f **Communication** *How awful! How fantastic!* **A** p.104 **B** p.109.

3 VIDEO HARRY FINDS OUT MORE ABOUT ROB

a **1 32))** Watch or listen to the after-dinner conversation. Does the evening end well or badly?

b Watch or listen again and answer the questions.
1 What school did Jenny go to?
2 Is Harry impressed by Rob's job? Why (not)?
3 What does Harry like doing in his free time?
4 Who are most of the photos in the dining room of?
5 Who are Miles Davis, John Coltrane, and Wynton Marsalis?
6 What surprises Harry about Rob?

c Look at the **Social English phrases**. Can you remember any of the missing words?

Social English phrases	
Harry	How do you _____ your career?
Rob	Not _____. I'm more of a writer.
Rob	Oh, you know, interviews, reviews, _____ like that...
Rob	I _____, I like photography.
Harry	That's _____ most of them are of Jenny.
Harry	How _____!
Rob	Well, he's a really nice _____.
Harry	Go _____, son!

d **1 33))** Watch or listen and complete the phrases.

e Watch or listen again and repeat the phrases. How do you say them in your language?

> **Can you...?**
> ☐ react to good news, bad news, unexpected news, and interesting news
> ☐ introduce yourself and other people
> ☐ use phrases that give you time to think, e.g., *you know, I mean,* etc.

G present perfect and simple past
V money
P the letter *o*

2A Spend or save?

Have you paid the phone bill yet?

Yes, I paid it yesterday.

1 VOCABULARY money

a ◁1 34◁)) Listen to a song about money. Fill in the blanks with phrases A–G.

A a material world
B comes with a fee
C foot the bill
D for free
E paper or plastic
F shopping sprees
G with money

b Listen again and read the lyrics. Which phrase (A–G) means…?

1 _____ rich
2 _____ cash or credit cards
3 _____ you have to pay for it
4 _____ pay the bill
5 _____ that you don't have to pay for
6 _____ buying a lot of things at one time
7 _____ a consumer society

c What do you think the song is saying? Do you think it is…?

- very cynical
- sad, but sometimes true
- offensive to women (and men)

d ▶ p.154 Vocabulary Bank *Money*.

Girls & Boys

Educated, ¹_____
He's well-dressed
Not funny
And not much to say in
Most conversations
But he'll ²_____ in
All situations
'Cause he pays for everything

Girls don't like boys, girls like cars and money
Boys will laugh at girls when they're not funny

³_____
Don't matter
She'll have it
Vacations
And ⁴_____
These are a few
Of her favorite things
She'll get what she wants
If she's willing to please
His type of girl
Always ⁵_____
Hey, now, there's nothing ⁶_____

Girls don't like boys, girls like cars and money
Boys will laugh at girls when they're not funny
And these girls like these boys like these boys like these girls
The girls with the bodies like boys with Ferraris
Girls don't like boys, girls like cars and money

All of these boys, yeah get all of these girls
Losing their souls in ⁷_____

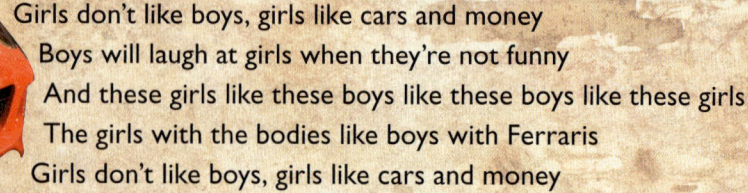

2 PRONUNCIATION the letter o

a Can you remember which word rhymes with *money* in the song *Girls & Boys*?

b Look at some more words with the letter *o*. Put them in the correct column.

clothes   dollar   done   honest   loan   money   go
nothing   owe   shopping   some   sold   won

c 1 38))) Listen and check.

d Look at some words with the letters *or*. How is *or* usually pronounced when it's stressed? Which two are different?

aff**or**d   **or**der   w**or**th   **or**ganized   m**or**tgage   st**or**e   w**or**k

e 1 39))) Listen and check.

f Practice saying these sentences.

Let's go shopping for clothes.
Can I borrow some money?
He won a million dollars.
They can't afford to pay the mortgage.
I work in a store.
I've done nothing wrong.

3 READING & SPEAKING

a Read the questionnaire and choose your answers.

b Compare your answers with a partner. Say why.

c ▶ **Communication** *Spender or saver? p.108.* Find out if you are a spender or a saver.

4 LISTENING

a 1 40))) Listen to six people answering the question *Are you a spender or a saver?* How many are savers?

b Listen again and match speakers 1–6 with A–F. Who…?

A ☐ always has money in the bank
B ☐ often ends up with no money
C ☐ thinks he / she is careful with money, but not cheap
D ☐ enjoys spending money on his / her hobby
E ☐ can save money if he / she needs to
F ☐ prefers to live now than worry about the future

ARE YOU A SPENDER OR A SAVER?

1 **You go shopping and you see something very expensive that you really want, but can't afford. You…**
   a buy it with your credit card. You can worry about the bill next month.
   b already have some money in the bank and plan to save for a couple of weeks and then buy the thing you want.
   c borrow the money and agree to pay back a small amount every week.

2 **You get $100 for your birthday. You…**
   a spend some of it and save some.
   b go straight to a shopping mall and spend it all.
   c put all of it in your bank account until you know what you want to spend it on.

3 **Do you always know how much money you have, how much money you have spent, and on what?**
   a Yes. I'm very organized and know exactly what I have and what I've spent.
   b No. I have no idea. When I have money, I usually just spend it.
   c I usually have a rough idea about what I spend my money on.

4 **You borrowed some money from a friend, but you don't think that you'll be able to pay it back by the time you promised to. You…**
   a don't worry about it. Hopefully your friend will forget about it, too!
   b figure out how much money you have and how much you owe. You speak to your friend and explain the situation and offer to pay the money back in small installments.
   c talk to your friend and promise that you'll pay him / her back, but it might take a little longer than you first thought.

5 **You have a friend who often borrows money from you and never pays you back. He / She wants to borrow $50. You…**
   a lend him / her the money. You can afford it, and it doesn't matter if you don't get it back.
   b say no; he / she owes you too much already.
   c lend the money, but explain that it is the last time, until he / she has paid back this loan.

5 GRAMMAR present perfect and simple past

a Read the conversation. What are they arguing about?

b 🔊 1 41)) Read the conversation again, and put the verbs in the present perfect or the simple past. Then listen and check.

David I ¹*haven't seen* (see) those shoes before. Are they new?
Kate Yes. I ² _____ (just buy) them. Do you like them?
D They're OK. How much ³ _____ they _____ (cost)?
K Oh, not much. They ⁴ _____ (be) a bargain. Under $100.
D You mean $99.99. That isn't cheap for a pair of shoes. Anyway, we can't afford to buy new clothes right now.
K Why not?
D ⁵ _____ you _____ (see) this?
K No. What is it?
D The phone bill. It ⁶ _____ (come) this morning. And we ⁷ _____ (not pay) the electricity bill yet.
K Well, what about the iPad you ⁸ _____ (buy) last week?
D What about it?
K You ⁹ _____ (not need) a new one. The old one ¹⁰ _____ (work) just fine.
D But I ¹¹ _____ (need) the new model.
K Well, I ¹² _____ (need) some new shoes.

c Do we use the present perfect (**PP**) or simple past (**SP**)…?

1 for a completed action in the past _____
2 for recent actions when we don't ask / say exactly when _____

d ▶ p.134 **Grammar Bank 2A.** Learn more about the present perfect and simple past, and practice them.

e In pairs, interview each other with the questions. Ask for more information.

HAVE YOU EVER…?

- bought or sold something on eBay or a similar site
- lost a credit card or your wallet
- saved for something for a long time

What?

- wasted money on something you've never used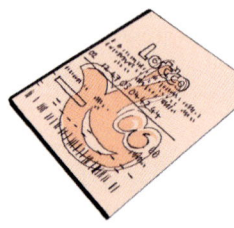
- won any money (e.g., in a lottery)
- lent money to someone who didn't pay you back

When?

- bought something online and then discovered that it was a scam
- been charged too much in a restaurant

How much? *What happened?*

Have you ever bought or sold something on eBay? *Yes, I sold my old computer.*

Who did you sell it to? How much did you sell it for?

6 READING & SPEAKING

a In pairs, answer the questions. Give as much information as you can.

1 Think of two people you know personally or have heard of who are very rich. Did they…?
   a earn their money (how?)
   b inherit their money (who from?)
   c win it (how?)

2 If they earned their money, was it because…?
   a they were very lucky
   b they worked very hard
   c they had a special talent

b Now read an interview with a billionaire. How did he become so rich? Why is his success surprising? What does he do to help homeless people?

c Now read the interview again and number the events in the order in which they happened.

A ☐ He was homeless again.
B ☐ He delivered newspapers.
C ☐ An investor didn't give him the money he had promised him.
D ☐ He sold encyclopedias from door-to-door.
E ☐ He left his wife.
F ☐ He was homeless.
G ☐ 1 He sold Christmas cards from door-to-door.
H ☐ He started a hair product company with $700.
I ☐ He was able to pay his bills on time.

d What do you think you can learn from John's story?

e Look at the **highlighted** words and phrases related to money and business. With a partner, try to figure out the meanings from context.

f Complete the questions with one of the **highlighted** words and phrases. Then ask and answer the questions with a partner.

1 What _brand_ of hair product do you use? How long have you used it?
2 Do you know anybody who sells encyclopedias or other products _____? What does he / she sell? Does he / she enjoy his / her job?
3 If you needed a _____ to lend you money to start a business, who would you ask? Why?
4 Have you ever experienced _____ from a boss, a teacher, etc.? How did you feel?
5 Do you know anybody who has tried to succeed in a difficult career (like acting), but who hasn't _____ yet? Is he / she still trying, or has he / she given up?

FROM THE STREETS TO SUCCESS!

John DeJoria, an American **billionaire** businessman, owns several companies, including John Paul Mitchell Systems, a successful **brand** of hair products. However, DeJoria was not always **wealthy**. He was the second son of immigrant parents and grew up in a very poor area of Los Angeles, California. Before forming his hair product company with only $700, he was a street gang member for some of his youth, he then worked at **low-paying** jobs including encyclopedia **salesman**, janitor, and insurance salesman, and he was homeless twice. DeJoria's **selfmade** rise is an inspiring story.

As a child, you were fairly entrepreneurial, weren't you?
My first job, at 9 years old, was selling Christmas cards door-to-door. At 10 years old, my brother and I had **paper routes**. We got up at 4 o'clock a.m., folded the papers, and delivered them, and then got ready for school.

As you got older, you continued to work. Is that right?
The job that was one of the most influential experiences you can imagine was **door-to-door** selling encyclopedias. Doors literally slam in your face—maybe 30, 40 doors before the first **customer** will actually talk to you and let you in.

You've been homeless, haven't you?
Twice. Once, when I was about 22 years old. The other time was when I started John Paul Mitchell Systems in 1980. I wasn't getting along with my wife at the time. So I had left and had given her all the money. We had a **backer** for John Paul Mitchell Systems **putting in a half-million dollars**. That money was supposed to arrive that day. I never got a penny. So I just slept in my car. And I slept in my car for the first two weeks when I started the company. So we started with humble beginnings.

Do memories of the streets motivate you?
It sure makes you very appreciative of what you have in your life. Those who are homeless—like people with kids who are homeless—I really have a heart for. So I participate in a lot of charitable organizations that take the homeless off the streets.

What are the biggest problems you've faced in business?
The biggest problem is **rejection**. Any business you start, be ready for it. The difference between successful people and unsuccessful people is that the successful people do all the things the unsuccessful people don't want to do. When 10 doors are slammed in your face, go to door number 11, with a smile.

When did you know you had made it?
I was in business two years, and we were able to pay every single **bill** on time. We had a couple of thousand dollars in the bank—$4,000, to be exact. And we said, "Man we made it; it's all downhill now." It was really hard. It took a couple years.

What was the first thing you bought yourself at that point?
I went to a restaurant. This is the first time I said I'm going to order off the left side of the menu, not the right side. The right side is where the prices are. Carne asada, guacamole, whatever I wanted. I didn't even look at the prices. That, to me, was a pretty big deal.

Adapted from Entrepreneur.com

G present perfect + *for* / *since*, present perfect continuous
V strong adjectives: *exhausted, amazed*, etc.
P sentence stress, stress on strong adjectives

How long have you been working here? For a long time! Since 2001.

2B Changing lives

1 LISTENING

a Look at the photos. Where do you think they were taken? What can you see in each photo?

b ◯ 1 45)) You are going to listen to an interview with Jane, talking about a trip she took in 2008. Listen to **Part 1**. Where did she go? What did she decide to do after the trip?

c Listen again. What does Jane say about:
1 her normal job
2 the vacation to Uganda
3 what happened when the lorry broke down
4 the condition of the school
5 the children
6 what the headmaster asked her for

> **Glossary**
> **holiday** *BritE* for vacation
> **lorry** *BritE* for truck
> **headmaster** *BritE* for principal

d ◯ 1 46)) Now listen to **Part 2**. Correct the wrong information in these sentences.
1 Jane's son chose the name *Adelante África*, which means "Go forward, Africa" in Spanish.
2 The new school opened in 2012.
3 Today the school has 75 children.
4 *Adelante África* has also been trying to improve the children's English.
5 They are building a home for the teachers.
6 Two of Jane's children have been helping in Uganda.
7 Jane says the school has changed children's lives because it has given them an education.
8 Jane thinks that she gives more than she gets.
9 The website has a video Jane's daughter took of her teaching the children.

e Compare your answers with a partner. Then listen again to check.

f Do you know anybody like Jane who does a lot of work for a charity? What do they do?

2 GRAMMAR present perfect + *for* / *since*, present perfect continuous

a Match the questions and answers.
1. How long has Jane been a writer? ____
2. How long has *Adelante África* had a website? ____
3. How long has she been working for *Adelante África*? ____

A Since 2008.
B For about 22 years.
C For four years.

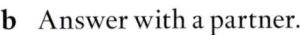

b Answer with a partner.
1. Are the three questions and answers in **a** about…?
   a a period of time in the past
   b a period of time from the past until now
   c a period of time in the present
2. What's the difference in form between the first two questions and question 3?

c ▶ **p.135 Grammar Bank 2B.** Learn more about the present perfect with *for* / *since* and the present perfect continuous, and practice them.

3 PRONUNCIATION sentence stress

a ⓘ 1 49))) Listen once and try to write down the stressed words in the large pink rectangles.

1. | How | long | | learning |
   | French | ? |

2. (empty boxes) .
3. (empty boxes) ?
4. (empty boxes) .
5. (empty boxes) ?
6. (empty boxes) .

b Look at the stressed words and try to remember what the unstressed words are. Then listen again to check and write them in.

c Listen again and repeat the sentences. Copy the rhythm.

d ⓘ 1 50))) Listen and make questions.

))) It's snowing. (How long has it been snowing?)

4 SPEAKING

a Look at the circles, and write something in as many as you can.

- A social networking site you use regularly
- A friend you know very well
- A sport you play regularly (or a kind of exercise you do regularly)
- The car / motorcycle / bike you have
- The place where you live
- A gadget you have that is very important to you
- A cafe or restaurant you often go to
- An organization, club, gym, etc. you are a member of
- Something you are learning (to do) 

b Compare circles with a partner. Ask your partner at least three questions about the things he or she has written. One question must be *How long have you…?*

How long have you been using Twitter? — For about a year.

Do you write things on it or do you just read other people's tweets?

Why did you buy a Nissan Juke? — Because it's small, and it's very "green."

How long have you had it?

5 READING & LISTENING

a In your country, are there charity events to raise money for a good cause? Have you ever taken part in one? What did you do? How much money did you raise?

b You're going to read an article about Helen Skelton, who agreed to kayak down the Amazon for charity. Read the introduction and answer the questions.

1 What did Helen do last year for charity?
2 What is she hoping to do this year?
3 What is dangerous about the trip?
4 What experience does she have?

c Before you read the texts of Helen's first three phone calls, imagine what kinds of problems you think she had on her trip. Then read and check. Were you right?

d (1 51)) Read **Phone calls 1–3** again and fill in the blanks with the correct word. Then listen and check.

1 a in front	b behind	c back
2 a freezing	b hot	c boiling
3 a exhausted	b angry	c lost
4 a down	b up	c over
5 a long	b wide	c short
6 a ice cream	b coffee	c chocolate
7 a sleep	b paddle	c rest
8 a boring	b interesting	c worrying
9 a being	b feel	c feeling
10 a sick	b well	c hard

e (1 52)) Now listen to the rest of Helen's trip down the Amazon. Did she manage to finish?

f Listen again. Then answer the questions.

Phone call 4
1 Why hasn't she had any music for three days?
2 What does she do to pass the time?
3 Why didn't she celebrate reaching the halfway point?

Phone call 5
4 What have been driving her crazy this week?
5 What wildlife has she seen?
6 Why is she starting to feel a little sad?

The 6:00 news
7 How many miles did she do altogether?
8 How long did the trip take?
9 What did Helen miss?
10 What is the first thing she is going to do when she gets home?

g Tell your partner about an adventure sport you've done or an exciting experience you've had. Was it a positive experience? Why (not)? How did you feel?

TV host's Amazon

Helen Skelton hopes to become the first woman to kayak down the Amazon River.

Helen Skelton is a 26-year-old TV host of *Blue Peter*, a show for young people. She has never been afraid of a challenge. Last year, she became the second woman to complete the 78-mile Ultra Marathon in Namibia, running the three consecutive marathons in 23 hours and 50 minutes. But when *Blue Peter* decided to do something to raise money for the charity Sports Relief (which sponsors projects around the world), Skelton said that she wanted an even bigger challenge. So they suggested that she kayak 1,998 miles down the Amazon from Nauta in Peru to Almeirim in Brazil.

This is a very risky trip. There are no roads and no towns, only rainforest and the river (which is sometimes more than 24 miles wide and infested with crocodiles). If she gets sick, it will take around 11 hours to fly her to a hospital.

Adapted from The Telegraph website

Phone call 1

"Everything went wrong. I only managed half a day on Wednesday, the first day, and on Thursday we started late, so I'm already ¹____. I've been suffering from the heat. It's absolutely ²____, and the humidity is 100% at lunchtime. I went the wrong way, and I had to paddle against the current. I was ³____! They asked me, 'Do you want to give ⁴____?' but I said, 'No!' Because I've also been having a wonderful time! There are pink dolphins – pink, not gray – that come close to the boat. I think that if I can do 62 miles a day, then I can make it."

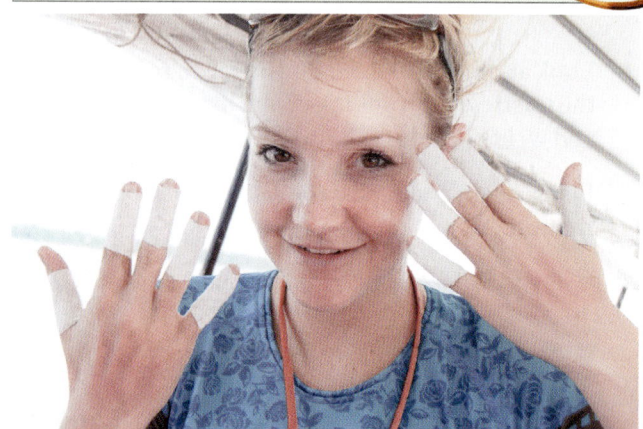

hallenge

Helen has only been kayaking once before in her life, so she has been training four hours a day. Last week, she arrived at the Amazon in Peru. After two days of kayaking, she made the first of her phone calls.

Phone call 2

"I've been on the Amazon for a week now, and I've been paddling for six out of the seven days. The river is incredibly ⁵____, and it's very hard to paddle in a straight line. The water is so brown that I can't see my paddle once it goes under the surface. It looks like melted ⁶____. I start at 5:30 in the morning, and I ⁷____ for at least 10 hours, from 5:30 a.m. until dark, with only a short break for lunch. My hands have been giving me problems – I have big blisters. I now have them bandaged in white tape.

I'm usually on the water for at least 10 hours; it's ⁸____ at times, and exciting at others. I listen to music on my iPod. I've been listening to *Don't Stop Me Now* by Queen to inspire me!"

Phone call 3

"I haven't been ⁹____ very well this week. The problem is heat exhaustion. They say it's because I haven't been drinking enough water. I've been traveling 62 miles a day, which is my target. But yesterday after 52 miles, I was feeling ¹⁰____, and my head was aching, and I had to stop and rest."

6 VOCABULARY & PRONUNCIATION
strong adjectives

> **Strong adjectives**
> Some adjectives have a strong meaning, e.g.,
> *I had to paddle against the current. I was **exhausted**!* (= very tired)
> *I've had a **fantastic** time!* (= very good)
> With strong adjectives you can use *absolutely* or *really*, but NOT *very*.
> *I've been suffering from the heat. It's **absolutely boiling**.* NOT *very boiling*.

a Complete the sentences with a regular adjective.

1 **A** Was Lisa's father *angry* about the car?
  B Yes, he was **furious**!
2 **A** Is Oliver's apartment _____?
  B Yes, it's really **tiny** – just a bedroom and a living room.
3 **A** Are you _____ of flying?
  B Yes, I'm **terrified**! I never fly anywhere.
4 **A** Was the food _____?
  B Yes, it was **delicious**.
5 **A** Are you very _____?
  B I'm **starving**! I haven't eaten all day.
6 **A** Is your parents' house _____?
  B It's **enormous**. It has seven bedrooms.
7 **A** Was it _____ in Moscow?
  B It was **freezing**! Minus 20 degrees.
8 **A** Was Jack's kitchen _____?
  B It was **filthy**. It took us three hours to clean it.
9 **A** Are your parents _____ about the wedding?
  B They're **excited**. In fact, they want to pay for everything!
10 **A** Was the movie _____?
  B It was **hilarious**. We laughed all the way through.
11 **A** Are you _____ you locked the door?
  B I'm **positive**. I remember turning the key.
12 **A** Were you _____ to hear that Ted is getting married?
  B I was absolutely **amazed**! I never thought it would happen.

b (1 53)) Listen and check. How are the strong adjectives pronounced? Practice the dialogues in pairs.

c ▶ **Communication** *Are you hungry?* **A** p.104 **B** p.109.

d Ask and answer with a partner. Ask for more information.

1 Have you ever been swimming in a place where the water was absolutely freezing?
2 Is there anything that makes you furious about car drivers or bike riders in your country?
3 Are there any animals or insects that you're terrified of?
4 What's the most delicious meal you've had recently?
5 Is there a comedian or a comedy series on TV in your country that you think is absolutely hilarious?

7 WRITING

▶ p.114 **Writing** *An informal email.* Write an informal email to thank somebody you have been staying with and to tell him or her what you have been doing recently.

1 & 2 Review and Check

GRAMMAR

Circle a, b, or c.

1. My sister _____ fish or seafood.
   a doesn't like   b don't like   c doesn't likes
2. I have a quick breakfast because _____ in a hurry.
   a I usually   b I usually am   c I'm usually
3. I _____ TV when I'm having a meal.
   a never watch   b don't never watch
   c am never watching
4. I usually drink a lot of diet soda, but right now _____ to cut down.
   a I try   b I'm trying   c I'm triing
5. _____ any brothers or sisters?
   a Are you having   b Are you have   c Do you have
6. What _____ when you graduate from school?
   a you are going to do   b are you going do
   c are you going to do
7. I can't see you this evening because _____ some friends.
   a I'm meeting   b I meet   c I'll meet
8. A Would you like something to drink?
   B Yes, _____ some orange juice, please.
   a I have   b I'm having   c I'll have
9. A I can't open this jar.
   B _____ help you.
   a I'll   b I'm   c I'd
10. That's a pretty dress. Where _____ it?
    a have you bought   b did you buy
    c did you bought
11. _____ good at saving money.
    a I've never been   b I haven't never been
    c I've never
12. I got $50 for my birthday, but I _____.
    a didn't spend it yet   b haven't spent it yet
    c yet I haven't spent it
13. I've had this computer _____.
    a for about three years   b since about three years
    c for about three years ago
14. A How long _____ in Paris?
    B Since last March.
    a is he living   b has he living   c has he been living
15. _____ the same gym for five years.
    a I'm going to   b I've been going to   c I go to

VOCABULARY

a Circle the word that is different.

1. shrimp   mussels   duck   squid
2. lamb   crab   beef   pork
3. cherry   pear   peach   beet
4. raspberry   cucumber   pepper   cabbage
5. fried   baked   chicken   roast

b Write the opposite adjective.

1. honest _____   4 hardworking _____
2. cheap _____   5 quiet _____
3. selfish _____

c Write verbs for the definitions.

1. to spend money on something that is not necessary _____
2. to receive money from somebody who has died _____
3. to get money by working _____
4. to get money from somebody that you will pay back _____
5. to keep money so that you can use it later _____

d Write the strong adjectives.

1. tired _____   3 cold _____   5 angry _____
2. hungry _____   4 dirty _____

e Complete the phrasal verbs.

1. Let's eat _____ tonight. I don't feel like cooking.
2. I'm allergic to milk, so I have to cut _____ dairy products from my diet.
3. We live _____ my salary. My wife is unemployed.
4. I'll lend you the money if you promise to pay me _____.
5. I took $200 _____ of my bank account.

PRONUNCIATION

a Circle the word with a different sound.

1. peach   steak   beef   steamed
2. money   shop   positive   honest
3. roast   sociable   owe   account
4. filthy   bill   tiny   chicken
5. afford   pork   worth   organized

b Underline the stressed syllable.

1. sal|mon   3 i|mma|ture   5 sen|si|ble
2. in|vest   4 de|li|cious

CAN YOU UNDERSTAND THIS TEXT?

a Read the article once. When did Bill Morgan's luck change?

When **bad luck** becomes good luck!

You've had a lot of bad luck in the past—a bad accident and some frightening health problems. Does that keep you from doing things in the future that involve luck, like buying a lottery ticket?

Anyone who has bought a ticket for the $500-million US Powerball jackpot can only dream of having as much luck as Australian truck driver Bill Morgan. In case you've never heard of Bill Morgan, his story actually begins with some very bad luck. First, he was almost crushed to death by a truck accident at work. The accident did not kill him, but it did leave Bill with a heart condition. When he was given medication for the heart condition, Bill had an allergic reaction that caused a powerful heart attack, which left him clinically dead for 14 minutes. After being revived by doctors, Morgan slipped into a coma for 12 days. During this time, his family was advised to unplug his life support system not once, but twice. Bill's luck began to change when he unexpectedly woke up from the coma without any permanent damage. Bill's bad luck was ending and his heartwarming story was just beginning.

After getting better, the 37-year-old Morgan found a new, higher-paying job, and asked his long-time girlfriend, Lisa Wells, to marry him. Lisa said yes. A week later, Morgan bought a scratch-off lottery ticket at his local newsstand. Bill scratched the ticket off and realized he had just won a brand new car! A local TV news station was so amazed by Bill's story that they sent a crew to do a human interest story on Bill and his lucky streak. The news crew thought it would be fun to re-create Bill's buying and scratching off the ticket right on camera. No one could have predicted what happened next. The ticket Bill bought for the re-enactment ended up being a $250,000 winner! And the best part is, it all happened on live TV (almost causing another heart attack).

Adapted from celebritynetworth.com

b Read the article again. Mark the sentences **T** (true), **F** (false), or **DS** (doesn't say).

1 Bill had a dream about winning the lottery.
2 Bill's heart condition was caused by the accident.
3 Bill was in a coma for 14 days.
4 Bill's new job was in an office.
5 The news crew bought Bill's lottery ticket for the re-enactment.
6 Winning $250,000 did not cause Bill to have another heart attack.

c Choose five new words or phrases from the article. Check their meaning and pronunciation, and try to learn them.

CAN YOU UNDERSTAND THESE PEOPLE?

1 54)) **On the street** Watch or listen to five people and answer the questions.

Max   Andrew   Samantha   Zenobia   Skylar

1 Max says he _____.
   a often made brownies for his sister in the past
   b doesn't mind sharing his brownies with friends who are also feeling down
   c hasn't eaten brownies in a long time
2 Andrew likes Asian restaurants because _____.
   a he doesn't like cooking
   b it's cheaper than eating at home
   c he can't cook that type of food at home
3 Samantha and her brother _____.
   a talk to each other a lot   b don't like each other at all
   c don't like each other as much after spending a lot of time together
4 Zenobia buys a bag _____.
   a if it's cheaper than usual   b every three months
   c if she needs a new one
5 Skylar took part in a charity event _____.
   a when she was 15   b for people who are sick with cancer
   c that raised money for captains

CAN YOU SAY THIS IN ENGLISH?

Do the tasks with a partner. Check (✓) the box if you can do them.

Can you…?

1 ☐ describe your diet and the typical diet in your country, and say how it is changing
2 ☐ agree or disagree with the following statement, and say why: *Our favorite food is usually something we liked when we were children.*
3 ☐ describe members of your family, saying what they look like and what they are like
4 ☐ describe some of your plans and predictions for the future (e.g., your education, your family life)
5 ☐ ask and answer the following questions:
   • Have you ever won any money? How much did you win? What did you do with it?
   • How long have you been learning English? Where did you first start learning?

 Short movies Goodwill Industries
VIDEO Watch and enjoy the movie.

G comparatives and superlatives
V transportation
P /ʃ/, /dʒ/, and /tʃ/, linking

3A Race across Miami

> What's the best way to get around New York City?

> Probably the subway, although taxis are more comfortable.

1 VOCABULARY & SPEAKING
transportation

a In pairs, can you think of four different forms of public transportation in towns and cities in your country?

b ▶ p.155 **Vocabulary Bank** *Transportation.*

2 PRONUNCIATION /ʃ/, /dʒ/, and /tʃ/

a (2 4))) Look at the pictures. What are the words and sounds? Listen and repeat.

/ʃ/	/dʒ/	/tʃ/

b Write three words from the list in each column.

adven**tu**re   bri**dge**   ca**tch**   **cr**a**sh**   **d**an**g**erous
ea**ch**   ru**sh**   **st**ation   traffic **j**am

c (2 5))) Listen and check. Practice saying the words.

d Look at the words in the columns. What are the typical spellings for these sounds? Go to the **Sound Bank p.167** and check.

e (2 6))) Listen to the pairs of words. Can you hear the difference? Practice saying them.

/tʃ/ and /dʒ/
1 a cheap   b jeep
2 a chain   b Jane
3 a choke   b joke

/ʃ/ and /tʃ/
4 a ship   b chip
5 a shoes   b choose
6 a wash   b watch

f (2 7))) Listen and circle the word you hear.

g (2 8))) Listen and write five sentences.

3 READING & LISTENING

a You are going to read about a race that the car show *Top Gear* organized across the US state of Florida. Read the introduction and answer the questions.
  1 Where do they have to go from? Where to?
  2 What are the three methods of transportation?
  3 Which one do you think will be the fastest? Why?
  4 In what order do you think the other two will arrive? Why?

TopGear Challenge
What's the fastest way to get across Florida?

On *Top Gear*, a very popular TV series about cars and driving, they decided to organize a race across Florida to find the quickest way to cross a busy state. The idea was to start from Miami, in the southwestern part of the tip of Florida, and to finish the race at the southern-most point of the US, Key West, a trip of 160 miles. Three possible forms of transportation were chosen: a motorboat, a car, and a combination of transportation. One of the show's hosts, **Rutledge Wood**, took the **motorboat** and his colleague **Adam Ferrera** took the **car** (a 2010 Lotus Evora). **Tanner Foust** took **different kinds of transportation**. His trip involved getting a taxi to the airport where he flew in a seaplane. Then he rented a scooter.
    They set off from Jones Boat Yard on the Miami River…

24

Rutledge in the motorboat

His trip began in the Miami River. For the first hour there was a speed limit of 7 miles an hour because of the enforced no-wake zone in the river. Once the boat passed through Biscayne Bay and went under the Rickenbacker Bridge, he entered open water. Rutledge increased the boat's speed to over 90 miles an hour and made up the time he lost on the Miami River. Approximately 60 miles from the finish line, Rutledge was ahead of Adam and Tanner, but he had to stop for gas if he wanted to reach the finish line in Key West. In the 15 minutes it took to refuel the boat, Adam passed Rutledge in the car and took the lead. Once Rutledge was back on the open water, there were a lot of big waves, but he was able to pass Adam near Seven Mile Bridge just outside of Key West. Unfortunately for both Rutledge and Adam, Tanner flew over both of them in the seaplane at about the same time. Now Tanner was in the best position to win. Each racer was only miles from the finish line in Key West. Who would win?

Adam in the car

Adam started off OK. He wasn't driving fast because he was going the speed limit. However, after an hour, Adam decided that he was going too slowly. He increased his speed to 75 miles an hour—20 miles an hour over the speed limit. As Adam passed through a small town, he was stopped by the police! They were angry that Adam was speeding, and it meant that Adam lost many valuable minutes! Another problem Adam had was that his GPS was programmed to give directions in Spanish instead of English. This made finding his way to Key West difficult. As Adam finally approached Key West, the traffic was getting worse. He was worried about getting stuck so close to the finish line. Only three miles to go…

b   Now read about the trips by motorboat and car. Do you still think your predictions in **3a** are right?

c   Read the two trips again and answer the questions with **R** (Rutledge) or **A** (Adam).

Who…?
1 ☐ went much faster in the later part of his trip
2 ☐ did something illegal
3 ☐ went more slowly in the later part of his trip
4 ☐ had to stop for more gas
5 ☐ couldn't understand the directions spoken by the GPS
6 ☐ was in the lead for most of the race

d   Look at the highlighted verbs and verb phrases. With a partner, figure out their meaning from context.

Tanner in the seaplane

e   **2 9))** Now listen to what happened to Tanner. Follow his route on the map.

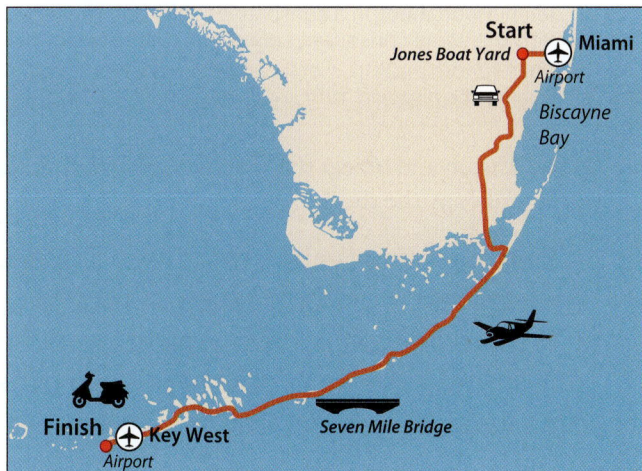

f   **2 10))** With a partner, write down the order in which you now think the three people arrived. Now listen to what happened. What order did they arrive in?

g   ▶ **Communication** *I'm a tourist – can you help me?* **A** p.104 **B** p.109.

> **Glossary**
> **1 mile** the unit of distance used in the US and the UK (=1.6 kilometers); 160 miles = 257 kilometers
> **seaplane** an airplane that can take off from the water or the land
> **no-wake zone** an area of water where boats must travel slowly to avoid making waves

4 GRAMMAR comparatives and superlatives

a Read the sentences. Are the highlighted phrases right or wrong? Write a check (✓) or an ✗ next to them and correct the wrong sentences.

1. ☐ What's the quicker way to get around Miami?
2. ☐ Driving is more boring than going by train.
3. ☐ The boat was almost as fast than the bike.
4. ☐ West Hollywood is the same distance from Los Angeles as South Gate.
5. ☐ There aren't as much trains as there were before on this line.
6. ☐ It was the more exciting trip I've ever taken.
7. ☐ The worst time of day to travel in New York City is between 7:30 a.m. and 9:30 a.m.
8. ☐ Women drive more careful than men.

b ▶ p.136 Grammar Bank 3A. Learn more about comparatives and superlatives, and practice them.

5 PRONUNCIATION linking

> 🔍 **Linking**
> We often link words together in English, especially when we speak fast. We link words:
> 1 when a word ends in a consonant sound and the next word begins with a vowel sound, e.g., *more‿exciting*
> 2 when a word ends in a consonant sound and the next word begins with the same consonant sound, e.g., *the fastest‿train*
> 3 when a word ends in /t/ or /d/ and the next word begins with /t/ or /d/, e.g., *the biggest‿dog*

a ②14))) Listen and repeat the sentences. Try to link the marked words and copy the rhythm.

1. Riding‿a motorcycle‿is more‿exciting than driving.
2. The fastest‿train‿only takes‿an‿hour‿and‿a half.
3. It's more difficult‿to drive‿at night than during the day.
4. My father's worse‿at‿driving than my mother.
5. The most‿dangerous road‿in my town‿is the freeway.

b Talk to a partner. For each group of three things compare them using the **bold** adjective, i.e., for 1 decide which is the most dangerous, and then compare the other two. Say why.

1 **dangerous:** riding a bike; riding a motorcycle; driving
2 **easy:** learning to drive; learning to ride a bike; learning to ride a horse
3 **relaxing:** flying; traveling by train; driving
4 **difficult:** sleeping on a train; sleeping in a plane; sleeping on a bus
5 **boring:** being stuck in a traffic jam; waiting at an airport; waiting for a bus

I think riding a bike is the most dangerous because sometimes drivers don't notice bike riders. Riding a motorcycle is more dangerous than driving.

6 LISTENING

a Read the text and then talk to a partner.

1 Which of these things do you (or people you know) do when you are driving?
2 Which do you think are the most dangerous? Number them 1–3 (1 = the most dangerous).
3 Which one do you think is the least dangerous?

b ②15))) Now listen to a safety expert. Number the activities 1–7. Were your top three right?

c Listen again for more information about each activity and why it is dangerous.

Which of these things is the most (and least) **dangerous** when you're driving a car?

A car magazine tested drivers in a driving simulator. The drivers had to drive in the simulator and do the things in the list below.

- ⚠ Eating or drinking ☐
- ⚠ Talking on a cell phone (not hands free) ☐
- ⚠ Setting or adjusting a GPS ☐
- ⚠ Listening to your favorite music ☐
- ⚠ Listening to music you don't know ☐
- ⚠ Sending or receiving text messages ☐
- ⚠ Doing your hair or putting on makeup ☐

7 SPEAKING

a Look at the statements below and decide whether you agree or disagree. Check (✓) the ones you agree with and put an ✗ next to the ones you disagree with. Think about your reasons.

| Slow drivers cause more accidents than fast drivers. |
| People who drink and drive should lose their driver's license for life. |
| Speed cameras do not stop accidents. |
| Drivers who are over 70 are as dangerous as young drivers. |
| Bike riders should have to wear helmets. |
| The minimum age for riding a motorcycle should be 25. |
| The speed limit on freeways should be lower. |

b In groups, give your opinions about each statement. Try to use expressions from the box. Do you agree?

🔍 **Agreeing and disagreeing**

I agree / don't agree	with this. / with Juan.
I think / don't think	you're right. / that's
I completely / totally	agree. / disagree.

8 WRITING

▶ p.115 Writing *An article for a magazine.* Write a magazine article about transportation in your town or city.

9 🎵 2 16))) SONG *500 Miles* 🎵

G articles: *a / an, the,* no article
V collocation: verbs / adjectives + prepositions
P /ə/, sentence stress, /ðə/ or /ði/?

3B Stereotypes – or are they?

Do you think women talk more than men?
Yes, in general I think they probably do.

1 READING & SPEAKING

a In pairs, answer the questions.
1 Are you a talkative or a quiet person?
2 Who is…?
   a the most talkative person in your family
   b the most talkative person you know
3 Do you think that, generally speaking, women are more talkative than men?
4 What topics do…?
   a men talk about more than women
   b women talk about more than men

b Look at the definition of *stereotype*. Then **A** read the article *Men talk just as much as women* and **B** read the article *Gossip with the girls?* Find answers to questions 1–4.

> **stereotype** /ˈstɛriətaɪp/ *noun* a fixed idea about a particular type of person or thing, which is often not true in reality. ▶ **stereotype** *verb* In advertisements, women are often stereotyped as housewives.

1 What was the stereotype that the researchers wanted to investigate?
2 Where was the research done?
3 How was the research done?
4 What did the research show?

c In pairs, tell each other about your article, using questions 1–4 to help you.

d Now read both articles again and look at the highlighted words and phrases, which are commonly used in articles about research. Match them with definitions 1–10.

1 *In fact* adverb really
2 _____ verb make less
3 _____ usually do it
4 _____ adverb a little bit
5 _____ linking word used to connect or contrast two facts
6 _____ verb say that something is true
7 _____ as said or shown by somebody
8 _____ verb include several different things in addition to the ones mentioned
9 _____ adverb nearly
10 _____ not completely believed, doubted

e Which of the two pieces of research do you think is…?
1 more credible
2 more important
3 more surprising

Men talk just as much as women – can it really be true?

Research by psychologists at the University of Arizona has shown that the stereotype that women talk more than men may not be true. In the study, hundreds of college students were fitted with recorders, and the total number of words they used during the day was then counted.

The results, published in the *New Scientist*, showed that women speak about 16,000 words a day and men speak only slightly fewer. In fact, the four most talkative people in the study were all men.

Professor Matthias Mehl, who was in charge of the research, said that he and his colleagues had expected to find that women were more talkative.

GOSSIP WITH THE GIRLS? JUST PICK ANY ONE OF FORTY SUBJECTS

Women are experts at gossiping – and they often talk about trivial things, or at least that's what men have always thought. However according to research done by Professor Petra Boynton, a psychologist at University College London, when women talk to women their conversations are not trivial at all, and cover many more topics (up to 40) than when men talk to other men.

Women's conversations range from health to their houses, from politics to fashion, from movies to family, from education to relationship problems. Almost everything, in fact, except soccer. Men tend to talk about fewer subjects, the most popular being work, sports, jokes, cars, and women.

However, they had been skeptical of the common belief that women use three times as many words as men. This idea became popular after the publication of a book called *The Female Brain* (2006) whose author, Louann Brizendine, claimed that "a woman uses about 20,000 words per day, whereas a man uses about 7,000."

Professor Mehl accepts that many people will find the results difficult to believe. However, he thinks that this research is important because the stereotype, that women talk too much and men keep quiet, is bad not only for women but also for men. "It says that to be a good male, it's better not to talk – that silence is golden."

Professor Boynton interviewed over 1,000 women for her study. She also found that women move quickly from one subject to another in conversation, whereas men usually stick to one subject for longer periods of time.

Professor Boynton also says that men and women talk for different reasons. In social situations, women use conversation to solve problems and reduce stress, while men talk to each other to laugh or to exchange opinions.

2 GRAMMAR articles: *a / an*, *the*, no article

a Complete 1–4 with *a / an*, *the*, or – (no article).

1 "Have you heard this joke? ___ hamburger and ___ French fry walk into a coffee shop. ___ waitress says, "I'm sorry. We don't serve ___ food here."
2 "I just read ___ article on ___ Internet about how eating ___ strawberries makes you look younger…"
3 "I'm sure there's something wrong between us because we never go out to ___ dinner or to ___ movies anymore."
4 "Did you watch ___ game ___ last night? I can't believe that ___ referee didn't see that it was ___ penalty…"

b According to the article *Gossip with the girls?*, who do you think would probably say 1–4, a man or a woman?

c ▶ p.137 Grammar Bank 3B. Learn more about articles and practice them.

3 PRONUNCIATION
/ə/, sentence stress, /ðə/ or /ði/?

a 2 20))) Listen and repeat the sound and words.

> a about anniversary complain credible
> problem talkative usually woman

b 2 21))) Listen and repeat the sentences. Then practice saying them with the /ə/ sound.

1 **What** are we **going** to **have** for **lunch today**?
2 I'd **like** to **see** a **good movie tonight**.
3 Please **stop complaining** about the **weather**.
4 The **woman** in the **kitchen** is very **talkative**.
5 There's a **problem** with the **computer**.

c 2 22))) Listen and underline five phrases where *the* is pronounced /ði/ (not /ðə/). Why does the pronunciation change?

> the movies   the end   the other day   the world   the sun
> the Internet   the kitchen   the answer   the Earth

4 SPEAKING

Prove that the research in *Gossip with the girls?* is wrong! Work in pairs or small groups.

> If you're a **woman**, try to talk for two minutes about:
>
> soccer   cars   computers
>
> If you're a **man**, try to talk for two minutes about:
>
> fashion   shopping   your family

5 READING & LISTENING

a Do you think it is a stereotype that women are better than men at taking care of small children? Do you know any men who stay at home and take care of their children? How do they manage?

b Look at an illustration based on a new book about taking care of young children. Can you name some of the things in the picture?

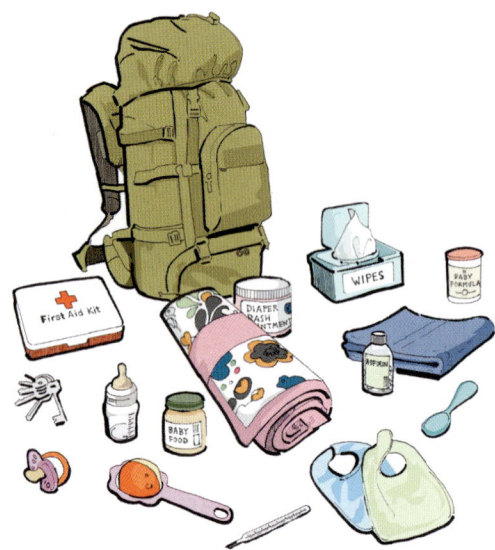

c Read the beginning of an article about the book. Why did Neil Sinclair write it? In what way is it different from other books about raising children?

d 2 23))) Listen to two men talking in the park about the book and mark the sentences **T** (true) or **F** (false).

1 Miranda is older than Stephen.
2 Miranda's father slept badly the night before.
3 Stephen's father recommends sleeping pills.
4 Stephen's father hasn't read *Commando Dad*.
5 He likes the website because he enjoys reading about other men's experiences.
6 Stephen's father really likes the book because it helps him and makes him laugh.
7 In *Commando Dad*, BT means Baby Trooper and Base Camp means the kitchen.
8 The author of *Commando Dad* thinks that women are only better than men when the baby is small.

e Listen again and correct the wrong information.

f Do you think it's a good idea to have a book and a website on childcare especially for men? Why (not)?

COMMANDO DAD

For six years Neil Sinclair served as a commando in the army. He had been in a lot of dangerous situations, but nothing prepared him for the day when he brought his first baby home from the hospital. "I put the car seat containing my two-day-old son Samuel down on the floor and said to my wife, 'What do we do now?'"

When he left the army, Sinclair and his wife agreed that he would stay at home and take care of the baby, while his wife went back to work.

"I have done a lot of crazy things, but when I put that baby down I thought: I have a tiny baby, and he is crying. What does he want? What does he need? I did not know. It was one of the most difficult days of my life."

It was at that moment that Sinclair had an idea. "I found myself thinking how much easier life would be if I had a basic training manual for my baby, like the manual you get when you join the army. I realized that somebody needed to write such a manual, and who better to write it than me? I had been a commando, but I was now a stay-at-home dad. I was the man for the job."

His book, *Commando Dad: Basic Training*, is a set of instructions that explains with military precision and diagrams how new fathers should approach the first three years of their child's life to become a first-rate father.

Adapted from *The Times*

Glossary
commando *noun* one of a group of soldiers who are trained to make quick attacks in enemy areas
stay-at-home dad *noun* a man who stays at home and takes care of the children while his wife goes to work

6 SPEAKING

a ➤ 2 24))) Listen to someone talking about men and women, and fill in the blanks.

> "Generally _____, I think women worry more about their appearance than men. They _____ to spend hours choosing what to wear, doing their hair, and putting on makeup. Women are also _____ better at making themselves look more attractive. But I think that in _____, men are more worried than women about their body image. They feel more insecure about their hair, for instance, especially when they're going bald."

b In small groups discuss if the statements about men and women are stereotypes or true. Try to use the highlighted expressions for generalizing from **a**.

MEN & WOMEN stereotypes or true?

- Women worry more about their appearance than men.
- Women spend more time than men on social networking sites.
- Men talk more about things; women talk more about people.
- Men are more interested than women in gadgets like phones and tablets.
- Women are better at multitasking than men.
- Men find it more difficult than women to talk to their friends or family if they have a problem.
- Women spend more time than men talking about celebrities and their lifestyles.
- Men are more interested than women in power.
- Women are less interested in sports than men.
- Men worry more about their health than women.

7 VOCABULARY

collocation: verbs / adjectives + prepositions

a Cover the statements above. Can you remember the missing prepositions?
   1 Men worry more ___ their health than women.
   2 Women are better ___ multitasking than men.
   3 Men are more interested than women ___ power.

b ➤ p.156 Vocabulary Bank *Dependent prepositions.*

> 🔍 **When are prepositions stressed?**
> Prepositions are usually only stressed when they are the last word, e.g., in a question. Compare:
>
> We **need** to **talk** about our **vacation**.
> **What** are you **talking about**?
>
> **Freddie** is **afraid** of **flying**.
> **What** are you **afraid of**?

c Complete the questions with a preposition.
   1 When you're with friends of the same sex, what do you usually talk ___?
   2 Are there any sports or games that you're good ___?
   3 Is there anything you're really looking forward ___?
   4 Who in your family are you closest ___?
   5 What kind of movies are you interested ___?
   6 Are there any animals or insects that you're afraid ___?
   7 What's your town famous ___?
   8 Are there any superstitions that you believe ___?

d ➤ 2 27))) Listen and check. Then ask and answer the questions with a partner.

Practical English A difficult celebrity EPISODE 2

1 🎥 ROB'S INTERVIEW

a **2 28))** Watch or listen to Rob interviewing Kerri. What is she happy / not happy to talk about?

b Watch or listen again. Mark the sentences **T** (true) or **F** (false). Correct the **F** sentences.
1 Kerri's song is about love.
2 Kerri plays in a band.
3 She used to go out with a member of the band.
4 Only one of her parents was a musician.
5 Kerri started playing the guitar when she was six.
6 Her new album is very different from the previous ones.
7 She's been recording and touring recently.
8 She's going to give a big concert in New York City.

2 🎥 GIVING OPINIONS

a **2 29))** Watch or listen to the conversation at lunch. What do they disagree about?

b Watch or listen again. Answer the questions.
1 What does Kerri think about…?
   a the waiters in New York City compared to London
   b people in New York City compared to London
2 Who agrees with Kerri? Who disagrees? What do they think?
3 Who calls Rob? What about?

c **2 30** Look at some extracts from the conversation. Can you remember any of the missing words? Watch or listen and check.

1 **Kerri** _____, I think people in London are a lot more easygoing. London's just not as hectic as New York.
Don Sure, we all like peace and quiet. But in my _____, New York is possibly… well, no, is definitely the greatest city in the world. Don't you _____?
Kerri To be _____, I definitely prefer London.
Don Come on, Rob. You've lived in both. What do you _____?

2 **Don** OK, I _____, London has its own peculiar charm. But if you _____ me, nothing compares with a city like New York. The whole world is here!
Kerri But that's the problem. It's too big. There are too many people. Everybody's so stressed out. And nobody has any time for you.
Jenny I don't think that's _____, Kerri. New Yorkers are very friendly.
Kerri Oh _____, they can sound friendly with all that "Have a nice day" stuff.

d **2 31** Watch or listen and repeat the highlighted phrases. Copy the rhythm and intonation.

e Practice the dialogues in **c** with a partner.

f In small groups, practice giving opinions. Discuss the following sentences.
 – The best place to live is in a big city.
 – Riding a bike is the most practical way to get around big cities.
 – You only get good service in expensive restaurants.
 – It's irritating when people in stores or restaurants say *Have a nice day!*

3 A SURPRISE FOR KERRI

a **2 32** Watch or listen to the end of the lunch. Why is Kerri surprised?

American and British English
cell phone = American English
mobile phone = British English

b Watch or listen again and complete the information.
 1 Kerri thinks the waitress is friendly when they leave because Don…
 2 Jenny is worried because she thinks Rob…
 3 Kerri thinks that the taxi driver is very…

c Look at the **Social English phrases**. Can you remember any of the missing words?

Social English phrases
Jenny Did you _____ what you said in the restaurant, Rob?
Jenny It's _____ that… you seemed homesick in there.
Rob Oh, _____ on a minute.
Rob Our taxi's come _____.
Kerri That was so _____ of him!

d **2 33** Watch or listen and complete the phrases.

e Watch or listen again and repeat the phrases. How do you say them in your language?

Can you…?
☐ interview someone or be interviewed
☐ give your opinion about something
☐ agree or disagree with other people's opinions

33

G can, could, be able to
V -ed / -ing adjectives
P sentence stress

> Can you speak French?
>
> No, I've never been able to learn a foreign language.

4A Failure and success

1 GRAMMAR can, could, be able to

a *If at first you don't succeed, try, try, try again* is a well-known saying. What does it mean?

b More recently other people have invented different ways of continuing the saying. Which one do you like best?

> **If at first you don't succeed,**
> …give up
> …blame your parents
> …destroy all the evidence that you tried
> …do it the way your mother told you to
> …skydiving is not for you

c Look at the definition of *be able to*. What other verb is it similar to?

> **be able to (do something)** to have the ability, opportunity, time, etc., to do something: *Will you be able to come to the meeting next week?*

d Read about three people who have tried (but failed) to learn something, and complete the texts with A–G.

A I was able to
B Not being able to
C I just wasn't able to
D I will never be able to
E I would suddenly be able to
F I've always wanted to be able to
G we would never be able to

e Read the article again. Why did they have problems? Have they completely given up trying? Have you ever tried to learn something and given up? Why?

f Look at phrases **A–G** again. What tense or form is *be able to* in each one? What tenses or forms does *can* have?

g ▶ **p.138 Grammar Bank 4A.** Learn more about *can, could,* and *be able to*, and practice them.

h ▶ **Communication** *Guess the sentence* **A** p.105 **B** p.109.

I've never been able to…

…scuba dive

I really wanted to learn. Maybe it was because of that scene in one of the very first James Bond movies, where a beautiful actress comes out of the ocean looking fabulous, with oxygen tanks on her back – I could see myself looking just like her. So, two years ago I booked a vacation that included a week-long intensive course. On the first day of the course, I was incredibly excited. First, we had two hours of theory, and then we went into the ocean to put it into practice. But as soon as I went under the water, I discovered that I suffered from claustrophobia. [1]_____ do it. After about half an hour I gave up. Every evening for the rest of my vacation I had to listen to my scuba-diving classmates talking about all the wonderful things they had seen that day on their diving excursions. [2]_____ join in the conversation was very frustrating.

I still love swimming and snorkeling, but I think that I have to accept that [3]_____ scuba dive.

Bea, the US

34

...learn to dance

⁴_____ dance salsa, and when I was working in Ecuador there were free classes, so I joined. But the art of salsa is to keep your arms still and move your hips, and I just couldn't do it. When I hear music my arms start moving, but my hips don't. After about ten hours of classes ⁵_____ do the basic steps, but I was dancing like a robot! I didn't give up, but soon everyone in the class was dancing, and I was just slowly moving from side to side and counting out loud "one, two, three, four." It was a little embarrassing. I was sure that one day ⁶_____ do it – but that never happened. I can still remember the first two steps, and I still try to dance when I hear a salsa tune – as long as nobody is watching!

Sean, Canada

...speak Japanese

I love manga – Japanese comics – and I tried to learn Japanese, but I found it incredibly difficult, and I gave up after two years. I think Asian languages, which have symbols instead of words, are extremely hard to learn for people who are more used to Roman letters. Also my teacher, a Japanese woman, didn't speak Spanish very well, which didn't help! She was a very charming woman, but she was a little disappointed with us, and you could see that she thought that ⁷_____ learn. However, one day she invited us to dinner and gave us some delicious traditional Japanese food, and since then I often go to Japanese restaurants. So I learned to love the food, if not to speak the language!

Joaquin, Argentina

2 PRONUNCIATION sentence stress

a 🔊 2 36 Listen and repeat the sentences. Copy the rhythm.

> 1 I'd **love** to be **able** to **ski**.
> 2 We **won't** be **able** to **come**.
> 3 I've **never** been **able** to **dance**.
> 4 She **hates not** being **able** to **drive**.

b 🔊 2 37 Listen again. Make new sentences with the verbs or verb phrases you hear.

> 🔊 I'd love to be able to ski. **Ride a horse**
> 💬 I'd love to be able to ride a horse.

> 🔊 We won't be able to come. **Park**
> 💬 We won't be able to park.

3 SPEAKING

a Look at the topics. Choose two or three and think about what you could say for them.

> Something you've tried to learn, but have never been able to do well.
>
> Something you learned to do after a lot of effort.
>
> Something you can do, but you'd like to be able to do better.
>
> Something new that you would like to be able to do.
>
> Something you are learning to do and that you hope you'll soon be able to do well.
>
> Something you think all young people should be able to do before they leave school.

b Work with a partner. Tell him / her about the things you chose in **a**. Give reasons or explanations for each one.

> 💬 I've never been able to ski, and now I don't think I'll ever learn. I always wanted to learn, but I don't live near mountains...

4 VOCABULARY -ed / -ing adjectives

a Look at the photo. Complete the sentences with *bored* or *boring*.

1 The movie was _____.
2 The audience was _____.

> **-ed and -ing adjectives**
> Many adjectives for feelings have two possible forms, either ending in *-ed* or in *-ing*, e.g., *frustrated* and *frustrating*.
> We use the adjective ending in *-ed* for the person who has the feeling (*I was very frustrated that I couldn't scuba dive.*). We use the adjective ending in *-ing* for a person or situation that produces the feeling (*I couldn't join in the conversation, which was very frustrating.*).

b Read the information box. Then complete the adjectives with *-ed* or *-ing*.

1 What do you think is the most **excit___** sport to watch?
2 What's the most **amaz___** scenery you've ever seen?
3 What music do you listen to if you feel **depress___**?
4 Have you ever been **disappoint___** by a birthday present?
5 Which do you find more **tir___**, speaking English or listening to English?
6 What's the most **embarrass___** thing that's ever happened to you?
7 Are you **scare___** of spiders?
8 Do you feel very **tir___** in the morning?
9 Who's the most **bor___** person you know?
10 Do you ever get **frustrat___** by technology?

c 2 38)) Listen and check. Underline the stressed syllable in the adjectives.

d Ask and answer the questions in pairs. Ask for more information.

5 READING & SPEAKING

a Do you know anybody who speaks more than two languages? Which languages do they speak? How did they learn?

b 2 39)) You are going to read an article about Alex Rawlings, who speaks 11 languages. Before you read, match the languages below with words 1–11. Then listen and check.

☐ English   ☐ Greek   ☐ German
☐ Spanish   ☐ Russian ☐ Dutch
1 Afrikaans ☐ French   ☐ Hebrew
☐ Catalan   ☐ Italian

c Read the article. Which language(s)…?

1 did he learn as a child
2 is he studying in college
3 does he like best
4 is he planning to learn next
5 did he wish he had been able to speak when he was a child
6 was the first one he taught himself
7 did he find the most difficult

1 Hallo
2 Guten Tag

He's only 20, but he can speak eleven languages

In a competition run by a dictionary publisher, college student Alex Rawlings was named the most multilingual student.

The German and Russian student, who is only 20 years old, can speak 11 languages fluently. In a video for a news website, he demonstrated his skills by speaking in all of them, changing quickly from one to another. Rawlings said that winning the competition was "a bit of a shock." He explained, "I saw the competition advertised, and I heard something about a free iPad. I never imagined that it would generate this amount of media attention."

As a child, Rawlings' mother, who is half Greek, used to speak to him in English, Greek, and French, and he often visited his family in Greece.

He said that he has always been interested in languages. "My dad worked in Japan for four years, and I was always frustrated that I couldn't speak to the kids because of the language barrier." After visiting Holland at the age of 14, he decided to learn Dutch with CDs and books. "When I went back I could talk to people. It was great."

He taught himself many of the languages with "teach yourself" books, but also by watching movies, listening to music, and traveling to the countries themselves.

d Look at the **highlighted** words and phrases related to language learning, and figure out their meaning from the context. Then ask and answer the questions with a partner.

1. Can you or anyone in your family speak another language fluently?
2. Do you know any basic phrases in any other languages?
3. Do you have a personal link to another country or language? Why?
4. Have you ever traveled to another country and felt that there was a real language barrier?
5. What other languages would you like to be able to speak? Why?

3 Bonjour
7 Geiá sou (γειά σου)
8 Bon dia
4 Shalom (שלום)
9 Hola
5 Privet (привет)
10 Goedendag
6 Hello
11 Ciao

Of all the languages he speaks, Rawlings says that Russian, which he has been learning for a year and a half, is the hardest. He said, "There seem to be **more exceptions than rules**!" He added, "I especially like Greek because I think it's beautiful and, because of my mother, I have a strong personal **link** to the country and to the language."

"Everyone should learn languages, especially if they travel abroad. If you make the effort to learn even the most **basic phrases** wherever you go, it instantly shows the person you're speaking to that you respect his or her culture. Going around speaking English loudly and getting frustrated with people is tactless and rude."

The next language Rawlings hopes to learn is Arabic, but "only once I've finished my degree and got some more time on my hands. For now I need to concentrate on my German and Russian, so I can prepare for my finals."

Glossary
Afrikaans a language that has developed from Dutch, spoken in South Africa
Catalan a language spoken in parts of northern Spain and southern France
finals the last exams that students take in college

Adapted from Cherwell.org

e Read the grammar information box. Then complete 1–5 with a reflexive pronoun.

> **Reflexive pronouns**
> He taught **himself** many of the languages with "teach yourself" books.
> We use reflexive pronouns (*myself, yourself, himself, herself, itself, ourselves, yourselves, themselves*) when the object of a verb is the same as the subject, e.g., *He taught himself Russian.* = He was his own teacher.
> We also use reflexive pronouns to emphasize the subject of an action, e.g., *We painted the kitchen ourselves.*

1. I always test _____ on new vocabulary. It's a good way to remember it.
2. My uncle built the house _____. It took him three years.
3. This light is automatic. It turns _____ on and off.
4. Did you fix the computer _____? Good job!
5. My sister's so vain! Everytime she passes a mirror, she looks at _____ in it!

6 LISTENING & SPEAKING

a 🔊 **2 40** You're going to listen to six advanced students of English giving a tip that has helped them to learn. Listen once and complete their tip. Then compare your notes with a partner.

TIP 1: Change the language to English on all the _____ you have, for example on your _____, or _____, or _____.

TIP 2: Do things that you _____ _____, but in English.

TIP 3: Try to find an English-speaking _____ or _____.

TIP 4: Get a _____ _____ app for your phone.

TIP 5: Book yourself a _____ in an _____-_____ _____.

TIP 6: Listen to as many _____ as possible in English, and then _____ _____ _____ them.

b Listen again. Try to add more details about each tip.

c Talk to a partner.
- Do you already do any of these things?
- Which do you think is the best tip?
- Which tip could you easily put into practice? Try it!
- What other things do you do to improve your English outside class (e.g., visit chat websites, listen to audio books)?

G modals of obligation: *must, have to, should*
V phone language
P silent consonants, linking

Do I have to bring a present?
Yes, I think you probably should.

4B Modern manners?

1 VOCABULARY & SPEAKING
phone language

a ⏵ 2 41 Listen and match the phone sentences with the sounds.
- A ☐ He's **dialing** a number.
- B ☐ She's **texting** / **messaging** a friend.
- C ☐ She just **hung up**.
- D ☐ She's choosing a new **ringtone**.
- E ☐ He's **calling back**.
- F ☐ She **left a message** on his **voicemail**.
- G ☐ The line's **busy**.

b Can you explain what these are?

Skype   a screensaver   silent / vibrate mode
quiet zones   instant messaging

c Use the questionnaire to interview another student. Ask for more information.

YOU AND YOUR PHONE

- 📱 What brand is your phone? How long have you had it?
- 📱 Would you like to get a new one? Why (not)?
- 📱 What ringtone do you have?
- 📱 What do you use your phone for (apart from talking)?
- 📱 Where and when do you usually turn off your cell phone?
- 📱 Have you ever…?
  - lost your phone
  - sent a message to the wrong person
  - forgotten to turn your phone off (with embarrassing consequences)

2 GRAMMAR
modals of obligation: *must, have to, should*

a Read the extract from Debrett's guide to cell phone etiquette. Then talk to a partner about questions 1–4.
1. Do you agree with what Debrett's says?
2. Do you ever do any of these things?
3. Are they a problem where you live?
4. Are there any other things people do with their phones that annoy you?

Debrett's, a well-known publisher, has been producing guides on how people should behave since the 1900s, including *Debrett's Etiquette and Modern Manners* and *The English Gentleman*. Nowadays it still offers advice on what (and what not) to do in social situations.

DEBRETT'S
guide to cell phone etiquette

1. *Think what your ringtone says about you*
   If you're sometimes embarrassed by your ringtone, it's almost certainly the wrong one and you should change it.

2. *When in doubt, use silent or vibrate mode*
   It may surprise your companions when you suddenly answer an invisible, silent phone, but at least they won't have to listen to your ringtone.

3. *Take notice of who is around you*
   Make sure your conversation is not disturbing other people. Intimate conversations are never appropriate in front of others.

b Read the text again. Match the highlighted phrases with their meaning. Two of the phrases match the same meaning.

A You don't need to do this. It isn't necessary.
B Don't do this. It isn't allowed / permitted.
C It's necessary or required to do this.
D It's a good idea to do this.

c ▶ p.139 Grammar Bank 4B. Learn more about *must*, *have to*, and *should*, and practice them.

4 *Respect quiet zones*
You must not use your phone in quiet zones on trains or in hotels. That is the reason why they exist.

5 *Never shout*
Your phone is not a megaphone. You don't have to shout. And don't shout because you think reception is poor. It won't make any difference.

6 *People with you deserve more attention than those at the end of a phone*
Wherever possible, turn off your phone in social situations and at mealtimes, or put it on vibrate. If you have to keep your phone on because you are expecting an important call, apologize in advance.

7 *Don't continue on with phone conversations when you are in the middle of something else*
This is especially true if you are in banks, stores, etc. It is insulting not to give the people who are serving you your full attention.

8 *Think about where you are calling from*
Don't make (or receive) calls in inappropriate places. Put your phone on vibrate in meetings, movies, etc. If you must take a call in the car, use a hands-free set.

Adapted from Debrett's Modern Manners

3 PRONUNCIATION & SPEAKING
silent consonants, linking

a Each of the words in the list has a silent consonant or consonants. With a partner, cross out the silent letters.

shou~~l~~d   talk   wrong   listen   half   dishonest
knowledge   design   whole   rhythm   doubt
foreign   calm   island

b 2 46))) Listen and check.

c 2 47))) Listen and repeat the sentences. Try to copy the rhythm and to link the marked words.

1 You must **turn off** your **phone** on a **plane**.
2 You should **only call him** in an **emergency**.
3 We **have** to **leave** at **eleven**.
4 You **must not open other people's emails**.
5 You **shouldn't talk loudly** on a **cell phone**.

d Read the definition of *manners*. Then make sentences using *should / shouldn't* for something that you think is a question of manners, and with *must / must not / have to* for something that is a law or rule.

manners /ˈmænərz/ *pl noun* a way of behaving that is considered acceptable in your country or culture

- turn off your phone in a theater
- talk loudly on your phone in public
- send text messages when you are driving
- reply to a message on your phone while you are talking to somebody face-to-face
- play noisy games on a phone in public
- use your phone at a gas station
- video people on your phone without their permission
- set your phone to silent mode on a train
- send or receive texts at the movies
- turn off your phone on a plane during take-off and landing

Online Practice 4B 39

4 READING

a Imagine that you have been invited to visit your partner's family. Think of <u>three</u> things that you feel would be bad manners to do.

b Read the article. Did Heidi do any of those things? What did she do wrong (according to Mrs. Bourne)? Whose side would you take?

News online

Two sides to every story

By NEWS ONLINE Reporter

Everyone knows it can be difficult to get along with your in-laws, but for 29-year-old **Heidi Withers**, it may now be impossible. Heidi was invited to spend the weekend with her fiancé Freddie's family at their house. But soon after they returned home, Heidi received a very nasty email from Carolyn Bourne, Freddie's stepmother, criticizing her manners.

✉

Here are a few examples of your lack of manners:

- *When you are a guest in another person's house, you should not declare what you will and will not eat – unless you are allergic to something.*
- *You should not say that you do not have enough food.*
- *You should not start before everyone else.*
- *You should not take extra helpings without being invited to by your host.*
- *You should not lie in bed until late morning.*
- *You should have sent a handwritten note after the visit. You have never written to thank me when you have stayed.*

Heidi was shocked, and immediately sent the email on to some of her close friends. Surprised and amused, the friends forwarded it to other people, and soon the email had been posted on several websites, with thousands of people writing comments about the mother-in-law.

Adapted from the Daily Mail website

c Find words or phrases in the article that mean…

1 _____ *noun* a man to whom you are going to be married
2 _____ *adj* unpleasant
3 _____ *verb* saying what is bad or wrong with somebody or something
4 _____ *noun* not having enough of something
5 _____ *noun* a person who you invite to your house
6 _____ *noun* a person who receives a visitor
7 _____ *verb* sent an email or message you received to another person

> **G should have**
> We use *should have* to talk about something that happened in the past that you think was wrong, e.g., *You should have written me a thank-you letter.* = you didn't write to me. I think this was wrong.

d Now read some of the comments that were posted on the Internet. Write **H** next to the ones that support Heidi and **C** next to the ones that support Carolyn.

1 Mrs. Bourne says Heidi should have sent a handwritten thank-you note… however, she sends this letter by email! We are in the 21st century. Nobody sends handwritten letters anymore. *07/13/2011 6:52 p.m.*

2 Why do we hear nothing about Freddie's role in all this? Why didn't he prepare Heidi? He must know what his stepmother is like. He could also have prepared his family by telling them about any eating problems his girlfriend has. *07/13/2011 4:25 p.m.*

3 The email was a private communication. I don't think Heidi should have sent it on to her friends. It makes me think that Mrs. Bourne might be right about her bad manners. *07/13/2011 12:40 p.m.*

4 The stepmother seems to be extremely jealous of Heidi. Maybe she wants to keep Freddie all to herself. If I were Heidi, I would leave him. *07/12/2011 10:15 a.m.*

5 The mother-in-law may have a few good points, but she should have spoken to Heidi face-to-face, and not sent her an email. *07/11/2011 6:50 p.m.*

6 I think that the one with the extremely bad manners is Mrs. Bourne. *07/11/2011 2:10 p.m.*

7 Mrs. Bourne, I agree with every word you say. Young people just don't have any manners nowadays. I hope Freddie comes to his senses and finds someone better. *07/11/2011 9:48 a.m.*

e Write your own comment. Then compare with a partner. Do you agree?

f ▶ **Communication** *The big day* p.105. Read about what Heidi and Freddie did next.

5 LISTENING

a (2 48)) Listen to Caroline Halloran, who is dating Jason Win, talking about the differences between Burmese manners and American manners. What was their problem when they first met? How have they managed to solve their differences about manners?

b Listen again and mark the sentences **T** (true) or **F** (false).

1. Jason thought Caroline was rude when she asked him to hang out with her.
2. In Burma it's OK to spend time alone with someone at the beginning of a romantic relationship.
3. Burmese culture is not as open as American culture is.
4. Jason wrote long responses to Caroline's Facebook romantic posts.
5. Caroline wants Jason to stop bragging about their relationship to his friends and family.
6. Jason sometimes gets confused about good and bad manners in the US.
7. Caroline and Jason don't argue about manners anymore.

c What would people from your country do in these situations?

6 SPEAKING

In groups, talk about each thing in the *Good Manners?* questionnaire. Do you think it's good manners, bad manners, or not important / not necessary. Why?

I think it's very rude to criticize the food if you are in somebody's house.

I think it depends. It's OK if you know the person very well or if it's a member of your family...

7 (2 49)) SONG *You Can't Hurry Love* ♪

GOOD MANNERS?
BAD MANNERS?
NOT IMPORTANT?

WHEN YOU ARE INVITED TO SOMEBODY'S HOUSE...
- [ ] criticize the food (e.g., if it is too cold, salty, etc.)
- [ ] take a present
- [ ] write an email to say thank you
- [ ] arrive more than ten minutes late for lunch or dinner

WHEN GREETING PEOPLE...
- [ ] use more formal language when speaking to an older person
- [ ] kiss a woman on the cheek when you meet her for the first time
- [ ] use your partner's parents' first names

MEN AND WOMEN – A MAN'S ROLE...
- [ ] pay for the meal on a first date
- [ ] wait for a woman to go through the door first
- [ ] accompany a woman home

WHEN YOU ARE HAVING A MEAL WITH FRIENDS IN A RESTAURANT...
- [ ] leave your cell phone on silent on the table in front of you
- [ ] answer or send a text or message
- [ ] make a phone call

ON SOCIAL NETWORKING SITES...
- [ ] post a private message or conversation on an Internet site
- [ ] post an embarrassing photo or video clip of a friend without asking his or her permission
- [ ] post all the details of your break-up with a partner

3 & 4 Review and Check

GRAMMAR

Circle a, b, or c.

1 I walk to work. It's _____ than driving.
   a healthyer   b as healthy   c healthier
2 Riding a bike isn't _____ people think.
   a as dangerous as   b as dangerous than   c so dangerous than
3 This is _____ time of day for traffic jams.
   a the most bad   b the worse   c the worst
4 My wife is a much safer driver than _____.
   a I   b me   c my
5 What _____ beautiful day!
   a a   b –   c an
6 I never drink coffee after _____ dinner.
   a –   b the   c an
7 _____ are usually good language learners.
   a The women   b Women   c Woman
8 We've decided to visit Peru _____.
   a the next summer   b next summer   c the summer next
9 We won't _____ come to the party.
   a can   b be able   c be able to
10 When he was five he _____ already swim.
   a can   b could   c was able
11 My mother has never _____ cook well.
   a been able to   b could   c be able to
12 Entrance is free. You _____ pay anything.
   a don't have to   b must not   c shouldn't
13 I'll _____ work harder if I want to pass.
   a must   b should   c have to
14 I don't think I _____ have a dessert. I've already eaten too much!
   a must   b should   c have to
15 You _____ turn on your phone until the plane has landed.
   a don't have to   b must not   c shouldn't

VOCABULARY

a Complete with a preposition.

1 We arrived _____ Vancouver at 5:30.
2 I apologized _____ being late.
3 I'm not very interested _____ horror movies.
4 My son is good _____ speaking languages.
5 This song reminds me _____ my vacation.

b Complete the compound nouns.

1 Slow down! The speed _____ on this road is 55 mph, not 65 mph.
2 I won't start the car until you have all put on your seat _____.
3 It's not a good town for bike riders – there are very few bicycle _____.
4 Try to avoid using the subway during _____ hour – between 8:00 and 9:30 in the morning.
5 There's a taxi _____ right next to the train station.

c Complete with the right word.

1 We were late because we got s_____ in a terrible traffic jam.
2 I'm moving into a new apartment next week. I've rented a v_____ so that I can take all my things there.
3 The next train to New Haven is now waiting at pl_____ 5.
4 We're going to s_____ off early because we want to get to the hotel before it gets dark.
5 How long does it t_____ to get from here to the airport?

d Circle the right adjective.

1 The game ended 0–0. It was really *bored* / *boring*.
2 It was the most *amazed* / *amazing* experience I've ever had.
3 We're very *excited* / *exciting* about our vacation!
4 I'm a little *disappointed* / *disappointing* with my exam results.
5 This show is too *depressed* / *depressing*. Turn it off.

e Complete the missing words.

1 I'm not in right now. Please l_____ a message.
2 The line's b_____. Please hold.
3 I was in the middle of talking to him, and he just h_____ up!
4 I love the scr_____ on your phone. Is it a photo of your kids?
5 I hate it when people have really loud r_____ on their cell phones!

PRONUNCIATION

a Circle the word with a different sound.

1 æ   language   want   manners   traffic
2   the moon   the sun   the beginning   the end
3   watch   cheap   machine   each
4   should   crash   permission   gossip
5   change   message   argue   apologize

b Underline the stressed syllable.

1 free|way   3 pe|des|tri|an   5 em|barr|ass|ing
2 dis|a|ppoint|ed   4 vi|brate

CAN YOU UNDERSTAND THIS TEXT?

a Read the article once. What kind of concert was it? What happened?

Turn it off!

Something historic happened at the New York Philharmonic on the evening of January 10, 2012, about an hour into Mahler's Ninth Symphony. During the beautiful fourth movement, an audience member's cell phone loudly rang. And rang. And rang again. It was the kind of marimba riff we've all heard on the street from a stranger's phone.

From my seat in Row L, I could see the horrified discomfort of the other audience members from their body language. We all wondered whether the conductor Alan Gilbert would react, and how. Suddenly there was silence. The orchestra had stopped playing. Mr. Gilbert had halted the performance. He turned to the man, who was seated in the front row, and said:

"Are you going to turn it off? Will you do that?"

There was some "discussion" between the conductor and the cell phone owner, but we couldn't hear it.

In the Avery Fisher Hall, many members of the audience stood and demanded that the man leave the hall. They were so furious that I could have imagined them dragging him from his seat on to the stage, tying him to a stake, and setting him alight!

When the "power off" button on the man's phone had finally been located and put to use, Mr. Gilbert turned to the audience. "Usually, when there's a disturbance like this, it's best to ignore it," he said. "But this time I could not allow it."

The audience applauded as if Mahler himself, the orchestra's conductor from 1909 to 1911, had suddenly been resurrected onstage. Mr. Gilbert neither smiled nor acknowledged the cheers. Instead he turned to the orchestra, instructing the players to resume, several bars back from the point at which he had stopped the performance. Just before, he raised his baton and turned again to the audience and said, this time with a smile, "We'll start again." A few seconds later, the fourth movement resumed.

Mr. Gilbert's brave decision that night brought new music to the Philharmonic.

Adapted from The New York Times

b Read the text again and answer the questions.

1 In what part of the symphony did the phone ring? What kind of ringtone was it?
2 Did the owner turn it off immediately?
3 How did the audience react a) to the phone ringing, and b) to what the conductor did?
4 Did the audience really drag the man onto the stage?
5 Did Mr. Gilbert restart the music from the same place where he had stopped?
6 Does the journalist think Mr. Gilbert made the right decision?

c Choose five new words or phrases from the text. Check their meaning and pronunciation and try to learn them.

CAN YOU UNDERSTAND THESE PEOPLE?

2 50))) **On the street** Watch or listen to five people and answer the questions.

Christopher   Maria   Harry   Skylar   Cristina

1 Christopher likes using the subway because _____.
   a he only needs to take one train
   b he gets to work in less than half an hour
   c it runs all day and night
2 Maria thinks that women are better than men at taking care of young children because _____.
   a they have had a lot of practice
   b they know when children are hungry
   c they know what to do when children are sick
3 Harry says that men in her family _____.
   a don't enjoy telling stories
   b talk about the same things as women
   c try to talk about things that interest them
4 Skylar _____.
   a still paints, but just as a free-time activity
   b paints very well
   c now does other things in her free time
5 It annoys Cristina when people _____.
   a check their phones for the time
   b don't interact with you while they're on the phone
   c use their phones when they are having dinner

CAN YOU SAY THIS IN ENGLISH?

Do the tasks with a partner. Check (✓) the box if you can do them.

Can you...?

1 ☐ compare different methods of public transportation in your town / country
2 ☐ agree or disagree with this statement, and say why: *All towns and cities should have a lot more bicycle lanes.*
3 ☐ talk about typical stereotypes about men and women, and say if you think they are true
4 ☐ describe something you would like to be able to do, but have never been able to
5 ☐ talk about things that are / aren't good manners in your country if you are staying with someone as a guest, and what you think is the right thing to do

Short movies Citi bikes
Watch and enjoy the movie.

G past tenses: simple, continuous, perfect
V sports
P /ɔr/ and /ər/

> Why did he lose the match?
>
> Because he wasn't feeling very well in the last set.

5A Sports superstitions

1 VOCABULARY sports

a Take the quiz in small groups.

SPORTS QUIZ
What sport do you associate with...?

b ▶ p.157 Vocabulary Bank *Sports*.

2 PRONUNCIATION /ɔr/ and /ər/

a Write the words in the correct column. Be careful with *or* (there are two possible pronunciations).

| court | four | girl | hurt | score | serve | shirt |
| sh**or**ts | sp**or**t | w**ar**m up | w**or**ld | w**or**se | w**or**k out |

/ɔr/	/ər/

b (3 6)) Listen and check.

c ▶ p.166 Sound Bank. Look at the typical spellings of these sounds.

d (3 7)) Listen and write six sentences.

3 SPEAKING

In pairs, interview your partner about sports using the questionnaire. Ask for more information.

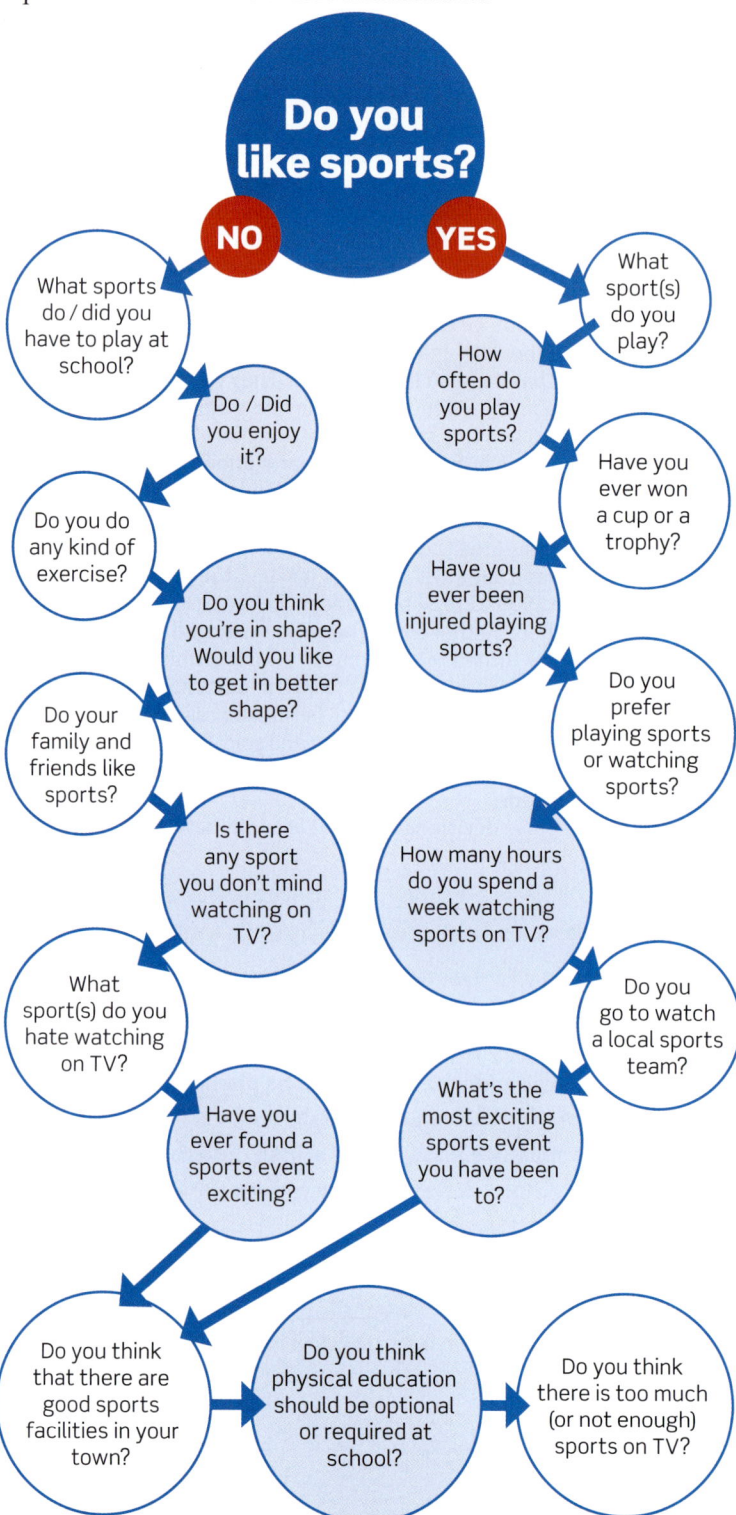

Do you like sports?

NO
- What sports do / did you have to play at school?
- Do / Did you enjoy it?
- Do you do any kind of exercise?
- Do you think you're in shape? Would you like to get in better shape?
- Do your family and friends like sports?
- Is there any sport you don't mind watching on TV?
- What sport(s) do you hate watching on TV?
- Have you ever found a sports event exciting?

YES
- What sport(s) do you play?
- How often do you play sports?
- Have you ever won a cup or a trophy?
- Have you ever been injured playing sports?
- Do you prefer playing sports or watching sports?
- How many hours do you spend a week watching sports on TV?
- Do you go to watch a local sports team?
- What's the most exciting sports event you have been to?

- Do you think that there are good sports facilities in your town?
- Do you think physical education should be optional or required at school?
- Do you think there is too much (or not enough) sports on TV?

4 READING

a Do you know of any sports players who are superstitious? What do they do?

b Read an article about sports superstitions and complete it with **A–F**.

A It is not only the players who are superstitious
B A good example is Serena Williams
C Superstitions and rituals are very common among fans
D After my wife had left the room, Murray lost the fourth set
E The superstitions and rituals are not confined to the court
F ~~Tennis players are strange people~~

c Read the article again. Who does the article say are superstitious: sports players, sports fans, TV spectators, or all of them?

d Underline five words or phrases you want to remember from the article.

e Look at the photos of four more famous sports people who are superstitious. Do you know what any of their superstitions are or were?

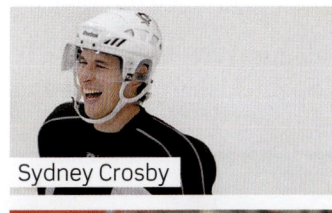

Sydney Crosby
Jason Terry
Kolo Touré
Alexander Wurz

f ▶ **Communication** *Other sports superstitions* **A** *p.104* **B** *p.108*. Read and tell each other about the people in the photos.

g Do *you* have any superstitions, e.g., when you are playing or watching sports, or before an exam?

If I bounce the ball five times…

MATTHEW SYED writes about sports superstitions

1 <u>Tennis players are strange people</u>. Have you noticed how they always ask for three balls instead of two; how they bounce the ball the same number of times before serving, as if any change from their routine might result in disaster?

2 _____, the number 1 female tennis player. When she was once asked why she had played so badly at the French Open she answered, "I didn't tie my shoe laces right, and I didn't bounce the ball five times, and I didn't bring my shower sandals to the court with me. I didn't have my extra dress. I just knew it was fate; it wasn't going to happen."

3 _____. Goran Ivanišević, Wimbledon champion in 2001, was convinced that if he won a match, he had to repeat everything he did the previous day, such as eating the same food at the same restaurant, talking to the same people, and watching the same TV shows. One year this meant that he had to watch *Teletubbies* every morning during his Wimbledon campaign. "Sometimes it got very boring," he said.

4 _____. As we were watching tennis player Andy Murray play the fourth set at Wimbledon, my wife suddenly got up and went to the kitchen. "He keeps losing games when I'm in the room," she said. "If I go out now, he'll win."

5 _____. Last year, a survey of British soccer supporters found that 21 percent had a lucky charm (anything from a scarf to a lucky coin), while another questionnaire revealed that 70 percent of Spanish soccer fans performed pre-match rituals (like wearing "lucky" clothes, eating the same food or drink, or watching games with the same people).

6 _____. She returned, and he won the fifth. I laughed at her, and then remembered my soccer team, Spurs, who were losing 1–0 in the Carling Cup. "If I leave the room now, Spurs will score," I told my kids, after 27 minutes of overtime. I left the room and they scored. Twice.

Glossary
Teletubbies a television series for very young children
Spurs Tottenham Hotspur, a London soccer team

Adapted from The Times

5 LISTENING

a In your country, are referees a) well-paid b) respected c) unpopular? Why do you think somebody would want to become a referee?

b 3 8))) You're going to hear an interview with an ex-Champions League soccer referee from Spain. Listen to **Part 1** and choose a, b, or c.

Juan Antonio Fernandez Marin refereed 200 league and 50 international games

1. Why did he become a referee?
    a His father was a referee.
    b He liked sports, but wasn't good at them.
    c He was always attracted by the idea.
2. What was the most exciting game he ever refereed?
    a His first professional game.
    b He can't choose just one.
    c Real Madrid against Barcelona.
3. The worst experience he ever had as a referee was when _____ attacked him.
    a a player b a woman c a child
4. Why does he think there is more cheating in soccer today?
    a Because soccer is big business.
    b Because the referees are worse.
    c Because soccer players are better at cheating.
5. How does he say soccer players often cheat?
    a They fall over when no one has touched them.
    b They accept money to lose games.
    c They touch the ball with their hands.

c 3 9))) Now listen to **Part 2**. Complete the sentences with one to three words.

1. The most difficult thing for him about being a referee is making _____ during a game.
2. One of the reasons why it's difficult is because soccer today is so _____.
3. Making correct decisions often depends on the referee's interpretation of _____.
4. He thinks that players who cheat are still _____.
5. A study that was done on Leo Messi shows that he can run exceptionally fast _____.
6. He thinks Messi isn't the _____ soccer player.

d Do you agree with the referee that there is more cheating in soccer than before? Is it true in other sports as well? Would *you* like to be a sports referee (or umpire)? Why (not)?

6 GRAMMAR past tenses: simple, continuous, perfect

a In your country, is cheating considered a serious problem in sports? In what sports do you think cheating is most common? What kinds of things do people do when they cheat?

b Read *Taking a Short Cut* about a marathon runner who cheated. How did she cheat?

c Look at the highlighted verbs in the text. Which of them are used for...?

1. a completed action in the past
2. an action that happened *before* the past time we are talking about
3. an action in progress (or not) at a particular moment in the past

d ▶ p.140 Grammar Bank 5A. Learn more about past tenses and practice them.

e Read *The Hand of God?* and complete it with the verbs in the right tenses.

Famous (cheating) moments in sports

Although it isn't true that everybody in sports cheats, it is certainly true that there are cheaters in every sport...

Taking a short cut

On April 21, 1980, 23-year-old Rosie Ruiz *was* the first woman to cross the finish line at the Boston Marathon. She *finished* the race in the third-fastest time for a female runner (two hours, 31 minutes, 56 seconds). But when the organizers congratulated Rosie after the race, they were surprised because she *wasn't sweating* very much. Some spectators who were watching the race told them what *had* really *happened*. During the last half mile, Rosie suddenly jumped out of the crowd and sprinted to the finish line. The marathon organizers took Ruiz's title away and awarded it to the real winner, Jacqueline Gareau. It was later discovered that three months earlier, Rosie *had also cheated* in the New York City Marathon where she *had taken* the subway!

The hand of God?

It was June 22, 1986. Argentina ¹*was playing* (play) England in the quarter-finals of the World Cup, and both teams ² _____ (play) well. The score ³ _____ (be) 0–0. In the 51st minute, the Argentinian captain, Diego Maradona, ⁴ _____ (score) a goal. The English players ⁵ _____ (protest), but the referee ⁶ _____ (give) the goal. However, TV cameras showed that Maradona ⁷ _____ (score) the goal with his hand! Maradona ⁸ _____ (say) the next day, "It was partly the hand of Maradona, and partly the hand of God."

Later in the game, Maradona ⁹ _____ (score) another goal, and Argentina ¹⁰ _____ (win) the game 2–1. They went on to win the World Cup.

7 SPEAKING

a You are going to tell your partner two anecdotes. Choose two of the topics below and plan what you are going to say. Ask your teacher for any words you need.

TELL YOUR PARTNER ABOUT...

- **a time you cheated (in a sport / game or on an exam)**
  When and where did this happen? What were you doing? Why did you cheat? What happened in the end?

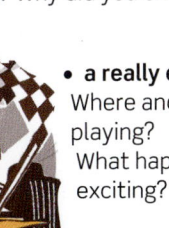

- **a really exciting sports event you saw**
  Where and when was it? Who was playing? What happened? Why was it so exciting?

- **a time you had an accident or got a sports injury**
  When and where did this happen? What were you doing? How did the accident happen? What part of your body did you hurt? What happened next? How long did it take you to recover?

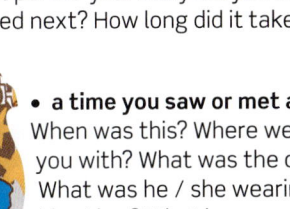

- **a time you saw or met a celebrity**
  When was this? Where were you? Who were you with? What was the celebrity doing? What was he / she wearing? Did you speak to him / her? What happened in the end?

- **a time you got lost**
  Where were you going? How were you traveling? Why did you get lost? What happened in the end?

b Work with a partner. Tell each other your two stories. Give as much detail as you can.

> **Starting an anecdote**
> I'm going to tell you about a time when...
> This happened a few years ago...
> When I was younger...

8 WRITING

▶ p.116 Writing *Telling a story*. Write a story about something that happened to you.

9 ⏵ 3 14 ⏴)) SONG *We Are the Champions* ♪

5A

G usually and used to
V relationships
P linking, the letter s

5B Love at Exit 19

> How do you usually get to work?
>
> I used to take the bus, but now I ride my bike.

1 READING

a How do you think people usually meet friends and partners nowadays? Number the phrases 1–5 (1 = the most popular). Then compare with a partner. Do you agree?

- A [2] at work
- B [3] at school or college
- C [1] on the Internet (e.g., on forums, on social networking sites, etc.)
- D [5] in a cafe, club, etc.
- E [4] through friends

b 3 15)) Read and listen to an article about Sonya Baker and Michael Fazio. Why did their relationship almost never happen?

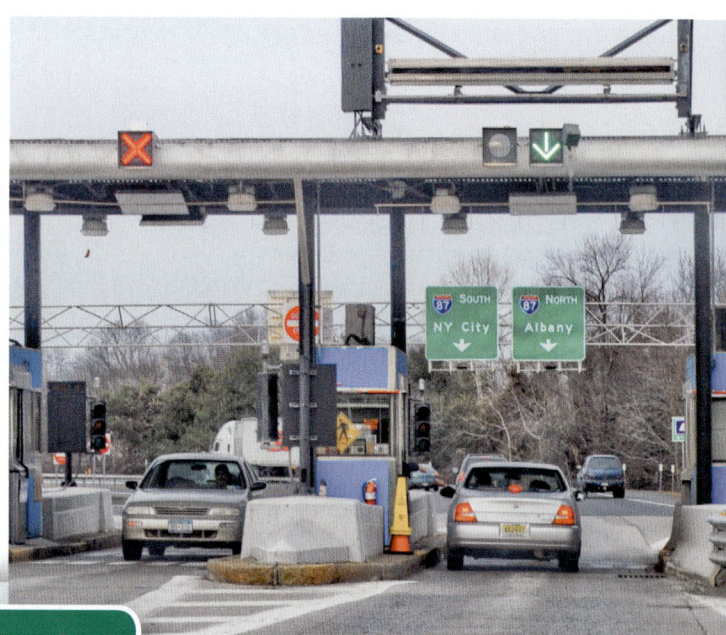

♥ Love at Exit 19

He was a tollbooth collector, and she was a soprano who sang in Carnegie Hall. Their eyes met at Exit 19 of the New York State Thruway, when he charged her 37¢. The romance that followed was even less likely than the plot of an opera!

Sonya Baker was a frequent commuter from her home in the suburbs to New York City. One day, when she was driving to an audition, she came off the Thruway and stopped at the tollbooth where Michael Fazio was working. She talked with him as she paid to go through, and thought he was cute. For the next three months, they used to exchange a few words as she handed him the money, and he raised the barrier to let her pass. "It was mostly 'What are you doing today? Where are you going?'" she said. They learned more about each other, for example that Sonya loved Puccini and Verdi, while Michael's love was the New York Yankees. But their conversations suddenly came to an end when Michael changed his working hours. "He used to work during the day," said Sonya, "but he changed to night shifts." Although Michael still looked out for Sonya's white Toyota Corolla, he did not see her again for six months.

When Michael's working hours changed back to the day shift, he decided to put a traffic cone in front of his lane. He thought, "It will be like putting a candle in a window." Sonya saw it, and their romance started up again. "I almost crashed my car on various occasions," she said, "trying to cross several lanes to get to his exit." Finally, she found the courage to give Michael a piece of paper with her phone number as she passed through the toll. Michael called her and for their first date they went to see the movie *Cool Runnings*, and then later they went to an opera, *La Bohème*, and to a Yankees game.

They are now married and living in Kentucky, where Sonya is a voice and music professor at Murray State College and Michael runs an activity center at a nursing home. It turned out that she had given him her number just in time. A short while later, she moved to New Jersey and stopped using the New York State Thruway. "I might never have seen him again," she said.

Glossary
a tollbooth a small building by the side of a road where you pay money to use the road
Carnegie Hall a famous concert hall in New York City
New York State Thruway a road
New York Yankees a baseball team based in the Bronx in New York City
a traffic cone a plastic object, often orange and white, used to show where vehicles can or can't go

Adapted from The Times

c Read the article again and number the events in the order they happened.

A [2] Michael changed his working hours.
B [5] Michael tried to find Sonya.
C [9] They got married.
D [8] Sonya moved to New Jersey.
E [6] Sonya gave Michael her phone number.
F [4] Michael changed his working hours again.
G [1] Sonya talked with Michael.
H [3] They stopped seeing each other.
I [7] They had their first date.
J [10] Sonya and Michael moved to Kentucky.

d Read the article again and look at the highlighted words and phrases. Try to figure out what they mean. Then match them with 1–10 below.

1 shift _____ a period of time worked by a group of workers
2 commuter _____ a person who travels into a city to work every day
3 cute _____ attractive, good-looking
4 it turned out _____ what had happened was
5 runs _____ manages
6 likely _____ probable
7 candle _____ something that is used to give light, made of wax
8 exchange a few words _____ have short conversations
9 _____ they looked at each other romantically
10 _____ was brave enough

2 GRAMMAR usually and used to

a Think of a couple you know well, e.g., your parents or friends. How did they meet? Do you know any couples who met under unusual circumstances?

b ▶3 16))) Listen to four people talking about where they met their partner. Match each one with a place from **1a**.

Speaker 1 ☐   Speaker 2 ☐   Speaker 3 ☐   Speaker 4 ☐

c Listen to each story again and take notes on how the people met. Compare your notes with your partner and listen again if necessary. Which meeting do you think was the most romantic?

d Look at two extracts from the listening. Answer the questions with a partner.

> We used to go to clubs together on Saturday night.
> It used to be difficult to meet people.

1 When do we use *used to*? How do you make negatives and questions?
2 How would you change these sentences (using *usually*) if you wanted to talk about present habits or situations?

e ▶ p.141 **Grammar Bank 5B**. Learn more about *usually* and *used to*, and practice them.

3 PRONUNCIATION & SPEAKING linking

> 🔍 **used to**
> Remember that *used to* and *use to* are usually linked and pronounced /ˈyustə/.

a ▶3 18))) Listen and repeat the sentences. Copy the linking and the sentence rhythm.

1 I **used** to **live** in Los Angeles.
2 She **didn't use** to **wear** glasses.
3 **Where** did you **use** to **work** before?
4 They **used** to **see** each **other** a lot.
5 **Didn't** you **use** to **have** a beard?

b In pairs, tell each other about *three* of the following. Give as much information as you can. How do you feel about these people and things now?

Is there...

- a kind of **food** or **drink** you didn't use to like at all, but that you now like?
- a **TV series** you used to be addicted to? Why did you like it?
- a **singer** or a **kind of music** you used to listen to a lot (but don't anymore)?
- a **sport** or **game** you used to play a lot, but that you've given up?
- a **place** you used to go during summer vacation, and that you'd like to go back to?
- a **machine** or **gadget** you used to use a lot, but that is now out of date?

I used to hate most vegetables, especially spinach and cauliflower, but now I love them and usually eat a lot of vegetables every day...

4 VOCABULARY relationships

a Explain the difference between these pairs of phrases.
1 to meet somebody and to know somebody
2 a colleague and a friend
3 to argue with somebody and to discuss something with somebody

b ▶ p.158 **Vocabulary Bank** *Relationships*.

c Think of one of your close friends. In pairs, ask and answer the questions.

- How long have you known him / her?
- Where did you meet?
- Why do you get along well?
- What do you have in common?
- Do you ever argue? What about?
- How often do you see each other?
- How do you keep in touch?
- Have you ever lost touch? Why? When?
- Do you think you'll stay friends?

5 PRONUNCIATION
the letter s

a **3 21))** Listen to the words in the list. How is the *s* (or *se*) pronounced? Write them in the correct columns.

| busy   close (*adj*)   close (*verb*)   conversation   decision |
| discuss   eyes   friends   lose   music   pleasure |
| promise   raise   school   somebody   sport   sugar |
| summer   sure   unusual   used to   usually   various |

s	z	ʃ	ʒ

b **3 22))** Listen and check.

c Answer with a partner.
1 How is *s* usually pronounced at the beginning of a word? What are the two exceptions?
2 What two ways can *s* (or *es*) be pronounced at the end of a word?
3 How is *s* pronounced in *-sion*?

6 LISTENING

a Talk to a partner. Do you think the following are **T** (true) or **F** (false)?
1 22-year-olds have an average of 1,000 friends.
2 Men have more online friends than women.
3 People who spend a lot of time on Facebook become more dissatisfied with their own lives.

b 3 23))) Listen to the introduction to a radio program. According to research, are 1–3 in **a** true or false?

c 3 24))) Listen to four people who call the program, Young, Beth, Emma, and Ned. Who is the most positive about Facebook? Who is the most negative?

d Listen again. Answer with **Y**oung, **B**eth, **E**mma, or **N**ed.

Which caller…?
1 ☐ does not want to share personal information with strangers
2 ☐ has fewer Facebook friends than he / she used to have
3 ☐ has over a thousand friends
4 ☐ uses it to keep in touch with friends who don't live close by
5 ☐ thinks people use Facebook to give themselves more importance
6 ☐ used to use Facebook more than he / she does now
7 ☐ uses Facebook instead of calling
8 ☐ does not use social networking sites

e Do you use Facebook or any other social networking sites? Do you agree with anything the speakers said?

7 SPEAKING

a Read sentences **A–F** below. Check (✓) the ones you agree with and put an ✗ next to the ones you don't agree with. Think about your reasons.

A ☐ You can only have two or three close friends.
B ☐ Nowadays people are in touch with more people but have fewer close friends.
C ☐ Men keep their friends longer than women.
D ☐ You should never criticize your friend's partner.
E ☐ You should never lend money to a friend (or borrow money).
F ☐ It's impossible to stay good friends with an ex-partner.

b In groups, compare opinions. Try to give real examples from your own experience or of people you know. Use the phrases below to help you.

> 🔍 **Giving examples**
> **For example**, I have a friend who I've known since I was five years old…
> **For instance**, I once lent some money to a cousin…

Practical English Old friends

EPISODE 3

1 VIDEO JENNY HAS COFFEE WITH A FRIEND

a (3 25) Watch or listen to Jenny and Monica. What's Monica's news?

b Watch or listen again and answer the questions.
1 Who's Scott?
2 When did they get engaged?
3 Who has Monica told the news to?
4 What did she use to do a lot at night? What does she do now?
5 Who's going to organize the wedding?
6 What does Jenny tell Monica about her relationship with Rob?
7 What does Monica think about Rob being British?

2 VIDEO PERMISSION AND REQUESTS

a (3 26) Watch or listen. What two favors does Rob ask Jenny?

b Watch or listen again. Mark the sentences **T** (true) or **F** (false). Correct the **F** sentences.
1 Rob orders a cappuccino. F
2 Rob says Monica looks different from her photos. F
3 Monica gets a good impression of Rob. T
4 Monica leaves because she has to go to work. F
5 Jenny says that most of their friends are in serious relationships. T
6 Paul is going to stay for two weeks. F
7 Paul used to be very quiet when they were younger. F
8 Jenny is excited to meet Paul. T

c **3 27** Look at some extracts from the conversation. Can you remember any of the missing words? Watch or listen and check.

Asking permission

1 Rob   Do you _mind_ if I join you?
  Monica Of _course_ not. Come on, sit down.

2 Rob   Is it _____ if we change our plans a bit this week?
  Jenny Uh...sure.

Requests: asking someone to do something

1 Rob   _Can_ you pass the sugar?
  Jenny _Sure_.

2 Rob   Could you do me a big _favor_? I have to work late this evening, so… would you mind _to meet_ him at the airport?
  Jenny _____ at all. I'd like to meet him.

3 Rob   And do you think you _____ take him to my flat? I'll give you the keys.
  Jenny No _problem_, Rob.

d Look at the highlighted phrases and answer the questions.
  1 How do you respond to *Do you mind if…?* and *Would you mind…?* when you mean *OK, no problem*?
  2 Which two forms of request should you use if you want to be very polite or are asking a very big favor?

e **3 28** Watch or listen and repeat the highlighted phrases. Copy the rhythm and intonation.

f Practice the dialogues in **c** with a partner.

g ▶ **Communication** *Could you do me a favor?* p.105.

3 PAUL ARRIVES

a **3 29** Watch or listen. How do Rob and Jenny feel about Paul's arrival?

b Watch or listen again and circle the right answer.
  1 Paul's appearance *has changed a lot / hasn't changed much*.
  2 His flight was *on time / late*.
  3 On the trip from the airport Paul *talked a lot about himself / asked Jenny a lot of personal questions*.
  4 Rob suggests *eating in / eating out*.
  5 Paul feels *exhausted / full of energy*.
  6 Jenny *feels like / doesn't feel like* going out.

c Look at the **Social English phrases**. Can you remember any of the missing words?

Social English phrases	
Paul	Hey _____!
Paul	It's _____ to see you, mate.
Rob	How _____ you're so late?
Paul	No _____, man!
Jenny	Rob, I think I'll go home if you don't_____.
Rob	Just like the old _____!
Paul	Rob, we've got a lot to talk _____!

d **3 30** Watch or listen and complete the phrases.

e Watch or listen again and repeat the phrases. How do you say them in your language?

Can you…?
- ☐ use different expressions to ask permission to do something and respond
- ☐ use different expressions to ask another person to do something and respond
- ☐ greet someone you haven't seen for a long time

Communication

PE1 HOW AWFUL! HOW FANTASTIC! Student A

a Read your sentences 1–9 to **B**. **B** must react with a phrase, e.g., *You're kidding, Oh, no!*, etc.

1. I collect funny salt-and-pepper shakers.
2. I spilled some coffee on my laptop last night, and now it doesn't work.
3. I'm going to New York City next weekend.
4. Someone stole my bike yesterday.
5. My dog can open the kitchen door by itself.
6. My father's going to be interviewed on TV tomorrow.
7. My grandmother just bought a sports car.
8. My parents met when they were only 15.
9. I just won $2,000 in the lottery!

b Listen to **B**'s sentences and react with a phrase.

c Tell **B** some real (or invented) news about you for **B** to react. React to **B**'s news.

5A OTHER SPORTS SUPERSTITIONS Student A

a Read about Sydney Crosby and Kolo Touré.

> **SIDNEY CROSBY** never calls his mother on a game day, even if it's her birthday. He believes that he gets injured on the days he calls his mother before a game.
>
> When **KOLO TOURÉ** played for Arsenal, he always insisted on being the last player to leave the dressing room after the half-time break. This was never usually a problem. However, in one game when William Gallas, his teammate, was injured and needed treatment at half-time during a match, Touré stayed in the dressing room until Gallas had been treated. This meant that Arsenal had to start the second half with only nine players.

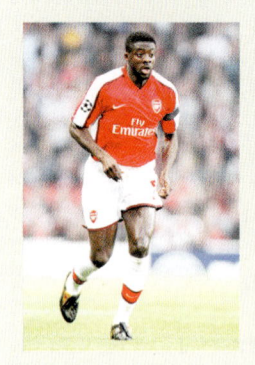

b Now cover the text and tell **B** about their superstitions from memory.

c Listen to **B** telling you about Jason Terry and Alexander Wurz's superstitions.

d Together decide which superstition you think is a) the strangest b) the most impractical.

2B ARE YOU HUNGRY? Student A

a Ask **B** your questions. He / She responds with the phrase in parentheses.

1. Is the water cold? (Yes, it's **freezing**.)
2. Was the movie good? (Yes, it was **fantastic**.)
3. Were you tired after the exam? (Yes, I was **exhausted**.)
4. Was the room dirty? (Yes, it was **filthy**.)
5. Is it a big house? (Yes, it's **enormous**.)
6. Were you surprised? (Yes, I was **amazed**.)
7. Are you sure? (Yes, I'm **positive**.)

b Respond to **B**'s questions. Say *Yes, it's… / I'm…*, etc. + the strong form of the adjective that **B** used in the question. Remember to stress the strong adjective.

Are you afraid of flying? — *Yes, I'm terrified.*

c Repeat the exercise. Try to respond as quickly as possible.

3A I'M A TOURIST – CAN YOU HELP ME? Student A

a Think of the town / city where you are, or the nearest big town. You are a foreign tourist, and you are planning to get around using public transportation. Ask **B** questions 1–5. Get as much information from **B** as you can.

1. What kind of public transportation is there?
2. What's the best way for me to get around the city?
3. Can I rent a bike? Are there any bicycle lanes?
4. Is it easy to find taxis? How expensive are they?
5. What's the best way to get to the airport from the center of town? How long does it take?

b Switch roles. **B** is a foreign tourist in the town who has rented a car. You live in the town. Answer **B**'s questions and give as much information as you can.

4A GUESS THE SENTENCE Student A

a Look at sentences 1–6 and think of the correct form of *be able to* + a verb. **Don't write anything yet!**

1 I'm sorry I won't _____ to your party next weekend.
2 It was August, but we _____ a hotel without any problems.
3 I used to _____ a little Japanese, but I can't now.
4 I love _____ in bed late on the weekend.
5 Will you _____ the work before Saturday?
6 I've never _____ fish well.

b Read your sentence 1 to **B**. If it isn't right, try again until **B** tells you, "That's right." Then write it. Continue with 2–6.

c Now listen to **B** say sentence 7. If it's the same as your sentence 7 below, say "That's right." If not, say "Try again" until **B** gets it right. Continue with 8–12.

7 It must be great to **be able to speak** a lot of languages.
8 I won't **be able to see** you tonight. I'm too busy.
9 My grandmother can't walk very well, but luckily we **were able to park** just outside the restaurant.
10 They haven't **been able to find** an apartment yet. They're still looking.
11 You should **be able to do** this exercise. It's very easy.
12 We really enjoy **being able to eat** outside in the summer.

PE3 COULD YOU DO ME A FAVOR?
Students A+B

a Look at the verb phrases below. Choose two things you would like somebody to do for you. Think about any details, e.g., what kind of dog it is, how much money you need, etc.

- **take care of** (your children, your dog for the weekend, your apartment while you're away, etc.)
- **lend you** (some money, their car, etc.)
- **give you a ride** (home, to the mall, etc.)
- **help you** (with a problem, with your homework, to paint your apartment, to choose some new clothes, etc.)

b Ask as many other students as possible. Be polite (*Could you do me a big favor? Would you mind…? Do you think you could…?*) and explain why you want the favor. How many people agree to help you?

4B THE BIG DAY Students A+B

Read a newspaper article about what happened at Heidi and Freddie's wedding. Do you think they behaved well or badly? Why?

News online

Two sides to every story
What happened next…

By **NEWS ONLINE Reporter**

Yesterday Heidi Withers married Freddie Bourne in a $40,000 ceremony at St. Mary the Virgin Church. It was followed by a reception at a 900-year-old castle. However, there was no sign of Carolyn, Freddie's stepmother, the woman who was ridiculed for the email she sent Heidi. She and her husband Edward, Freddie's father, were not invited.

Heidi arrived almost 25 minutes late for the ceremony, which was due to begin at 2:45 p.m. Perhaps, as Carolyn suggested was her habit, she had been in bed until the last possible minute. She arrived at the church with security guards holding umbrellas to prevent onlookers from seeing her, and with her head covered. This is a well-known tactic for celebrities, but for a 29-year-old secretary it seemed, in the words of one onlooker, "a bit ridiculous."

Edward and Carolyn admitted to being disappointed at not receiving an invitation. They spent the weekend on vacation with friends. They have had no contact with the couple since the saga began, and did not even know the date of the wedding.

Communication

5A OTHER SPORTS SUPERSTITIONS
Student B

a   Read about Jason Terry and Alexander Wurz.

JASON TERRY, an American basketball player, wears the colors of his team's opponents the night before a game. If the team he's playing the next day wears black and white, then Terry wears black and white to bed the night before. He's been doing this since his playing days in college.

ALEXANDER WURZ, an Austrian racing driver, used to race with odd-colored shoes, the left one red and the right one blue. It came about when he lost a shoe before a big race and had to borrow one of a different color. After winning the race, he decided it was a lucky omen.

b   Now listen to **A** telling you about Sydney Crosby and Kolo Touré's superstitions.

c   Cover the text and tell **B** about Jason Terry and Alexander Wurz's superstitions from memory.

d   Together decide which superstition you think is a) the strangest b) the most impractical.

1B PERSONALITY   Students A+B

Read the explanation and compare with a partner. Do you agree with your results?

> The activity you have just done is a personality test. The first adjective you wrote down is how you see yourself, the second is how other people see you, and the third is what you are really like.

2A SPENDER OR SAVER?   Students A+B

Check your results. Then compare with a partner. Do you agree with your results?

Mostly a answers
You can't be trusted with your own money! You definitely need someone to help you to manage your finances better. Why not speak to an organized friend about how to plan? This will help you to make your money go further and stop you from getting into debt.

Mostly b answers
Although you understand how to manage your money, sometimes you need to be a little more organized. Try setting yourself a weekly or monthly budget, and then stick to it. You will then know how much money you have, what you spend it on, and how much you can save.

Mostly c answers
Congratulations! It sounds like you really know what you are doing when it comes to managing your money. You know how important it is to keep track of your spending and are responsible with your money.

PE1 HOW AWFUL! HOW FANTASTIC! Student B

a Listen to **A**'s sentences and react with a phrase, e.g., *You're kidding, Oh, no!*, etc.

b Read your sentences 1–9 for **A** to react.
1 I failed my driving test yesterday.
2 I lost my wallet on the way to class.
3 I met George Clooney at a party last week.
4 I think I saw a ghost last night.
5 I won a salsa competition last weekend.
6 I'm going to be on a new edition of *Big Brother*.
7 My dog died yesterday.
8 My grandfather has a black belt in karate.
9 My uncle is 104.

c Tell **A** some real (or invented) news about you for **A** to react. React to **A**'s news.

2B ARE YOU HUNGRY? Student B

a Respond to **A**'s questions. Say *Yes, it's… / I'm…*, etc. + the strong form of the adjective that **A** used in the question. Remember to stress the strong adjective.

Is the water cold?) (*Yes, it's freezing.*

b Ask **A** your questions. He / She responds with the phrase in parentheses.

1 Are you afraid of flying? (Yes, I'm **terrified**.)
2 Is the soup hot? (Yes, it's **boiling**.)
3 Was the teacher angry? (Yes, he / she was **furious**.)
4 Is the bedroom small? (Yes, it's **tiny**.)
5 Are the children hungry? (Yes, they're **starving**.)
6 Is the chocolate cake good? (Yes, it's **delicious**.)
7 Was she happy with the present? (Yes, she was **excited**.)

c Repeat the exercise. Try to respond as quickly as possible.

3A I'M A TOURIST – CAN YOU HELP ME? Student B

a Think of the town / city where you are, or the nearest big town. **A** is a foreign tourist who is planning to get around using public transportation. You live in the town. Answer **A**'s questions and give as much information as you can.

b Switch roles. You are a foreign tourist in the town. You have rented a car. Ask **A** questions 1–5. Get as much information from **A** as you can.

1 What time is rush hour in this town?
2 Where are there usually traffic jams?
3 What's the speed limit in the town? Are there speed cameras anywhere?
4 What will happen if I park somewhere illegal?
5 Where's the nearest tourist attraction outside the city? How long does it take to drive there from here?

4A GUESS THE SENTENCE Student B

a Look at sentences 7–12 and think of the correct form of *be able to* + a base form verb. **Don't write anything yet!**

7 It must be great to _____ a lot of languages.
8 I won't _____ you tonight. I'm too busy.
9 My grandmother can't walk very well, but luckily we _____ just outside the restaurant.
10 They haven't _____ an apartment yet. They're still looking.
11 You should _____ this exercise. It's very easy.
12 We really enjoy _____ outside in the summer.

b Now listen to **A** say sentence 1. If it's the same as your sentence 1 below, say "That's right." If not, say "Try again" until **A** gets it right. Continue with 2–6.

1 I'm sorry I won't **be able to come** to your party next weekend.
2 It was August, but we **were able to find** a hotel without any problems.
3 I used to **be able to understand** a little Japanese, but I can't now.
4 I love **being able to stay** in bed late on the weekend.
5 Will you **be able to finish** the work before Saturday?
6 I've never **been able to cook** fish well.

c Read your sentence 7 to **A**. If it isn't right, try again until **A** tells you, "That's right." Then write it. Continue with 8–12.

Writing

1 A DESCRIPTION OF A PERSON

a Read the two Facebook messages once and answer the questions.

1. Why has Angela written to Sofia?
2. Does Sofia recommend her friend to Angela?

Messages + New Message

Angela Vernon

Hi Sofia,

I hope you're well.

I'm looking for an au pair to look after Austin and Melissa, and I remembered your Peruvian friend Marisol, who I met last summer. She said she might be interested in working in the US as an au pair, so I thought I would write and ask her. The thing is, I don't really know her, so before I write and suggest it, could you tell me a little about her (age, personality, etc., and what she likes doing) so that I can see if she would fit in with the family? Please be honest!

Angela

Sofia Lugo

Hi Angela,

Marisol is one of my best friends, so of course I know her *very* well. She's 22, and she just graduated from college with a degree in economics, but she doesn't have a job yet, and I'm sure she would be interested in going to the US. Her parents are both doctors, and she has two younger brothers. She gets along very well with them, and they are a very close family.

Marisol's an intelligent girl and very hardworking. She can be *really* shy at first, but when she gets to know you she's *incredibly* friendly. She loves children – she often takes care of her brothers – so she has a lot of experience, and she's also very responsable.

In her free time she likes going to the movies, listening to music, and she's also very good at fotography – she always has her camera with her. She's *really* independant and happy to do things on her own, so you won't have to worry about taking her to places.

The only problem with Marisol is that she's *a little* forgetfull... she sometimes loses things, like her keys, or her phone. Also, to be honest her English isn't great, but I'm sure she'll improve very quickly. I think Austin and Melissa will love her.

I hope this helps! Let me know if you need anything else.

Love,

Sofia

b The computer has found five spelling mistakes in Sofia's email. Can you correct them?

c Read both emails again. Then cover them and answer the questions from memory.

1. What five + adjectives describe Marisol's personality?
2. What does she like doing in her free time?
3. What negative things does Sofia say about Marisol?
4. Does Sofia think Marisol will get along with Angela's family?

d Look at the highlighted expressions we use to modify adjectives. Put them in the correct place in the chart.

Marisol is _____ / _____ / *very* / _____ forgetful.

> **Useful language: describing a person**
> He's *really* / *very*, etc. + positive adjective (e.g., *friendly*, *outgoing*, etc.)
> She's *a little* + negative adjective (e.g., *messy*, *shy*, etc.)
> He likes / loves / doesn't mind + verb + -ing
> She's happy to + base form
> He's good | **with** children
> | **at** making new friends

e Imagine you received Angela's message asking about a friend of yours. **Write** an email to answer it. **Plan** what you're going to write using the paragraph headings below. Use the **Useful language** box and **Vocabulary Bank** *Personality p.153* to help you.

Paragraph 1	age, family, work / study
Paragraph 2	personality (good side)
Paragraph 3	hobbies and interests
Paragraph 4	any negative things?

f **Check** your email for mistakes (grammar, vocabulary, punctuation, and spelling).

◀ p.11

2 AN INFORMAL EMAIL

a Marisol went to the US and stayed for six months with a couple, Angela and Matt, working as an au pair. After going back to Peru, she sent them an email. Look at the list of things she says in her email. Number them in a logical order 1–6.

- [ ] She promises to send some photos.
- [ ] She thanks them for her stay and says how much she enjoyed it.
- [ ] She talks about what she's been doing recently.
- [ ] She apologizes for not writing before.
- [ ] She thanks them again and invites them to stay.
- [ ] She talks about the nice things that happened when she was with them.

b Now read Marisol's email and check your answers to **a**.

c Correct eight mistakes in the email (grammar, vocabulary, punctuation, and spelling.)

> **Useful language: informal emails**
>
> **Beginnings**
> *Hi* + name (or *Dear* + name if you want to be a little more formal)
> *Sorry for not writing sooner, but...*
> *Thank you / Thanks (so much) for (your letter, having me to stay, etc.)...*
> *It was great to hear from you...*
>
> **Endings**
> *That's all for now.*
> *Hope to hear from you soon. / Looking forward to hearing from you soon.*
> *(Give my) regards / love to...*
> *Best wishes / Love (from)*
> *P.S. (when you want to add a short message at the end of an email) I've attached a photo...*

d Imagine you have some American friends in the US, and you stayed with them for a week last month. **Write** an email to say thank you. **Plan** what you're going to say. Use 1–6 in **a** and the **Useful language** box to help you.

e **Check** your email for mistakes (grammar, vocabulary, punctuation, and spelling).

◀ p.21

From: Marisol [marisol_new@gmail.com]
To: Angela [angelav1970@yahoo.com]
Subject: Thanks

Hi Angela,

I'm really sorry for not writing sooner, but I am very busy since I got back!

Thanks for a wonderful six months. I loved being in Colorado, and I had a great time. I also think my english got a little better... dont you think?

It was so nice to take care of Austin and Melissa. I thought they were adorable, and I think we had a fantastic time together. I have really good memories – for example our travel to Denver and the amusement park there!

I've been a little stressed these last few weeks, because I've started working at a restaurant, while I look for a full-time job. Be a waitress is very hard work, but I can now afford to rent an apartment with Sofia and two other friends, and I'm saving for to buy a car! I've also spent a lot of time with my family – my brothers have changed so much over the past six months!

I've had several mesages from Austin and Melissa since I've been back! Please tell them from me that I miss them and that I send them some photos very soon.

That's all for now. Thanks again for everything. And I hope you know you're welcome in Lima any time – my family would love to meet you. Summer here is usually beautiful.

Hope to hear from you soon. Give my regards to Matt!

Best wishes,

Marisol

P.S. I've attached a photo I took of me with the kids. I hope you like it!

Writing

3 AN ARTICLE FOR A MAGAZINE

a Look at the four forms of public transportation in New York City. Which one do you think is probably…?

- the least expensive
- the healthiest
- the best if you want to see the sights of New York City
- the safest to use at night

subway · double-decker bus · bike · taxi

b Read an article from an online magazine for foreign students about public transportation in New York City and check your answers to **a**. Then answer these questions from memory.

1. What can you use a MetroCard for?
2. What kind of money do you have to use if you want to pay cash to ride a New York City bus?
3. What's the difference between a taxi and car service?

c Read the article again and fill in the blanks with a preposition from the list.

around   at   in   next to   on (x2)   on the top of   with

> **Useful language: transportation in your town**
> You can buy MetroCards at many places in New York City.
> You need a ticket or card before you get on the subway.
> (*You* = people in general)
>
> **Comparatives and superlatives:**
> Buses aren't as quick as trains.
> Riding a bike is the cheapest way to get around.

d Write an article about transportation in your nearest town or city for foreign students. **Plan** what headings you're going to use and what to say about each form of transportation.

e Check your article for mistakes (grammar, vocabulary, punctuation, and spelling).

◀ p.27

Transportation in New York City

The Subway This is the quickest way to get [1]*around* the city, and there are many subway stations all over New York City. The cheapest way to use the subway is to get a MetroCard. This is like a phone card. You put money on it, and you can add more when you need to. Then you use it every time you get [2]_____ the subway. You can buy MetroCards at subway stations, newsstands, and even from your employer.

Buses They can be quicker than the subway if there isn't too much traffic. The easiest way to use the buses, like the subway, is to just use your MetroCard. You can buy a single-ride ticket from machines [3]_____ some, but not all bus stops. You can also pay cash (but no pennies and no paper money) when you get [4]_____ the bus. Traveling [5]_____ a private double-decker bus is also a good way to see New York City.

Bikes Bikes are starting to become more popular in New York City, especially [6]_____ tourists and people who want to travel to parts of the city, like the waterfront areas, where subways don't usually go. One of the newest bike-share programs is called Citi Bike. When you rent a bike from Citi Bike, you get a key that looks like a flash drive. You can use the key at any Citi Bike kiosk and get a bike to ride for the day.

Taxis and Car Service New York City's yellow taxis are expensive, but they are comfortable, and the taxi drivers know shortcuts through the city to get you to places quickly. You usually tell the driver where you want to go when you get [7]_____ the taxi. Car service is made up of normal cars that work for a company, and you have to call them ahead of time to pick you up. They are more expensive than taxis. Taxis and car service are probably the safest way to travel late [8]_____ night.

4 TELLING A STORY

a A magazine asked its readers to send in stories of a time they got lost. Read the story once. Why did Bethany and her husband get lost? What else went wrong?

b Read the story again and complete it with a connecting word or phrase from the list.

| although | as soon as | because | but |
| instead of | so | ~~then~~ | when |

> **Useful language: getting lost**
> We were going in the wrong direction.
> We took the wrong exit / turn.
> We turned right instead of left.
> We didn't know where we were.
> We had to turn around and go back in the opposite direction.

c **Write** about a trip where you got lost (or invent one) to send to the magazine. **Plan** what you're going to write using the paragraph headings below. Use the **Useful language** to help you.

Paragraph 1	When was the journey? Where were you going? Who with? Why?
Paragraph 2	How did you get lost? What happened?
Paragraph 3	What happened in the end?

d **Check** your story for mistakes (grammar, vocabulary, punctuation, and spelling).

◀ p.47

DISASTROUS TRIPS!

We asked you to tell us about a time you got lost. **Bethany** from the US wrote to us...

This happened a few years ago. My husband and I had rented a house in Galicia for a summer vacation. We were going to first drive to Tarragona, to stay for a few days with some friends, and ¹ _then_ drive from Tarragona to Galicia.

The first part of the trip was fine. We were using our new GPS for the first time, and it took us right to the door of our friends' house. Three days later, ² _____ we continued our trip, we put in the name of the small town in Galicia, Nigrán, which was our final destination. We started off, obediently following the instructions, but after a while we realized that ³ _____ driving west toward Lérida, we were going north. In fact, soon we were very close to Andorra. I was sure we were going in the wrong direction, ⁴ _____ my husband wanted to do what the GPS was telling us – it was his new toy! It was only when we started seeing mountains that even he admitted this couldn't be the right way. ⁵ _____ we stopped, got out an old map, and then turned around! We had wasted almost two hours going in the wrong direction!

It was an awful trip ⁶ _____ as well as getting lost, when we were almost at our destination we had another problem. We stopped for a coffee, but ⁷ _____ we got back onto the road, we realized that we had left our dog under the table in the cafe! For the second time that day we had to turn around and go back. Luckily, the dog was still there! However, ⁸ _____ the beginning of our trip was a disaster, we had a wonderful vacation!

Listening

1 6))

A I usually have meat or seafood. Usually shrimp or something as an appetizer and then maybe lamb for the main course.

B I often have ready-made vegetable soups that you just have to heat up – in fact, they're the only vegetables I ever eat! And I usually have a couple of frozen pizzas in the freezer for emergencies. I don't really order take-out when I'm on my own, but if I'm with friends in the evening, we sometimes order Chinese food for dinner.

C Eggs and soda. I have eggs for breakfast at least twice a week, and I drink a couple of cans of soda every day.

D If I'm feeling down, chicken soup, with nice big pieces of chicken in it. It's warm and comforting. Uh, I usually have a banana before going to the gym. If I know I'm going to have a really long meeting, I usually have a coffee and a cupcake because I think it will keep me awake and give me energy.

E Fruit – cherries, strawberries, raspberries, and apples. Vegetables – peppers, tomatoes, and cucumbers. The only thing I really don't like is zucchini. I can't even stand the smell of it.

1 7))
Part 1
Interviewer What was your favorite food when you were a child?
Steve Well, I always liked unusual things, at least things that most English children at the time didn't like. For instance, when I was six or seven my favorite things were snails, oh and prawns with garlic.
Interviewer Funny things for a six-year-old English boy to like!
Steve Well, the thing is my parents liked traveling and eating out a lot, and I first tried snails in France, and the prawns, my first prawns I had at a Spanish restaurant in the town where we lived.
Interviewer So you were interested in Spanish food right from the start. Is that why you decided to come to Spain?
Steve Partly, but of course, I suppose like a lot of British people I wanted to see the sun! The other thing that attracted me when I got here were all the fantastic ingredients. I remember going into the market for the first time and saying "Wow!"
Interviewer When you opened your restaurant, how did you want it to be different from typical Spanish restaurants?
Steve Well, when I came to Spain, all the good restaurants were very formal, very traditional. In London then, the fashion was for informal places where the waiters wore jeans, but the food was amazing. So I wanted a restaurant a bit like that. I also wanted a restaurant where you could try more international food, but made with some of these fantastic local ingredients. For example, Spain's got wonderful seafood, but usually here it's just grilled or fried. I started doing things in my restaurant like cooking Valencian mussels in Thai green curry paste.
Interviewer What do you most enjoy cooking?
Steve What I most enjoy cooking, I think, are those traditional dishes which use quite cheap ingredients, but they need very long and careful cooking, and then you turn it into something really special... like a really good casserole, for example.
Interviewer And is there anything you don't like cooking?
Steve Maybe desserts. You have to be very very precise when you're making desserts. And that's not the way I am.

1 8))
Part 2
Interviewer What's the best thing about running a restaurant?
Steve I think the best thing is making people happy. That's why even after all this time I still enjoy it so much.
Interviewer And the worst thing?
Steve That's easy, it has to be the long hours. This week for example, I'm cooking nearly every day. We usually close on Sundays and Mondays, but this Monday is a public holiday, when lots of people want to eat out, so we're open.
Interviewer Seu Xerea is in all the British restaurant guides now. Does that mean you get a lot of British customers?
Steve Yes, we get a lot of British people, especially at the weekends, but then we get people from other countries, too.
Interviewer And are the British customers and the Spanish customers very different?
Steve Yes, I think they are. The British always say that everything is lovely, even if they've only eaten half of it. The Spanish, on the other hand, are absolutely honest about everything. They tell you what they like; they tell you what they don't like. I remember when I first opened, I had sushi on the menu, which was very unusual at that time, and I went into the dining room, and I said to people, "So what do you think of the sushi" And the customers, who were all Spanish, said "Oh, it was awful! It was raw fish!" Actually, I think I prefer that honesty, because it helps us to know what people like.
Interviewer What kind of customers do you find difficult?
Steve I think customers who want me to cook something in a way that I don't think is very good. Let's see, a person who asks for a really well-done steak, for instance. For me that's a difficult customer. You know, they'll say, "I want steak," so I give them a really really well-done steak, and then they say "It's tough." And I think well, of course it's tough. It's well done! Well-done steak is always tough.
Interviewer People say that the Mediterranean diet is very healthy. Do you think people's eating habits in Spain are changing?
Steve Well, I think they are changing. Unfortunately, I think they're getting worse. People are eating more unhealthily.
Interviewer How do you notice that?
Steve I see it with, especially with younger friends. They often eat in fast-food restaurants, they don't cook... and actually the younger ones come from a generation where their mothers don't cook either. That's what's happening now, and it's a real pity.

1 27))
Interviewer This morning we're talking about family and family life, and now Danielle Barnes is going to tell us about a book she has just read called *Birth Order* by Linda Blair. So what's the book about, Danielle?
Danielle Well, it's all about how our position in the family influences the kind of person we are. I mean whether we're first born, a middle child, a youngest child, or an only child. Linda Blair argues that our position in the family is possibly the strongest influence on our character and personality.
Interviewer So tell us more about this, Danielle. What about the oldest children in a family, the first-born?
Danielle Well, first-born children often have to take care of their younger brothers and sisters, so they're usually sensible and responsible as adults. They also tend to be ambitious, and they make good leaders. Many US Presidents and British Prime Ministers, including for example Abraham Lincoln were oldest children.
On the negative side, oldest children can be insecure and anxious. This is because when the second child was born, he or she lost some of his or her parents' attention and maybe he or she felt rejected.
Interviewer That's very interesting. What about the middle child?
Danielle Middle children are usually more relaxed than oldest children. That's probably because the parents are more relaxed themselves by the time the second child arrives. They are usually very sociable – the kind of people who get along with everybody, and they're also usually sensitive to what other people need. Now, this is because they grew up between older and younger brothers and sisters. For the same reason they're often good at sorting out arguments, and they're always sympathetic to the ones on the losing side, or in general to people who are having problems. On the other hand, middle children can sometimes be unambitious, and they can lack direction in life.
Interviewer And youngest children?
Danielle I was very interested in this part of the book because I'm a youngest child myself. It seems that youngest children are often very outgoing and charming. This is the way they try to get the attention of both their parents and their older brothers and sisters.
They are often more rebellious, and this is probably because it's easier for the youngest children to break the rules – by this time their parents are more relaxed about discipline. On the negative side, youngest children can be immature and disorganized, and they often depend too much on other people. This is because they have always been the baby of the family.
Interviewer Fascinating. And finally, what about only children?
Danielle Only children usually do very well at school because they have a lot of contact with adults. They get a lot of love and attention from their parents, so they're typically self-confident. They're also independent because they're used to being by themselves. And because they spend a lot of time with adults they're usually very organized.
Interviewer I'm an only child myself and people always think that I must be spoiled. Is that true, according to Linda Blair?
Danielle Well, it's true that only children can sometimes be spoiled by their parents because they're given everything they ask for. Also, on the negative side, only children can be selfish, and they can also be impatient, especially when things go wrong. This is because they're not used to sorting out problems with other brothers and sisters.

1 28))
Jenny My name's Jenny Zielinski. And New York is my city. I live here and I work for a magazine, *NewYork24seven*.
Rob My name's Rob Walker. I'm a writer on *NewYork24seven*. You can probably tell from my accent that I'm not actually from New York. I'm British, and I came over to the States a few months ago.

Jenny I met Rob in London when I was visiting the UK on a work trip. He was writing for the London edition of *24seven*. We got along well right away. I really liked him.
Rob So why am I in New York? Because of Jenny, of course. When they gave me the opportunity to work here for a month, I took it immediately. It gave us the chance to get to know each other better. When they offered me a permanent job I couldn't believe it!
Jenny I helped Rob find an apartment. And now here we are. Together in New York. I'm so happy. I just hope Rob's happy here, too.
Rob I really loved living in London. A lot of my friends and family are there, so of course I still miss it. But New York's a fantastic city. I've got a great job and Jenny's here, too.
Jenny Things are changing pretty fast in the office. We have a new boss, Don Taylor. And things are changing in my personal life, too. This evening's kind of important. I'm taking Rob to meet my parents for the very first time. I just hope it goes well!

🔊 **1 29**
Jenny I can't believe we got here so late.
Rob I'm sorry, Jenny. I had to finish that article for Don.
Jenny Don't forget the chocolates.
Rob OK.
Rob Oh, no!
Jenny I don't believe it. Don't tell me you forgot them!?
Rob I think they're still on my desk.
Jenny You're kidding.
Rob You know what my desk's like.
Jenny Yeah, it's a complete mess. Why don't you ever tidy it?
Rob We could go and buy some more.
Jenny How can we get some more? We're already late!
Jenny Hi, there!
Harry You made it!
Jenny Sorry we're late. So, this is my mom and dad, Harry and Sally. And this, of course, is Rob.
Rob Hello.
Sally It's so nice to meet you at last.
Harry Yes, Jenny's finally decided to introduce you to us.
Sally Come in, come in!
Jenny Mom, I'm really sorry – we bought you some chocolates, but we left them at the office.
Sally What a pity. Never mind.
Harry Yeah, don't worry about it. We know what a busy young woman you are. And your mom has made way too much food for this evening anyway.
Sally Oh, Harry.
Jenny But I also have some good news.
Sally Really? What's that?
Jenny Well, you know we have a new boss? He's still new to the job and needs support, so today he made me the managing editor of the magazine.
Sally So you've got a promotion? How fantastic!
Harry That's great news! Hey, does that mean Jenny's going to be your boss, Rob?
Rob Uh… yes, I guess so.
Jenny Well, not exactly. I'm a manager, but I'm not Rob's manager.
Sally Let's go and have dinner.
Jenny What a great idea!

🔊 **1 32**
Harry You know, our Jenny has done incredibly well, Rob. She's the first member of our family to study at Harvard. She's a very capable and ambitious young woman.
Jenny Oh, Dad.
Rob No, it's true, Jenny.
Harry But what about you, Rob? How do you see your career? Do you see yourself going into management?
Rob Me? No. Not really. I'm more of a… a writer.
Harry Really? What kind of things do you write?
Rob Um… you know, interviews, reviews… things like that… and I'm doing a lot of work for the online magazine…

Jenny Rob's a very talented writer, Dad. He's very creative.
Harry That's great, but being creative doesn't always pay the bills.
Jenny You know, my dad's a very keen photographer. He took all of these photos.
Harry Oh, Rob won't be interested in those.
Rob But I am interested. I mean, I like photography. And I think I recognize some of these people…
Harry That's because most of them are of Jenny.
Rob But there are some great jazz musicians, too. That's Miles Davis… and isn't that John Coltrane? And that's Wynton Marsalis.
Harry You know about Wynton Marsalis?
Rob Know about him? I've interviewed him!
Harry How incredible! I love that guy. He's a hero of mine.
Rob Well, he's a really nice guy. I spent a whole day with him, chatting and watching him rehearse.
Harry Really? I want to hear all about it.
Sally Have a cookie, Rob.
Harry Go ahead, son! Sally makes the best cookies in New York!

🔊 **1 40**
1 I'm a spender, I think. I try to save, but something always seems to come along that I need to buy, and I end up broke. I can get by with very little money for myself when I need to, but I don't seem to be good at holding on to it. Also, if my kids ask to borrow some money, I always say yes.
2 I would say that I'm a spender. I spend money on things like concerts or on trips because I like having the experience and the memories. I know that I should spend my money on things that last, or save for the future, but I don't want to miss all those good things that are happening right now.
3 I consider myself a spender. I don't have much money, but when I do have some there's always something I need or want to spend it on. I love computers and computer games, so I buy things to make sure my computer's always up to date. I know it's not very sensible, but it's important to me.
4 That's hard to say. I can save money if there's something I really, really want, but usually my money disappears as soon as I get it. I get some money from my parents every week, so I have just enough money to go to the movies with my friends and to buy something for myself, maybe a book or a DVD or some makeup… I usually end up buying something. But, for example, if I want to go on a trip with my friends, then I can make an effort and save some money for a few weeks.
5 Since I was little, I've always saved about a third of the money I get. I would never think of spending all the money I have. You could say that I'm careful about money. When I want to buy something that's expensive, I don't use a credit card. I take the money out of the bank so I never have to worry about getting into debt.
6 I'd say a saver, definitely. I like having some money saved in case I have an emergency. I also think very carefully before I buy something, and I always make sure it's the best I can buy for that price. But I wouldn't describe myself as cheap. I love buying presents for people, and when I do spend my money I like to buy nice things, even if they're more expensive.

🔊 **1 45**
Part 1
Interviewer Jane, you're an elementary school teacher, and a writer. What kind of books do you write?
Jane Well, I write books for children who are learning English as a foreign language.
Interviewer How long have you been a writer?
Jane Uh, let me see, since 1990. So for about 22 years.
Interviewer Tell us about the trip that changed your life. Where were you going?

Jane Well, it was in the summer of 2008, and my family - my husband and I and our three children - decided to have a holiday of a lifetime, and to go to Africa. We went to Uganda and Rwanda, to see the mountain gorillas. It was something we'd always wanted to do. Anyway, about halfway through the trip, we were in Uganda, and we were traveling in a lorry when the lorry broke down. So the driver had to find a mechanic to come and help fix it.
Interviewer And then what happened?
Jane Well, as soon as we stopped, lots of children appeared and surrounded us. I could see some long buildings quite near, so I asked the children what they were, and they said in English "That's our school." And I was very curious to see what a Ugandan school was like, so I asked them to show it to me.
Interviewer What was it like?
Jane I was shocked when I first saw it. The walls were falling down, the blackboards were broken, and there weren't many desks. But the children were so friendly, and I asked them if they would like to learn a song in English. They said yes, and I started teaching them some songs, like *Heads, Shoulders, Knees, and Toes* a song I've used all over the world to teach children parts of the body. Almost immediately the classroom filled up with children of all ages, and they all wanted to learn. I was just amazed by how quickly they learned the song!
Interviewer Did you meet the teachers?
Jane Yes, we did, and the headmaster, too. He explained that the school was called St. Josephs, and it was a community school for orphans, very poor children and refugees. I asked him what the school needed. I thought that he might say, "We need books, or papers," and then later we could send them to him. But actually he said, "What we need is a new school." And I thought yes, of course he's right. These children deserve to have better conditions than this to learn in. So when I got back home, my husband and I, and other people who were with us on the trip decided to set up an organization to get money to build a new school.

🔊 **1 46**
Part 2
Interviewer So *Adelante África* was born. Why did you decide to call it that?
Jane Well, we wanted a name that gave the idea of Africa moving forward, and my husband is Spanish, and he suggested *Adelante África*, because in Spanish Adalante means "go forward," and *Adelante África* sort of sounded better than "Go Forward, Africa."
Interviewer How long did it take to raise the money for the new school?
Jane Amazingly enough, not long really, only about two years. The school opened on the 14th March 2010 with 75 children. Today, it has nearly 500 children.
Interviewer That's great! I understand that since the new school opened you've been working on other projects for these children.
Jane Yes. When we opened the school we realized that although the children now had a beautiful new school, they couldn't really make much progress because they were suffering from malnutrition, malaria, things like that. So we've been working to improve their diet and health, and at the moment we're building a house where children who don't have families can live.
Interviewer And are your children involved in *Adelante África* too?
Jane Yes, absolutely! They all go out to Uganda at least once a year. My daughter Tessie runs the *Facebook* page, and my other daughter Ana runs a project to help children to go to secondary school, and Georgie, my son, organizes a football tournament there every year.
Interviewer And how do you think you have most changed the children's lives?

Jane I think the school has changed the children's lives because it has given them hope. People from outside came and listened to them and cared about them. But it's not only the children whose lives have changed. *Adelante África* has also changed me and my family. We have been very lucky in life. I feel that life has given me a lot. Now I want to give something back. But it's not all giving. I feel that I get more from them than I give! I love being there. I love their smiles and how they have such a strong sense of community, and I love feeling that my family and the other members of *Adelante África* are accepted as part of that community.
Interviewer And do you have a website?
Jane Yes, we do. It's www.adelanteafrica.com. We've had the website for about four years. It was one of the first things we set up. If you'd like to find out more about *Adelante África*, please go there and have a look. There are lots of photos and even a video my son took of me teaching the children to sing on that first day. Maybe it will change your life too, who knows?

🔊 **1 52**

Phone call 4
I haven't had any music for the last three days, because my iPod broke, so paddling has been getting more boring. To pass the time I count or I name countries in my head, and sometimes I just look up at the sky. Sometimes the sky is pink with clouds that look like cotton, and other times it's dark like the smoke from a fire, and sometimes it's bright blue. The day that I reached the halfway point in my trip, the sky was bright blue. I'm superstitious so I didn't celebrate – there's still a very long way to go.

Phone call 5
This week the mosquitoes have been driving me crazy. They obviously think I'm easy food! They especially like my feet. I wake up in the night when they bite me, and I can't stop scratching my feet.
  But I'm feeling happier now than I've been feeling for weeks. I've seen a lot of amazing wildlife this week. One day, I found myself in the middle of a group of dolphins. There were about six pairs jumping out of the water. I've also seen enormous butterflies, iguanas, and vultures that fly above me in big groups. Yesterday, a fish jumped into my kayak. Maybe it means I'm going to be lucky. I am starting to feel a little sad that this adventure is coming to an end.

The six o'clock news
And finally on the news, TV host Helen Skelton has successfully completed her 1,998-mile trip down the Amazon River in a kayak. She left from Nauta in Peru six weeks ago on a trip that many people said would be impossible. But yesterday, she crossed the finish line at Almeirim in Brazil to become the first woman to paddle down the Amazon. Here's Helen: "It's been hard, but I've had an amazing time. The only thing I've really missed is my dog Barney. So the first thing I'm going to do will be to pick him up and take him for a nice long walk."

🔊 **2 9**

Tanner took a taxi from the the boat yard to the airport where the seaplane was leaving from. It took 45 minutes to get from the boat yard to the airport. Once he got on the seaplane, Tanner quickly made up the time he spent riding in the taxi. With the plane flying close to 100 miles an hour, Tanner caught up to Rutledge and Adam near Seven Mile Bridge. After landing at the airport in Key West, Tanner rented a scooter for the last three miles of the race. Just a few more minutes until he arrived at the southern-most point of the US.

🔊 **2 15**

Host And on tonight's program we talk to Tom Dixon, who is an expert on road safety. Tom, new technology like GPS devices has meant new distractions for drivers, hasn't it?
Tom That's right, Nicky, but it isn't just technology that's the problem. Car drivers do a lot of other things while they're driving that are dangerous and that can cause accidents. Remember, driver distraction is the number one cause of road accidents.
Host Now I know you've been doing a lot of tests with simulators. According to your tests, what's the most dangerous thing to do when you're driving?
Tom The tests we did in a simulator showed that the most dangerous thing to do while you're driving is to send or receive a text message. This is incredibly dangerous, and it is, of course, illegal. In fact, research done by the police shows that this is more dangerous than drinking and driving.
Host Why is that?
Tom Well, the reason is obvious – many people use two hands to text, one to hold the phone and the other to type. Which means that they don't have their hands on the wheel, and they're looking at the phone, not at the road. Even for people who can text with one hand, it's still extremely dangerous. In the tests we did in the simulator, two of the drivers crashed while texting.
Host And which is the next most dangerous?
Tom The next most dangerous thing is to set or adjust your GPS. This is extremely hazardous too because although you can do it with one hand, you still have to take your eyes off the road for a few seconds.
Host And number three?
Tom Number three was putting on makeup or doing your hair. In fact, this is something that people often do, especially women, of course, when they stop at traffic lights, but if they haven't finished when the lights change, they often continue when they start driving again. It's that fatal combination of just having one hand on the steering wheel, and looking in the mirror, not at the road.
Host And number four?
Tom In fourth place, there are two activities that are equally dangerous. One of them is making a phone call on a cell phone. Our research showed that when people talk on the phone, they drive more slowly (which can be just as dangerous as driving fast), but their control of the car gets worse, because they're concentrating on the phone call and not on what's happening on the road. But the other thing, which is just as dangerous as talking on your cell phone, is eating and drinking. In fact, if you do this, you double your chance of having an accident because eating and drinking always involves taking at least one hand off the steering wheel. And the thing that's most worrying here is that people don't think of this as a dangerous activity at all, and it isn't even illegal.
Host And in fifth, well actually sixth place. It must be listening to music, but what kind?
Tom Well, it's listening to music you know.
Host Oh, that's interesting.
Tom We found in our tests that when drivers were listening to music they knew and liked, they drove either faster or slower depending on whether the music was fast or slow.
Host So fast music made drivers drive faster.
Tom Exactly. And a study in Canada also found that if the music was very loud, then drivers' reaction time was 20% slower. If you're listening to very loud music you're twice as likely to go through a red light.
Host So the safest of all of the things on the list is to listen to music we don't know.
Tom Exactly. If we don't know the music, then it doesn't distract us. In this part of the tests all drivers drove safely.

🔊 **2 23**

A Excuse me, is this seat empty?
B Yes, sure sit down. Ah, he's cute. Is he yours?
A Yes, yes. Actually, he's a she. Miranda.
B Oh. Three months?
A Three and a half. How about yours?
B Stephen. He's four months. Did you have a bad night?
A Yes, Miranda was crying all night. You know, that noise gets to you. It drives me crazy.
B Do you know what you need? These.
A What are they? Earplugs?
B Yes. Earplugs! When the baby starts crying you just put these in. You can still hear the crying, but the noise isn't so bad, and it's not so stressful.
A That's a great idea! Who told you to do that?
B It's all in this book I read. You should get it.
A Yeah? What's it called?
B It's called *Commando Dad*. It was written by an ex-soldier. He was a commando in the army, and it's especially for men with babies or small children. It's pretty good.
A Really? So what's so good about it?
B Well, it's like a military manual. It tells you exactly what to do with a baby in any situation. It makes everything easier. There's a website, too, that you can go to – commandodad.com. It has a lot of advice about taking care of babies and small kids, and I really like the forums where men can write in with their problems or their experiences.
A What kind of things does it help you with?
B All kinds of things. How to change diapers – he has a really good system, how to dress the baby, how to get the baby to sleep, the best way to feed the baby, how to know if the baby is sick. It's really useful and it's pretty funny, too, I mean he uses a kind of military language, so for example he calls the baby a BT which means a baby trooper, and the baby's bedroom is base camp, and taking the baby for a walk is maneuvers, and taking the diapers to the trash is called bomb disposal.
A What else does it say?
B Well, it has all kinds of stuff about...
A And what does he think about men taking care of children? Does he think we do it well?
B He thinks that men are just as good as women at taking care of children in almost everything.
A Almost everything?
B Yeah, he says the one time when women are better than men is when the kids are sick. Women kind of understand better what to do. They have an instinct. Oh. Now it's my turn. OK, I know exactly what that cry means. It means he's hungry.
A Wow! What was that book called?

🔊 **2 28**

Kerri (singing) You work hard, but your money's all spent
Haven't got enough to pay the rent
You know it's not right and it makes no sense
To go chasing, chasing those dollars and cents
Chasing, chasing those dollars and cents...
Rob That was great, Kerri.
Kerri Thanks.
Rob Kerri, you used to be in a band, now you play solo. Why did you change?
Kerri What happened with the band is private. I've already said I don't want to talk about it in interviews. All I'll say is that I have a lot more freedom this way. I can play – and say – what I want.
Rob Did your relationship with the band's lead guitarist affect the break up?
Kerri No comment. I never talk about my private life.
Rob Your dad was in a famous punk band, and your mom's a classical pianist, have they influenced your music?
Kerri Of course they have – what do you think? Isn't everyone influenced by their parents?
Rob When did you start playing?
Kerri I started playing the guitar when I was about four.
Rob Four? That's pretty young.
Kerri Yeah, the guitar was nearly as big as me!
Rob I think that your new album is your best yet. It's a lot quieter and more experimental than your earlier albums.
Kerri Thank you! I think it's my best work.
Rob So what have you been doing recently?

124 Listening

Kerri Well, I've been writing and recording some new songs. And I've played at some of the summer festivals in the UK.
Rob And what are you doing while you're in the States?
Kerri I'm going to play at some clubs here in New York, then I'm doing some small gigs in other places. I just want to get to know the country and the people. It's all very new to me.
Jenny Good job, Rob. She isn't the easiest person to interview.
Rob She's OK. And this video clip will work great online.
Don Well, thank you for coming in today, Kerri. Now I suggest we have some lunch. Rob, could you call a taxi?
Rob Uh, sure.

2 29))

Don So when will you be coming back to New York, Kerri?
Kerri Oh, I don't know.
Waitress Hi, guys. Is everything OK?
Don Yes, it's delicious, thank you.
Waitress That's great!
Kerri New York waiters never leave you alone! I really don't like all this "Hi guys! Is everything OK?" stuff.
Don What? You mean waiters aren't friendly in London?
Rob Oh, they're very friendly!
Kerri Yes, they're friendly, but not too friendly. They don't bother you all the time.
Waitress Can I get you anything else? More drinks, maybe?
Don No thanks. We're fine.
Waitress Fantastic.
Kerri See what I mean? Personally, I think people in London are a lot more easygoing. London's just not as hectic as New York.
Don Sure, we all like peace and quiet. But in my opinion, New York is possibly... well, no, is definitely the greatest city in the world. Don't you agree?
Kerri To be honest, I definitely prefer London.
Don Come on, Rob. You've lived in both. What do you think?
Rob Um, well, I have to say, London's very special. It's more relaxed, it's got great parks and you can cycle everywhere. It's dangerous to cycle in New York!
Don Why would you cycle when you can drive a car?
Kerri You can't be serious.
Don OK, I agree, London has its own peculiar charm. But if you ask me, nothing compares with a city like New York. The whole world is here!
Kerri But that's the problem. It's too big. There are too many people. Everybody's so stressed out. And nobody has any time for you.
Jenny I don't think that's right, Kerri. New Yorkers are very friendly...
Kerri Oh sure, they can sound friendly with all that "Have a nice day" stuff. But I always think it's a little bit... fake.
Don You've got to be kidding me!
Rob I'm sorry. I'll just have to take this... Hello?... Yes... You're who?... The taxi driver?... What did she leave? ... Her cell phone... right. OK. Yes, we're still at the restaurant. See you in about five minutes.

2 32))

Kerri Thank you for a nice lunch, Don.
Don You're welcome.
Waitress Thanks for coming, guys! Have a nice day.
Don See? Nice, friendly service.
Kerri Maybe. But I think she saw the big tip you left on the table!
Jenny Did you mean what you said in the restaurant, Rob?
Rob Did I mean what?
Jenny About missing London?
Rob Sure, I miss it, Jenny.
Jenny Really?
Rob But hey, not that much! It's just that moving to a new place is always difficult.
Jenny But you don't regret coming here, do you?
Rob No ... no ... not at all.
Jenny It's just that... you seemed homesick in there. For the parks, the cycling ...
Rob Well there are some things I miss but – Oh, hang on a minute. Look over there. Our taxi's come back.
Taxi driver Excuse me, Ma'am.
Kerri Who me? What is it?
Taxi driver I believe this is your cell phone. You left it in my cab.
Kerri What?... Oh, wow... thank you!
Taxi driver Have a nice day!
Kerri That was so kind of him!
Don See? New Yorkers are really friendly people.

2 40))

1 One very easy thing you can do is just change the language to English on all the gadgets you have, for example on your phone, or laptop, or tablet. That way you're reading English every day and without really noticing you just learn a whole lot of vocabulary, for example the things you see on your screen like "Are you sure you want to shut down now?," things like that.
2 My tip is to do things that you like doing, but in English. So for example, if you like reading, then read in English, if you like movies, watch them in English with subtitles, if you like computer games, play them in English. But don't do things you don't enjoy in your language, I mean if you don't like reading in your language, you'll enjoy it even less in English, and so you probably won't learn anything.
3 What really helped me to improve my English was having an American boyfriend. He didn't speak any Japanese – well, not many foreigners do – so we spoke English all the time, and my English improved really quickly. We broke up when he went back to the US, but by then I could speak pretty fluently. We didn't exactly end up as friends, but I'll always be grateful to him for the English I learned. So my tip is try to find an English-speaking boyfriend or girlfriend.
4 I've always thought that learning vocabulary is very important, so I bought a vocabulary flashcard app for my phone. I write down all the new words and phrases I want to remember in French and in English, and then when I get a quiet moment I test myself. It really helps me remember new vocabulary. So that's my tip. Get a vocabulary learning app for your phone.
5 I think one of the big problems when you're learning something new is motivation, something to make you continue and not give up. So my tip is to book yourself a vacation in an English-speaking country or a country where people speak very good English, like the Caribbean, as a little reward for yourself, and so you can actually practice your English. It's really motivating when you go somewhere and find that people understand you and you can communicate! Last year, I went to the Bahamas for a weekend, and I had a great time, and I spoke a lot of English.
6 If you love music, which I do, my tip is to listen to as many songs as possible in English and then learn to sing them. It's so easy nowadays with *YouTube*. First, I download the lyrics and try to understand them. Then I sing along with the singer and try to copy the way he or she sings – this is fantastic for your pronunciation. Then once I can do it well, I go back to *YouTube* and get a karaoke version of the song, and then I sing it. It's fun and your English will really improve as a result.

2 48))

I always thought that good manners were good manners wherever you were in the world. But that was until I met my boyfriend Jason, who is from Burma—also known as Myanmar. We met in upstate New York, when we were both students in college. When we first got to know each other, we were always surrounded by a group of friends. I liked Jason because he was funny and kind, and I could tell he liked me, but we never spent any time alone.

The first time I suggested that we hang out without our friends, he said no without an explanation, which I thought was kind of rude. My feelings were hurt, so I didn't talk to him as much. The next time I saw Jason in our big group, he was just as friendly and happy as usual. I was confused. Finally, I asked him why he wouldn't hang out with me. He apologized and then he told me that in Burma, it's custom to "date" in a group situation. Since he had only been in the US for a few years, he was still having trouble navigating the two cultures he lived in—the more reserved Burmese culture and the more open American culture.

A few months later, after we we started dating, I asked him why he never responded to my cute, romantic *Facebook* posts with more than "cool" or "thanks." It seemed weird to me that his responses weren't romantic. And honestly, I was a little jealous of the sweet posts my American friends' boyfriends left on their *Facebook* pages.

But Jason told me in Burma, it's considered bragging to express your feelings in public, especially on a social networking site. He didn't want his family and friends to think he was bragging about his American girlfriend. From an American point of view, I thought he was being a bit cold; however from a Burmese point of view, he was actually being respectful.

As confused as I was about what's considered good and bad manners in Jason's culture, he felt the same way about American culture. He thought it was bad manners to refer to have a "best friend," and he would argue with me whenever I called my friend Rachel, my best friend. Jason said there is no such thing as a "best friend" in Burmese culture. There are only "close friends." It would be inconsiderate to name one person as a "best friend" because your other friends would feel offended.

Anyway, we've been together for two years, and we still have disagreements. But, we've learned that as long as we're a couple, we'll never completely agree about whether our manners are good or bad, and that most importantly...it's OK to agree to disagree!

3 8))

Part 1
Interviewer What made you want to become a soccer referee, or football referee as you would call it?
Juan My father was a referee, but that didn't influence me – in fact, the opposite because I saw all the problems that he had as a referee. But as a child I was always attracted by the idea of being a referee, and at school I used to referee all kinds of sports, basketball, handball, volleyball, and of course, football. I was invited to join the Referee's Federation when I was only 14 years old.
Interviewer Were you good at sports yourself?
Juan Yes, I was a very good handball player. People often think that referees become referees because they are frustrated sportsmen, but this is just not true in most cases in my experience.
Interviewer What was the most exciting match you ever refereed?
Juan It's difficult to choose one match as the most exciting. I remember some of the Real Madrid–Barcelona matches, for example the first one I ever refereed. The atmosphere was incredible in the stadium. But really it's impossible to pick just one – there have been so many.
Interviewer What was the worst experience you ever had as a referee?
Juan The worst? Well, that was something that happened very early in my career. I was only 16, and I was refereeing a match in a town in Spain, and the home team lost. After the match, I was attacked and injured by the players of the home team and by the spectators. After all these years I can still remember a mother, who had a little baby in her arms, who was trying to hit me. She was so

angry with me that she nearly dropped her baby. That was my worst moment, and it nearly made me stop being a referee.

Interviewer Do you think that there's more cheating in soccer than in the past?

Juan Yes, I think so.

Interviewer Why?

Juan I think it's because there's so much money in football today that it's become much more important to win. Also football is much faster than it used to be, so it's much more difficult for referees to detect cheating.

Interviewer How do soccer players cheat?

Juan Oh, there are many ways, but for me the worst thing in football today is what we call "simulation." Simulation is when a player pretends to have been fouled when in fact he hasn't. For example, sometimes a player falls over in the penalty area when, in fact, nobody has touched him and this can result in the referee giving a penalty when it wasn't a penalty. In my opinion, when a player does this he's cheating not only the referee, not only the players of the other team, but also the spectators, because spectators pay money to see a fair contest.

3 9))
Part 2
Interviewer What's the most difficult thing about being a referee?

Juan The most difficult thing is to make the right decisions during a match. It's difficult because you have to make decisions when everything's happening so quickly – football today is very fast. You must remember that everything is happening at 100 kilometres an hour. Also important decisions often depend on the referee's interpretation of the rules. Things aren't black and white. And of course making decisions would be much easier if players didn't cheat.

Interviewer Do you think that the idea of fair play doesn't exist any more?

Juan Not at all. I think fair play does exist – the players who cheat are the exceptions.

Interviewer Finally, who do you think is the best player right now?

Juan I think most people agree that the best footballer today is Leo Messi.

Interviewer Why do you think he's so good?

Juan It's hard to say what makes him so special, but a study was done on him which showed that Messi can run faster with the ball than many footballers can do without the ball. Apart from his great ability, what I also like about him is that he isn't the typical superstar footballer. You can see that he enjoys playing football, and he behaves in public and in his personal life in a very normal way. That's unusual when you think how famous he is. And what's more he doesn't cheat – he doesn't need to!

3 23))
Host Hello, and welcome to *Forum*, the program that asks you what you think about current topics. Today Martha Park will be talking about the social networking site *Facebook*, how we use it, how much we like it – or dislike it. So get ready to call us, or text us and tell us what you think. The number as always is 555-4318. Martha.

Martha Hello. Since *Facebook* was first launched in 2004, a lot of research has been done to find out what kind of people use it, what they use it for, and what effect it has on their lives. According to a recent study by consumer research specialist Intersperience, the average 22 year old in Britain has over 1,000 online friends. In fact, 22 seems to be the age at which the number of friends peaks. It also appears that women have slightly more online friends than men. And another study from an American university shows that people who spend a lot of time on *Facebook* reading other people's posts tend to feel more dissatisfied with their own lives, because they feel that everyone else is having a better time than they are. So, over to you. Do you use *Facebook*? How do you feel about it? Can you really have 1,000 friends? Are social networking sites making us unhappy? Call in and share your experiences…

3 24))
Host And our first caller is Young. Go ahead, Young.

Young Hi. Uh, yeah, I use *Facebook* a lot, every day. I think it's a great way to, uh, organize your social life and keep in touch with your friends. I have a lot of friends.

Martha How many friends do you have, Young?

Young Right now, I have 1,042.

Martha And how many of them do you know personally?

Young About half maybe?

Martha And what do you use *Facebook* for?

Young For me, it's a good way to get in touch with my friends without having to use the phone all the time. When I'm having a busy week at school, I can change my status so I can let my friends know I can't go out. That's a lot easier than wasting time telling people "Sorry, I'm too busy to get together." It's just easier and quicker than using the phone.

Host Thanks, Young. We have another caller. It's Beth. Hello, Beth.

Beth Hi. Uh, I don't use *Facebook* or any other social networking site.

Martha Why's that Beth?

Beth Well, two reasons. First, I don't spend much time online. I play a lot of sports – I'm on a hockey team, so I meet my teammates almost every day, and we don't need to communicate on *Facebook*.

Martha And the other reason?

Beth I just don't really like the whole idea of social networking sites. I mean, why would I want to tell the whole world everything that I'm doing? I don't want to share my personal information with the world and become friends with people I don't even know. And I don't want to read what other people had for breakfast or lunch or dinner or what they're planning to do this weekend.

Host Thanks for that, Beth. Our next caller is Emma. It's your turn, Emma.

Martha Hi, Emma.

Emma Hi, Martha.

Martha And do you use *Facebook*, Emma?

Emma I use it once in a while, but not very much. I only really use it to keep up with friends who have moved abroad or live too far away for us to meet regularly. For example, one of my best friends recently moved to Canada, and we chat on *Facebook*. But I never add friends who are people I hardly know. I just can't understand those people who collect hundreds or even thousands of *Facebook* friends! I think it's just competition, people who want to make it seem that they're more popular than everybody else.

Martha So you think the *Facebook* world is kind of unreal?

Emma Absolutely. I think people write things and post photos of themselves just to show everyone they know what a fantastic time they're having and what exciting lives they lead. But they're probably just sitting at home in front of the computer all the time.

Host Thanks for that, Emma. We have time for one more caller before the news, and it's Ned. Hi, Ned. You'll have to be quick.

Martha Hi, Ned.

Ned Hi. When I started off with *Facebook*, I thought it was great, and I used it to communicate with close friends and with family, and I got back in touch with old friends from school. It was good because all the people I was friends with on *Facebook* were people I knew, and I was interested in what they were doing. But then I started adding friends, people I hardly knew who were friends of friends, people like that – in the end, I had more than 1,000 – and it just became too much. It was just too many people leaving updates, writing messages on my wall. So last month I decided to delete most of them. It took me about half an hour to delete, and in the end, the only people I left were actual, real-life friends and family, and old school friends. I got it down to 99. It was really liberating.

Host Thanks, Ned, and we'll be back after the news, so keep those calls coming.

3 25))
Jenny Monica!
Monica Jenny!
Jenny Wow! How are you? You look great!
Monica Thanks, Jenny! You look really good, too.
Jenny Hey, why don't we get some coffee?
Monica I'd love to, but I'm on the way to meet… oh, come on. Five minutes!
Jenny So, how is everything?
Monica Oh, great. Things couldn't be better actually. Scott and I … we're getting married!
Jenny You're what? Congratulations!
Monica Thank you!
Jenny When did you get engaged?
Monica Only a few days ago. I'm glad I saw you actually. I was going to call you. We've only told family so far.
Jenny I can't believe it. Monica the wife! And to think you used to go clubbing every night!
Monica Well, that was a few years ago! All I want to do now is stay in and read wedding magazines.
Jenny And how are the plans coming along?
Monica I haven't done anything yet. My mom and Scott's mom want to organize the whole thing themselves!
Jenny That's what mothers are for!
Monica True. But what about you? You look fantastic.
Jenny Well, I guess I'm kind of happy, too.
Monica Uh-huh. What's his name?
Jenny Rob.
Monica You've been keeping him very quiet! Is it serious?
Jenny Um, it's kind of, you know…
Monica So it is!
Jenny It's still early. We haven't been together for long. He only moved here from London a few months ago…
Monica What? He's British? And you think you can persuade him to stay in New York? That won't be easy!
Jenny I think he likes it here. You know how guys are, you never know what they're thinking.
Monica When can I meet him?
Jenny Uh… that's him now.

3 26))
Rob Do you mind if I join you?
Monica Of course not. Come on, sit down.
Rob Thank you.
Monica I have to leave in a minute anyway.
Rob Could I have a large latte, please?
Waiter Of course.
Jenny Rob, this is Monica.
Monica Nice to meet you, Rob.
Rob You too, Monica. You know, Jenny talks about you a lot. And I've seen college photos of you two together. At Jenny's parents' house.
Jenny Of course you have. My dad's photos.
Rob You've hardly changed at all.
Monica What a nice man! I can see why you like him, Jenny. The perfect English gentleman.
Waiter Your latte.
Rob Oh, thanks. Can you pass the sugar?
Jenny Sure.
Monica Sorry guys, but I have to go.
Rob You're sure I haven't interrupted anything?
Monica Not at all. It's just that I have to meet someone. But let's get together very soon.
Jenny We will!
Monica Bye, Rob. Nice meeting you.
Rob Bye.
Jenny Bye. Talk soon.
Rob She seems like a happy person.
Jenny She is, especially right now - she's getting married.
Rob That's fantastic news!
Jenny Yeah, it is. I guess we're at that age now. When most of our friends are settling down and getting married.

Rob Yeah... Oh, speaking of friends, I want to ask you a favor. Is it OK if we change our plans a bit this week?
Jenny Uh... sure. What's up?
Rob I've just had a call from an old friend of mine, Paul. I haven't seen him since we were at university, and he's traveling around the States at the moment. Anyway, he's arriving in New York this evening and, uh... I've invited him to stay for the week.
Jenny Cool! It'll be fun to meet one of your old friends! What's he like?
Rob Oh, Paul's a laugh. He used to be a bit wild, but that was a long time ago. He's probably changed completely.
Jenny Well, I'm looking forward to meeting him.
Rob Just one other thing. Could you do me a big favor? I have to work late this evening so... would you mind meeting him at the airport?
Jenny Not at all. I'd like to meet him.
Rob And do you think you could take him to my flat? I'll give you the keys.
Jenny No problem, Rob.
Rob Thanks so much, Jenny. You're a real star.

(3) 29))

Paul Hey, man!
Rob Paul!
Paul It's great to see you, mate.
Rob You too, Paul. It's been years. You haven't changed at all.
Paul Just got better looking!
Rob How come you're so late?
Jenny Paul's flight from LA was delayed. And then the traffic coming back was just awful.
Paul But that gave us time to get to know each other.
Jenny Yeah. Paul told me all about his travels. Every detail.
Paul And look at this. Your own New York flat. How cool is that?
Rob It's good. Really good. But – do you want something to eat? I got some things on my way home.
Paul Stay in? It's my first night in the Big Apple! Let's go out and have a pizza or something.
Rob I thought you'd be tired after the flight.
Paul No way, man! I'm ready for action.
Rob Great! I'll get my jacket...
Jenny Rob, I think I'll go home if you don't mind. I, uh, I'm exhausted.
Rob Oh, OK then.
Paul So it's a boys' night out!
Rob Just like the old days!
Paul And after the pizza we can go on somewhere else. Rob, we've got a lot to talk about!

1A

simple present and continuous, action and nonaction verbs

simple present: *I live, he works,* etc.

> 1 I **work** in a bank. She **studies** Russian. (1 10))
>   We **don't have** any pets. Jack **doesn't wear** glasses.
>   Where **do** you **live**? **Does** your brother **have** a car?
> 2 She usually **has** cereal for breakfast.
>   **I'm** never late for work.
>   We only **eat out** about once a month.

1 We use the simple present for things that are always true or happen regularly.
   - Remember the spelling rules for third person singular, e.g., *lives, studies, watches*.
   - Remember the word order for questions: (question word), auxiliary, subject, base form of verb. *Do you know David? What time does the movie start?*
2 We often use the simple present with adverbs of frequency, e.g., *usually, never*, or expressions of frequency, e.g., *every day, once a week*.
   - Adverbs of frequency go <u>before</u> the main verb, and <u>after</u> *be*.
   - Expressions of frequency usually go at the end of the sentence or verb phrase.

present continuous: *be* + verb + *-ing*

> A Who **are** you **waiting** for? (1 11))
> B **I'm waiting** for a friend.
> A **Is** your sister still **going out** with Adam?
> B No, they broke up. She **isn't going out** with anyone right now.

- We use the present continuous (not the simple present) for actions in progress at the time of speaking, e.g., things that are happening now or around now. These are usually temporary, not habitual actions.
- Remember the spelling rules, e.g., *living, studying, getting*.
- We also use the present continuous for future arrangements (see **1B**).

action and nonaction verbs

> A What **are** you **cooking**? (1 12))
> B **I'm making** pasta.
> A Great! I **love** pasta.
> A What **are** you **looking** for?
> B My car keys.
> A I'll help you in a minute.
> B But I **need** them now!

- Verbs that describe **actions**, e.g., *cook, make*, can be used in the simple present or continuous. *I'm making* lunch. *I usually make* lunch on the weekend.
- Verbs that describe **states** or **feelings** (not actions), e.g., *love, need, be, are* **nonaction verbs**. They are not usually used in the present continuous, even if we mean "now."
- Common nonaction verbs are *agree, be, believe, belong, depend, forget, hate, hear, know, like, love, matter, mean, need, prefer, realize, recognize, remember, seem, suppose*.

> 🔍 **Verbs than can be both action and nonaction**
> A few verbs have an action and a nonaction meaning, e.g., *have* and *think*.
> *I have a cat now.* = possession (nonaction)
> *I can't talk now. I'm having lunch.* = an action
> *I think this music's great.* = opinion (nonaction)
> *What are you thinking about?* = an action

---

a Complete the sentences with the simple present or present continuous forms of the verbs in parentheses).

   We *don't go* to Chinese restaurants very often. (not go)
1 These days, most children _____ too many sugary snacks. (have)
2 _____ you _____ any vitamins right now? (take)
3 Don't eat that spinach if you _____ it. (not like)
4 _____ your boyfriend _____ how to cook fish? (know)
5 We _____ take-out pizzas during the week. (not get)
6 What _____ your mother _____? It smells great! (make)
7 You look sad. What _____ you _____ about? (think)
8 The diet in my country _____ worse. (get)
9 How often _____ you _____ seafood? (eat)
10 I _____ usually _____ fish. (not cook)

b (Circle) the correct form, simple present, or continuous.
   (*I don't believe*) / *I'm not believing* that you cooked this meal yourself.
1 Come on, let's order. The waiter *comes* / *is coming*.
2 Kate *doesn't want* / *isn't wanting* to have dinner now. She isn't hungry.
3 The head chef is sick, so he *doesn't work* / *isn't working* today.
4 The check *seems* / *is seeming* very high to me.
5 We've had an argument, so we *don't speak* / *aren't speaking* to each other right now.
6 My mom *thinks* / *is thinking* my diet is awful these days.
7 *Do we need* / *Are we needing* to go shopping today?
8 Can I call you back? *I have* / *I'm having* lunch right now.
9 I didn't use to like oily fish, but now *I love* / *I'm loving* it!
10 What *do you cook* / *are you cooking*? It smells delicious!

◀ p.7

1B GRAMMAR BANK

future forms

be going to + base form

future plans and intentions 🔊 1 17

My sister **'s going to adopt** a child.
Are you **going to buy** a new car or a used one?
I**'m not going to go** to New York City tomorrow. The meeting is canceled.

predictions 🔊 1 18

The Yankees **are going to win**. They're playing really well.
Look at those black clouds. I think it**'s going to rain**.

- We use *going to* (NOT *will / won't*) when we have already decided to do something. NOT ~~My sister will adopt a child~~.
- We also use *going to* to make a prediction about the future, especially when you can see or have some evidence (e.g., black clouds).

present continuous: be + verb + -ing

future arrangements 🔊 1 19

Lorna and James **are getting** married in October.
We**'re meeting** at 10:00 tomorrow in Jack's office.
Jane**'s leaving** on Friday and **coming back** next Tuesday.

- We often use the present continuous for future arrangements.
- There is very little difference between the present continuous and *going to* for future plans / arrangements, and often you can use either.

- *going to* shows that you have made a decision. *We're going to get married next year.*
- the present continuous emphasizes that you have made the arrangements. *We're getting married on October 12th.* (= we've ordered the invitations, etc.)
- We often use the present continuous with verbs relating to travel arrangements, e.g., *go, come, arrive, leave*, etc. *I'm going to Tokyo tomorrow and coming back on Tuesday.*

will + base form

instant decisions, promises, offers, predictions, 🔊 1 20
future facts, suggestions

I**'ll have** the steak. (instant decision)
I **won't tell** anybody where you are. (promise)
I**'ll carry** that bag for you. (offer)
You**'ll love** New York City! (prediction)
I**'ll be** home all afternoon. (future fact)

We use *will / won't* (NOT the simple present) for instant decisions, promises, offers, and suggestions. NOT ~~I carry that bag for you~~.

- We can also use *will / won't* for predictions, e.g., *I think the Yankees will win,* and to talk about future facts, e.g., *The election will be on March 1st.*

---

a (Circle) the correct form. Check ✓ the sentence if both are possible.

My grandparents *are going to retire | will retire* next year. ✓

1 *We'll invite | We're going to* invite your parents for Sunday lunch?
2 *I'm going to make | I'll make* a cake for your mom's birthday, if you want.
3 *I'm not having | I'm not going to have* dinner with my family tonight.
4 The exam *will be | is being* on the last Friday of the semester.
5 You can trust me. *I'm not telling | I won't tell* anyone what you told me.
6 My cousin *is arriving | will arrive* at 5:30 p.m.
7 I think the birthrate *will go down | is going to go down* in my country in the next few years.
8 *I'm not going to go | I won't go* to my brother-in-law's party next weekend.
9 *I'm going to help | I'll help* you with the dishes.

b Complete B's replies with a correct future form.

A What's your stepmother going to do about her car?
B She*'s going to buy* a used one. (buy)
1 A I'm going to miss you.
B Don't worry. I promise I _____ every day. (write)
2 A What are Alan's plans for the future?
B He _____ a degree in engineering. (earn)
3 A Can I see you tonight?
B No, I _____ late. How about Saturday? (work)
4 A What would you like for an appetizer?
B I _____ the shrimp, please. (have)
5 A There's nothing in the refrigerator.
B OK. _____ we _____ some take-out Mexican food? (get)
6 A I don't have any money, so I can't go out.
B No problem, I _____ you some. (lend)
7 A Can we have a barbecue tomorrow?
B I don't think so. On the radio they said that it _____. (rain)
8 A We land at about eight o'clock.
B _____ you _____ a ride from the airport? (need)

◀ p.9

2A

present perfect and simple past

present perfect: have / has + past participle (worked, seen, etc.)

1. **past experiences**
   I**'ve been** to Miami but I **haven't been** to Tampa.
   Have you ever **lost** your credit card?
   Sally **has** never **met** Bill's ex-wife.

2. **with yet and already (for emphasis)**
   I**'ve** already **seen** this movie twice. Can't we watch another one?
   My brother **hasn't found** a job yet. He's still looking.
   Have you **finished** your homework yet? No, not yet.

1 We use the present perfect for past experiences when we don't say exactly when they happened.
   - We often use *ever* and *never* when we ask or talk about past experiences. They go <u>before</u> the main verb.
2 In American English, we use the present perfect and the simple past with *yet* and *already*.
   - *already* is used in + sentences and goes <u>before</u> the main verb.
   - *yet* is used with − sentences and ?. It goes <u>at the end</u> of the phrase.
   - For irregular past participles see **Irregular verbs** *p.165*.

simple past (worked, stopped, went, had, etc.)

They **got** married last year.
What time **did** you **wake up** this morning?
I **didn't have** time to do my homework.

- Use the simple past for finished past actions (when we say, ask, or know when they happened).

present perfect or simple past?

I**'ve been** to Miami twice.
 (= in my life up to now)
I **went** there in 1998 and 2002.
 (= on two specific occasions)

- Use the simple past (NOT the present perfect) to ask or talk about finished actions in the past, **when the time is mentioned or understood**. We often use a past time expression, e.g., *yesterday, last week*, etc.

---

a Complete the mini dialogues with the present perfect form of the verb in parentheses and an adverb from the list. You can use the adverbs more than once.

already   ever   never   yet

   A _____ you _____ the lottery _____? (play)
   B That's why I'm smiling – I won $50!
1 A _____ you _____ _____ a flight online? (book)
   B Yes, of course. I've done it many times.
2 A When are you going to buy a motorcycle?
   B Soon. I _____ _____ almost $1,000. (save)
3 A _____ you _____ the electricity bill _____? (pay)
   B No, sorry. I forgot.
4 A _____ your parents _____ _____ you money? (lend)
   B Yes, but I paid it back as soon as I could.
5 A How does eBay work?
   B I don't know. I _____ _____ _____ it. (use)
6 A _____ you _____ _____ to Thailand? (be)
   B No, I haven't. But I'd like to some day.
7 A Why don't you have any money?
   B I _____ _____ my salary. I bought a new tablet last week. (spend)
8 A Do you like Hugh Jackman?
   B Yes, I _____ _____ his new movie twice! (see)

b Right or wrong? Write a check ✓ or an ✗ next to the sentences. Correct the wrong sentences.

   I've never been in debt. ✓
   How much has your new camera cost? ✗
   How much did your new camera cost?

1 Dean inherited $5,000 from a relative.
2 Did your sister pay you back yet?
3 We booked our vacation online a month ago.
4 When have you bought that leather jacket?
5 They've finished paying back the loan last month.
6 We haven't paid the gas bill yet.
7 Have you ever wasted a lot of money on something?
8 I'm sure I haven't borrowed any money from you last week.
9 I spent my salary really quickly last month.
10 Have you seen the Batman movie on TV yesterday?

◀ *p.16*

2B GRAMMAR BANK

present perfect + *for* / *since*, present perfect continuous

present perfect + *for* / *since*

They've **known** each other for ten years.
Julia **has had** that bag since she was in college.
A How long **have** you **worked** here?
B Since 1996.
A How long **has** your brother **had** his motorcycle?
B For about a year.

- We use the present perfect + *for* or *since* with **nonaction verbs** (e.g., *like*, *have*, *know*, etc.) to talk about something that started in the past and is still true now.
  They've known each other for ten years. (= they met ten years ago, and they still know each other today)
- We use *How long…?* + present perfect to ask about an unfinished period of time (from the past until now).
- We use *for* + a period of time, e.g., *for two weeks*, or *since* + a point of time, e.g., *since 1990*.
- Don't use the simple present with *for* / *since*, NOT ~~They know each other for a long time.~~

present perfect continuous: *have* / *has been* + verb + *-ing*

1. How long **have** you **been learning** English?
   Nick **has been working** here since April.
   They**'ve been going out** together for about three years.
2. Your eyes are red. **Have** you **been crying**?
   No, I**'ve been cutting** onions.

1. We use the present perfect continuous with *for* and *since* with **action verbs** (e.g., *learn*, *work*, *go*, etc.) to talk about actions that started in the past and are still true now.
   - Don't use the present continuous with *for* / *since*, NOT ~~I am working here for two years.~~
2. We can also use the present perfect continuous for continuous or repeated actions that have been happening very recently. The actions have usually just finished.

I've (I have) You've (You have) He / She / It's (He has) We've (We have) They've (They have)	been working here for two years.
I haven't (I have not) You haven't He / She / It hasn't We haven't They haven't	been working here for two years.
Have you been working here for two years?	Yes, I have.	No, I haven't.
Has she been working here for two years?	Yes, she has.	No, she hasn't.

> 🔍 **work and live**
> *Work* and *live* are often used in either present perfect or present perfect continuous with the same meaning.
> *I've lived here since 1980.*
> *I've been living here since 1980.*

---

a Correct the mistakes.

Harry is unemployed since last year.
Harry has been unemployed since last year.

1. We've had our new apartment since six months.
2. Hi, Jackie! How are you? I don't see you for ages!
3. How long are you knowing your husband?
4. Emily has been a volunteer for ten years ago.
5. Paul doesn't eat anything since yesterday because he's sick.
6. It hasn't rained since two months.
7. How long has your parents been married?
8. They're having their dog since they got married.
9. I haven't gotten any emails from my brother for last winter.
10. My grandmother lives in the same house all her life.

b Make sentences with the present perfect or present perfect continuous (and *for* / *since* if necessary). Use the present perfect continuous if possible.

I / work for a charity / eight years
I've been working for a charity for eight years.

1. we / know each other / we were children
2. the children / play computer games / two hours
3. your sister / have that hairstyle / a long time?
4. I / love her / the first day we met
5. my Internet connection / not work / yesterday
6. how long / you / wait?
7. I / be a teacher / three years
8. it / snow / five o'clock this morning
9. Sam / not study enough / recently
10. you / live in Chicago / a long time?

◀ p.19

3A

comparatives and superlatives: adjectives and adverbs

comparing two people, places, things, etc.

1 My sister is a little **taller than** me.
San Francisco is **more expensive than** Chicago.
This test is **less difficult than** the last one.
Olive oil is **better** for you **than** butter.
2 The new sofa isn't **as comfortable as** the old one.
I don't have **as many** books **as** I used to.

1 We use comparative **adjectives** to compare two people, places, things, etc.
- Regular comparative adjectives: spelling rules
  old > old**er**   big > big**ger**   easy > eas**ier**
  modern > **more** modern   difficult > **more** difficult
- Irregular comparative adjectives:
  good > better   bad > worse   far > farther / further
- One-syllable adjectives ending in -ed:
  bored > **more** bored   stressed > **more** stressed   tired > **more** tired

2 We can also use (not) as + adjective + as to make comparisons.

> 🔍 **Object pronouns (me, him, etc.) after than and as**
> After *than* or *as* we can use an object pronoun (*me, him, her*, etc.) or a subject pronoun (*I, he, she*, etc.) + auxiliary verb.
> She's taller than me. OR She's taller than I am. NOT ~~She's taller than I.~~
> They're not as busy as us. OR They're not as busy as we are. NOT ~~They're not as busy as we.~~
>
> **the same as**
> We use *the same as* to say that two people, places, things, etc. are identical.
> Her dress is the same as mine.

comparing two actions

1 My father drives **faster than** me.
You walk **more quickly** than I do.
Atlanta played worse today **than** last week.
2 Max doesn't speak English **as well as** his wife does.
I don't earn **as much as** my boss.

1 We use comparative **adverbs** to compare two actions.
- Regular comparative adverbs: spelling rules
  fast > fast**er**   slowly > **more** slowly   carefully > **more** carefully
- Irregular comparatives:
  well > better   badly > worse

2 We can also use (*not*) *as* + adverb + *as* to make comparisons.

superlatives

Kevin is **the tallest** player on the team.
Tokyo is **the most expensive** city in the world.
The small bag is **the least expensive**.
Lucy is the **best student** in the class.
Who dresses **the most stylishly** in your family?
That's **the worst** we've ever played.

- We use superlative **adjectives** and **adverbs** to compare people, things, or actions with all of their group.
- Form superlatives like comparatives, but use *-est* instead of *-er* and *most / least* instead of *more / less*.
- We usually use **the** before superlatives, but you can also use possessive adjectives, e.g., **my** best friend, **their** most famous song.
- We often use a superlative with present perfect + *ever*, e.g., It's the best book I've ever read.

> 🔍 **in after superlatives**
> Use *in* (NOT *of*) before places after a superlative.
> It's the longest bridge **in** the world. NOT ~~of the world~~
> It's the best beach **in** Florida. NOT ~~of Florida~~

---

a Complete with the comparative or superlative of the **bold** word (and *than* if necessary).

What's *the fastest* way to get around Miami? **fast**
1 I think skiing is _____ horseback riding. **easy**
2 A motorcycle is _____ a scooter. **powerful**
3 I think that traveling by train is _____ form of transportation. **relaxing**
4 You walk _____ I do. **slowly**
5 _____ time to travel is on holiday weekends. **bad**
6 _____ I've ever driven is from Washington, D.C. to Chicago. **far**
7 The London Underground is _____ the subway in New York City. **old**
8 This is _____ bus I've ever been on. **hot**
9 Of all my family, my mom is _____ driver. **good**

b Complete with one word.

Going by motorboat is *more* exciting than traveling by ferry.
1 A bus isn't as comfortable _____ a train.
2 It's _____ most expensive car we've ever bought.
3 The traffic was worse _____ we expected.
4 This is the longest trip I've _____ been on.
5 He gets home late, but his wife arrives later than _____.
6 The _____ interesting place I've ever visited is Venice.
7 I leave home at the same time _____ my brother.
8 He drives _____ carefully than his girlfriend – he's never had an accident.
9 We don't go abroad _____ often as we used to.
10 What's the longest freeway _____ the US?

◀ p.26

3B GRAMMAR BANK

articles: a / an, the, no article

a / an

1 I saw **an old man** with **a dog**.
2 It's **a nice house**. She's **a lawyer**.
3 What **an awful day**!
4 I have classes three times **a week**.

- We use *a / an* with singular countable nouns:
  1 the first time you mention a thing / person.
  2 when you say what something is or what somebody does.
  3 in exclamations with *What…!*
  4 in expressions of frequency.

the

1 I saw an old man with **a dog**.
  The dog was barking.
2 My father opened **the door**.
  The children are at school.
3 **The moon** goes around **the Earth**.
4 I'm going to **the movies** tonight.
5 It's **the best** restaurant in town.

- We use *the*:
  1 when we talk about something we've already mentioned.
  2 when it's clear what you're referring to.
  3 when there's only one of something.
  4 with places in a town, e.g., *movies* and *theater*.
  5 with superlatives.

no article

1 **Women** usually talk more than **men**.
  Love is more important than **money**.
2 She's not **at home** today.
  I get back **from work** at 5:30.
3 I never have **breakfast**.
4 See you **next Friday**.

- We don't use an article:
  1 when we are speaking in general (with plural and uncountable nouns). Compare:
  I love *flowers*. (= flowers in general)
  I love **the flowers** in my garden. (= the specific flowers in my garden)
  2 with some nouns, (e.g., *home, work, school*) after *at / to / from*.
  3 before meals, days, and months.
  4 before *next / last* + day, week, etc.

---

a Circle the correct answers.

I love *weddings* / *the weddings*!

1 Jess is *nurse* / *a nurse* in a hospital. *A hospital* / *The hospital* is far from her house.
2 What *a horrible day* / *horrible day*! We'll have to have our picnic in *the car* / *a car*.
3 My wife likes *love stories* / *the love stories*, but I prefer *the war movies* / *war movies*.
4 We go to *theater* / *the theater* about *once a month* / *once the month*.
5 I'm having *dinner* / *the dinner* with some friends *the next Friday* / *next Friday*.
6 My boyfriend is *chef* / *a chef*. I think he's *the best cook* / *best cook* in the world.
7 I'm not sure if I closed *the windows* / *windows* before I left *the home* / *home* this morning.
8 In general, I like *dogs* / *the dogs*, but I don't like *dogs* / *the dogs* that live next door to me.
9 I got to *the school* / *school* late every day *the last week* / *last week*.
10 I think *happiness* / *the happiness* is more important than *success* / *the success*.

b Complete with *a / an*, *the*, or – (= no article).

A We're lost. Let's stop and buy *a* map.
B No need. I'll put *the* address in *the* GPS.

1 A How often do you go to _____ gym?
  B About three times _____ week. But I never go on _____ Fridays.
2 A What time does _____ train leave?
  B In ten minutes. Can you give me _____ ride to _____ station?
3 A What _____ beautiful dress!
  B Thanks. I bought it on _____ sale _____ last month.
4 A What's _____ most interesting place to visit in your town?
  B Probably _____ museum. It's _____ oldest building in town.
5 A What should we do _____ next weekend?
  B Let's invite some friends for _____ lunch. We could eat outside in _____ yard.
6 A Do you like _____ dogs?
  B Not really. I prefer _____ cats. I think they're _____ best pets.
7 A Is your mom _____ housewife?
  B No, she's _____ teacher. She's always tired when she gets home from _____ work.
8 A Have you ever had _____ problem in your relationship?
  B Yes, but we got over _____ problem, and we got married _____ last year.
9 A When is _____ meeting?
  B They've changed _____ date. It's _____ next Tuesday now.

◀ p.29

4A

can, could, be able to (ability and possibility)

can / could

I **can** speak three languages fluently.
Jenny **can't** come tonight. She's sick.
My cousin **could** play the violin when she was three.
They **couldn't** wait because they were in a hurry.
Could you open the door for me, please?

- *can* is a modal verb. It only has a present form (which can be used with future meaning) and a past or conditional form (*could*).
- For all other tenses and forms, we use *be able to* + base form.

be able to + base form

1 Luke **has been able to** swim since he was three.
I'd like **to be able to** ski.
I love **being able to** stay in bed late on Sunday morning.
You'**ll be able to** practice your English in the US.
2 Fortunately, I **am able to** accept your invitation.
My colleagues **weren't able to** come to yesterday's meeting.

1 We use *be able to* + base form for ability and possibility, especially where there is no form of *can*, e.g., future, present perfect, infinitive and gerund, etc.
2 We sometimes use *be able to* in the present and past (instead of *can / could*), usually if we want to be more formal.

a Complete with the correct form of *be able to* (+, −, or ?).

I'*ve* never *been able to* scuba dive.
1 Her cell phone has been turned off all morning, so I _____ talk to her yet.
2 I don't like noisy restaurants. I like _____ have a conversation without shouting.
3 I _____ leave home when I get a job.
4 We're having a party next Saturday. _____ you _____ come?
5 You need _____ swim before you can go in a canoe.
6 I'm going to France next week, but I don't speak French. I hate _____ communicate with people.
7 Fortunately, firefighters _____ rescue all of the people trapped inside the burning house.
8 I'm very sorry, but we _____ go to your wedding next month. We'll be on vacation.
9 I'm feeling a little worse. _____ you _____ contact the doctor yet?
10 The manager _____ see you right now because he's in a meeting.

b Circle the correct form. Check ✓ if both are possible.

I've always wanted to *can* / **be able to** dance salsa.
1 My little boy *couldn't* / *wasn't able to* speak until he was almost two years old.
2 She's much better after her operation. She'll *can* / *be able to* walk again in a few months.
3 He hasn't *could* / *been able to* fix my bike yet. He'll do it tomorrow.
4 It's the weekend at last! I love *can* / *being able to* go out with my friends.
5 When we lived on the coast, we used to *can* / *be able to* go to the beach every day.
6 I *can't* / *'m not able to* send any emails right now. My computer isn't working.
7 I *could* / *was able to* read before I started school.
8 We won't *can* / *be able to* go on vacation this year because we need to spend a lot of money on the house.
9 Linda *hasn't been able to* / *couldn't* find a job.
10 Alex *can* / *is able to* speak Korean fluently after living in Seoul for ten years.

◀ p.34

4B GRAMMAR BANK

have to, must, should

have to / must (+ base form)

1 You **have to** wear a seat belt in the car. (2 42)
  Do you **have to** work on Saturdays?
  I **had to** wear a uniform at my elementary school.
  I'**ll have to** get up early tomorrow. My interview is at 9:00.
2 You **must** be on time tomorrow because there's a test.
  You **must** remember to call Emily – it's her birthday.
3 I love the Louvre! You **have to** go when you're in Paris.
  You **must** see this movie – it's amazing!

- *have to* and *must* are usually used to talk about obligation or something that is necessary to do.
1 *have to* is a normal verb and it exists in all tenses and forms, e.g., also as a gerund or infinitive.
2 *must* is a modal verb. It only exists in the present, but it can be used with a future meaning.
3 You can also use *have to* or *must* for strong recommendations.

> **have to or must?**
> *Have to* and *must* have a very similar meaning, and you can usually use either form.
> *Have to* is more common for general, external obligations, for example rules and laws.
> *Must* is more common for specific (i.e., on one occasion) or personal obligations. Compare:
> *I have to wear a shirt and tie at work.* (= It's the rule in this company.)
> *I must buy a new shirt – this one is too old now.* (= It's my own decision.)
>
> **have got to**
> *Have got to* is often used instead of *have to* in spoken English, e.g., *I've got to go now. It's very late.*

don't have to

You **don't have to** pay – this museum is free. (2 43)
You **don't have to** go to the party if you don't want to.

must not

You **must not** park here. (2 44)

- We use *don't have to* when there is no obligation to do something, and *must not* when something is prohibited.
- *don't have to* and *must not* are completely different. Compare:
  You don't have to drive – we can take a train. (= You can drive if you want to, but it's not necessary / obligatory.)
  You must not drive along this street. (= It's prohibited, against the law, NOT ~~You don't have to drive along this street.~~)
- You can often use *can't* or *not allowed to* instead of *must not*.
  You **must not** / **can't** / **'re not allowed to** park here.

should / shouldn't (+ base form)

You **should** take warm clothes with you to Quito. (2 45)
It might be cold at night.
You **shouldn't** drink so much coffee. It isn't good for you.
I think the government **should** do something about unemployment.

- *should* is not as strong as *must* / *have to*. We use it to give advice or an opinion – to say if we think something is the right or wrong thing to do.
- *should* is a modal verb. The only forms are *should* / *shouldn't*.

---

a Complete with the correct form of *have to* (+, –, or ?).

I'*ll have to* call back later because the line's busy. +

1 Passengers _____ turn off their laptops during take-off. +
2 _____ you _____ do a lot of homework when you were in school? ?
3 My sister is a nurse, so some weeks she _____ work nights. +
4 _____ you ever _____ have an operation? ?
5 Saturdays are the best day of the week. I love _____ get up early. –
6 I _____ leave a message on her voicemail because she wasn't in. +
7 In the future, people _____ go to school; they'll all study at home. –
8 With old cell phones, you used to _____ charge the battery more often. +
9 _____ your boyfriend _____ answer his work emails on weekends? ?
10 The exhibition was free, so I _____ pay. –

b Circle the correct form. Check ✓ if both are possible.

You *don't have to* / **must not** use your phone in quiet zones.

1 Do you think we *should* / *have to* text Dad to tell him we'll be late?
2 You *don't have to* / *must not* send text messages when you are driving.
3 A pilot *has to* / *must* wear a uniform when he's at work.
4 You *shouldn't* / *must not* talk on your cell phone when you're filling up the car with gas.
5 I *have to* / *should* speak to my phone company. My last bill was wrong.
6 We *don't have to* / *shouldn't* hurry. We have plenty of time.

◀ p.39

5A

past tenses

simple past: *worked, stopped, went, had,* etc.

> She **was** born in Seoul.
> They **got** married last year.
> On the way to Rome we **stopped** in Florence for the night.
> The plane **didn't arrive** on time.
> What time **did** you **get up** this morning?

- We use the simple past for finished actions in the past (when we say, ask, or know when they happened).
- Remember **Irregular verbs** p.165.

past continuous: *was / were* + verb + *-ing*

> 1 What **were** you **doing** at six o'clock last night?
> 2 I **was driving** along the freeway when it started snowing.
> 3 While I **was doing** the housework the children **were playing** in the yard.
> 4 It was a cold night and it **was raining**. I **was watching** TV in the living room…

1 We use the past continuous to talk about an action in progress at a specific time in the past.
2 We often use the past continuous to describe a past action in progress that was interrupted by another action (expressed in the simple past).
3 We often use the past continuous with *while* for two actions happening at the same time.
4 We often use the past continuous to describe the beginning of a story or anecdote.

past perfect: *had* + past participle

> When they turned on the TV, the game **had** already **finished**.
> As soon as I shut the door, I realized that **I'd left** my keys on the table.
> We couldn't get a table in the restaurant because we **hadn't booked** one.

- We use the past perfect when we are talking about the past and we want to talk about an earlier past action. Compare:
  When John arrived, they **went out**. (= first John arrived and then they went out)
  When John arrived, they **had gone out**. (= they went out <u>before</u> John arrived)

using narrative tenses together

> It was a cold night and it **was raining**. I **was watching** TV in the living room. Suddenly I **heard** a knock at the door. I **got up** and **opened** the door. But there was nobody there. The person who **had knocked** on the door **had disappeared**…

- Use the past continuous (*was raining, was watching*) to set the scene.
- Use the simple past (*heard, got up,* etc.) to say what happened.
- Use the past perfect (*had knocked, had disappeared*) to say what happened <u>before</u> the previous past action.

---

a Circle the correct form.

The teacher gave Robbie a zero because he *cheated /* (*had cheated*) on the exam.
1 They didn't win the game although they *were training / had trained* every evening.
2 Mike had an accident while he *drove / was driving* to work.
3 I *cleaned / had cleaned* the house when I got home. It looked great.
4 When we arrived, the game *started / had started*. We got there just in time and saw the whole game!
5 The captain *didn't score / hadn't scored* any goals when the referee ejected him.
6 My son got injured while he *played / was playing* basketball last Saturday.
7 Luckily, we *stopped / had stopped* skiing when the snowstorm started. We were already back at the hotel.
8 The Lakers *weren't losing / hadn't lost* any of their games during their trip to the East Coast.
9 The referee suspended the game because it *was raining / rained* too hard to play.

b Complete with the simple past, past continuous, or past perfect.

The marathon runner <u>was sweating</u> when she <u>crossed</u> the finish line. (sweat, cross)
1 The accident _____ when they _____ home. (happen, drive)
2 The crowd _____ when the referee _____ the final whistle. (cheer, blow)
3 I _____ her at first because she _____ so much. (not recognize, change)
4 The police _____ her on the freeway because she _____ a seat belt. (stop, not wear)
5 Some of the players _____ while the coach _____ to them. (not listen, talk)
6 We _____ use the ski slope because it _____ enough. (not can, not snow)
7 They _____ play tennis because they _____ a court. (not able to, not book)
8 The player _____ a yellow card because he _____ his shirt. (get, take off)

◀ p.46

5B

present and past habits and states: *usually* and *used to*

> 1. I **usually get up** at 8:00 during the week.
>   I **don't normally go out** during the week.
>   Houses in the suburbs **usually have** yards.
>   **Do** you **normally walk** to work?
> 2. We **used to go** to the beach for our vacations when I was a child.
>   He **didn't use to do** any exercise, but now he runs marathons.
>   I **never used to like** hockey, but I watch it every week now.
>   We **used to be** close friends, but we don't talk to each other anymore.
>   That building **used to be** a restaurant, but it closed down last year.
>   **Did** they **use to live** downtown?
>   **Didn't** you **use to have** long hair?

1. For present habits we can use *usually* or *normally* + simple present.
   NOT ~~I used to get up at 8:00.~~
2. For past habits we use *used to* / *didn't use to* + base form.
   - *used to* does not exist in the present tense. NOT ~~I use to get up at 8:00 during the week.~~
   - We use *used to* for things that were true over a period of time in the past. *Used to* often refers to something that is not true now.
     I used to play a lot of sports. (= I played a lot of sports for a period of time in the past, but now I don't.)
   - *used to* / *didn't use to* can be used with action verbs (e.g., *go, do*) and nonaction verbs (e.g., *be, have*).
   - We can also use the simple past to describe past habits (often with an adverb of frequency).
     We (often) went to the beach for our vacations when I was a child.
     I lived downtown until I got married.

GRAMMAR BANK

> **used to or simple past?**
> We can use *used to* or simple past for repeated actions or states, and the meaning is the same.
> *I used to live in Miami as a child. / I lived in Miami as a child.*
> But if the action happened only once, or we mention exact dates or number of times, we have to use simple past.
> *I went to Paris last year.* NOT ~~I used to go to Paris last year.~~
> *Jack caught the train to Chicago four times last week.* NOT ~~Jack used to catch the train to Chicago four times last week.~~
>
> **anymore and any longer**
> We often use *not...anymore / any longer* (= not now) with the simple present to contrast with *used to.*
> *I used to go to the gym, but I don't (go) anymore / any longer.*
>
> **be used to and get used to**
> Don't confuse *used to* / *didn't use to* (do something) with *be used to* or *get used to* (doing something).
> *I am used to getting up early every day.* (= I am accustomed to it. I always do it, so it is not a problem for me.)
> *Lola can't get used to living in the US.* (= She can't get accustomed to it. It is a problem for her.)

a Complete with *used to* (+, -, or ?) and a verb from the list.

argue	be	get along	go out	have
like	~~live~~	speak	spend	wear	work

Sonya *used to live* in New York City, but later she moved to New Jersey. +

1. We _____ a lot in common, but now we're completely different. +
2. I _____ much time online, but now I'm addicted to Facebook. -
3. _____ your fiancé _____ glasses? He looks different now. ?
4. I _____ with my classmates, but now I spend all my time with my boyfriend. +
5. Where _____ your husband _____ before he got the job in the bank? ?
6. My sister lost a lot of weight. She _____ so slim. -
7. _____ you _____ a lot with your parents when you were a teenager? ?
8. I _____ Japanese food, but now I eat a lot of sushi. -
9. Laura _____ well with her roommate, but now they don't talk to each other. +
10. My ex _____ to me, but now he calls me a lot. -

b Are the highlighted verb forms right ✓ or wrong ✗? Correct the wrong ones.

Sonya **use to see** Michael every day. ✗ *used to see*

1. His parents **used to split up** after he was born.
2. **Do you usually tell** a close friend about your problems?
3. My sister **didn't use to want** children, but now she has four!
4. I **didn't used to like** my math teacher when I was in school.
5. They **used to go** on vacation every year.
6. That couple has three kids, so they **don't use to go** out at night.
7. Where **did your parents use to meet** when they first went out?
8. My husband **use to work** for a bank, but now he's unemployed.
9. We love the theater. We **usually go** to a play at least once a month.

◀ p.49

Food and cooking

VOCABULARY BANK

1 FOOD

a Match the words and pictures.

Fish and seafood
- *1* crab /kræb/
- mussels /ˈmʌslz/
- salmon /ˈsæmən/
- shrimp /ʃrɪmp/
- squid /skwɪd/
- tuna /ˈtunə/

Meat
- beef /bif/
- chicken /ˈtʃɪkən/
- duck /dʌk/
- lamb /læm/
- pork /pɔrk/

Fruits and vegetables
- beet /bit/
- cabbage /ˈkæbɪdʒ/
- cherries /ˈtʃɛriz/
- cucumber /ˈkyukʌmbər/
- eggplant /ˈɛgplænt/ (*BritE* aubergine)
- grapes /greɪps/
- green beans /grin binz/
- lemon /ˈlɛmən/
- mango /ˈmæŋgoʊ/
- melon /ˈmɛlən/
- peach /pitʃ/
- pear /pɛr/
- raspberries /ˈræzbɛriz/
- red pepper /rɛd ˈpɛpər/
- zucchini /zuˈkini/ (*BritE* courgette)

b 1 2)) Listen and check.

c Are there any things in the list that you…?
  a love
  b hate
  c have never tried

d Are there any other kinds of fish, meat, or fruits and vegetables that are very common in your country?

2 COOKING

a Match the words and pictures.

- *4* boiled /bɔɪld/
- roasted /ˈroʊstɪd/
- baked /beɪkt/
- grilled /grɪld/
- fried /fraɪd/
- steamed /stimd/

b 1 3)) Listen and check.

c How do you prefer these things to be cooked?

eggs	chicken
potatoes	fish

> 🔍 **Phrasal verbs**
>
> Learn these phrasal verbs connected with food and diet.
>
> I **eat out** a lot because I don't really have time to cook. (= eat in restaurants)
>
> I'm trying to **cut down on** coffee right now. I'm only having one cup at breakfast. (= have less)
>
> The doctor told me I had very high cholesterol and that I should completely **cut out** all high-fat cheese and dairy products from my diet. (= eliminate)

◀ p.4

Personality

VOCABULARY BANK

1 WHAT ARE THEY LIKE?

a Complete the definitions with the adjectives.

| affectionate /əˈfɛkʃənət/ aggressive /əˈgrɛsɪv/ |
| ambitious /æmˈbɪʃəs/ anxious /ˈæŋkʃəs/ bossy /ˈbɔsi/ |
| charming /ˈtʃɑrmɪŋ/ competitive /kəmˈpɛtətɪv/ |
| independent /ˌɪndɪˈpɛndənt/ jealous /ˈdʒɛləs/ |
| moody /ˈmudi/ rebellious /rɪˈbɛlyəs/ reliable /rɪˈlaɪəbl/ |
| selfish /ˈsɛlfɪʃ/ sensible /ˈsɛnsəbl/ sensitive /ˈsɛnsətɪv/ |
| sociable /ˈsoʊʃəbl/ spoiled /spɔɪld/ stubborn /ˈstʌbərn/ |

1 _Selfish_ people think about themselves and not about other people.
2 A _____ person always wants to win.
3 _____ children behave badly because they are given everything they want.
4 An _____ person gets angry quickly and likes fighting and arguing.
5 _____ people have an attractive personality and make people like them.
6 A _____ person has common sense and is practical.
7 A _____ person is friendly and enjoys being with other people.
8 _____ people are often worried or stressed.
9 A _____ person is happy one minute and sad the next, and is often bad-tempered.
10 _____ people like doing things on their own, without help.
11 A _____ person likes giving orders to other people.
12 An _____ person shows that he or she loves or likes people very much.
13 A _____ person thinks that someone loves another person more than him or her, or wants what other people have.
14 A _____ person can be easily hurt or offended.
15 An _____ person wants to be successful in life.
16 A _____ person is someone who you can trust or depend on.
17 A _____ person doesn't like obeying rules.
18 A _____ person never changes his (or her) opinion or attitude about something.

b ((1 23)) Listen and check.

c Cover the definitions and look at the adjectives. Remember the definitions.

2 OPPOSITES

a Match the adjectives and their opposites.

| cheap /tʃip/ hardworking /ˈhɑrdˌwərkɪŋ/ |
| outgoing /ˈaʊtˌgoʊɪŋ/ self-confident /ˈsɛlf ˈkɑnfədənt/ |
| stupid /ˈstupəd/ talkative /ˈtɔkətɪv/ |

	Opposite
generous	_____
insecure	_____
lazy	_____
quiet	_____
shy	_____
smart	_____

b ((1 24)) Listen and check. Then cover the opposites and test yourself.

c With a partner, look at the adjectives again in **1** and **2**. Do you think they are positive, negative, or neutral characteristics?

3 NEGATIVE PREFIXES

a Which prefix do you use with these adjectives? Put them in the correct column.

| ~~ambitious~~ clean friendly honest imaginative |
| kind mature organized patient reliable |
| responsible selfish sensitive sociable |

un- / dis-	im- / ir- / in-
unambitious	

b ((1 25)) Listen and check. Which of the new adjectives has a positive meaning?

c Cover the columns. Test yourself.

> **False friends**
>
> Some words in English are very similar to words in other languages, but have different meanings.
>
> **Sensible** looks very similar to *sensible* in Spanish and French, but in fact in English it means someone who has common sense and is practical. The Spanish / French word *sensible* translates as **sensitive** in English (to describe a person who is easily hurt).
>
> **Sympathetic** does not mean the same as *sempatik* in Turkish (which mean **nice, friendly**). In English, **sympathetic** means a person who understands other people's feelings, e.g., *My best friend was very sympathetic when I failed my exam last week.*

◀ p.11

Money

VOCABULARY BANK

1 VERBS

a Complete the sentences with a verb from the list.

be worth /bi wərθ/   borrow /ˈbɑroʊ/   can't afford /kænt əˈfɔrd/   charge /tʃɑrdʒ/   cost /kɔst/   earn /ərn/
inherit /ɪnˈhɛrət/   invest /ɪnˈvɛst/   lend /lɛnd/   owe /oʊ/   raise /reɪz/   save /seɪv/   waste /weɪst/

1 My uncle died and left me $2,000.   I'm going to _inherit_ $2,000.
2 I put some money aside every week for my next vacation.   I _____ money every week.
3 My brother promised to give me $50.   He promised to _____ me $50.
4 I need to ask my mom to give me $20.   I need to _____ $20 from my mom.
5 I often spend money on stupid things.   I often _____ money.
6 I don't have enough money to buy that car.   I _____ to buy that car.
7 I usually have to pay the mechanic $400 to fix my car.   The mechanic _____ me $400.
8 These shoes are very expensive. They are $200.   They _____ $200.
9 Jim gave me $100. I haven't paid him back yet.   I _____ Jim $100.
10 I want to put money in a bank account. They'll give me 5% interest. I want to _____ some money.
11 I work in a supermarket. They pay me $1,600 a month.   I _____ $1,600 a month.
12 I could sell my house for about $200,000.   My house _____ about $200,000.
13 We need to get people to give money to build a new hospital.   We want to _____ money for the new hospital.

b 🔊 1 35)) Listen and check. Cover the sentences on the right. Try to remember them.

2 PREPOSITIONS

a Complete the **Preposition** column with a word from the list.

by   for (x2)   from   in (x2)   into   on   to

		Preposition
1	Would you like to pay ___ cash or ___ credit card?	in, by
2	I paid ___ the dinner last night. It was my birthday.	
3	I spent $50 ___ books yesterday.	
4	My uncle invested all his money ___ real estate.	
5	I don't like lending money ___ friends.	
6	I borrowed a lot of money ___ the bank.	
7	They charged me $120 ___ a haircut!	
8	I never get ___ debt. I hate owing people money.	

b 🔊 1 36)) Listen and check.

c Cover the **Preposition** column. Look at the sentences and remember the prepositions.

3 NOUNS

a Match the nouns and definitions.

ATM (BritE cash machine) /eɪ ti ˈɛm/   bill /bɪl/
coin /kɔɪn/   loan /loʊn/   mortgage /ˈmɔrgɪdʒ/
salary /ˈsæləri/   tax /tæks/

1 _coin_   a piece of money made of metal
2 _____   a piece of paper that shows how much money you have to pay for something
3 _____   the money you get for the work you do
4 _____   money that you pay to the government
5 _____   money that somebody (or a bank) lends you
6 _____   money that a bank lends you to buy a house
7 _____   a machine where you can get money

b 🔊 1 37)) Listen and check. Cover the words and look at the definitions. Try to remember the words.

> 🔍 **Phrasal verbs**
>
> I **took out** $200 from an ATM. (= took from my bank account)
> When can you **pay** me **back** the money I lent you? (= return)
> I have to **live off** my parents while I'm in college. (= depend on financially)
> It's difficult for me and my wife to **live on** only one salary. (= have enough money for basic things you need to live)

◀ p.14

Transportation

VOCABULARY BANK

1 PUBLIC TRANSPORTATION AND VEHICLES

a Match the words and pictures.

- ☐ bus /bʌs/
- ☐ freeway /ˈfriweɪ/
- ☐ light rail /laɪt reɪl/
- **1** platform /ˈplætfɔrm/
- ☐ scooter /ˈskutər/
- ☐ subway /ˈsʌbweɪ/ (*BritE* the underground)
- ☐ train /treɪn/
- ☐ truck /trʌk/
- ☐ van /væn/

b 🔊 2 2))) Listen and check.

c Cover the words and look at the pictures. Try to remember the words.

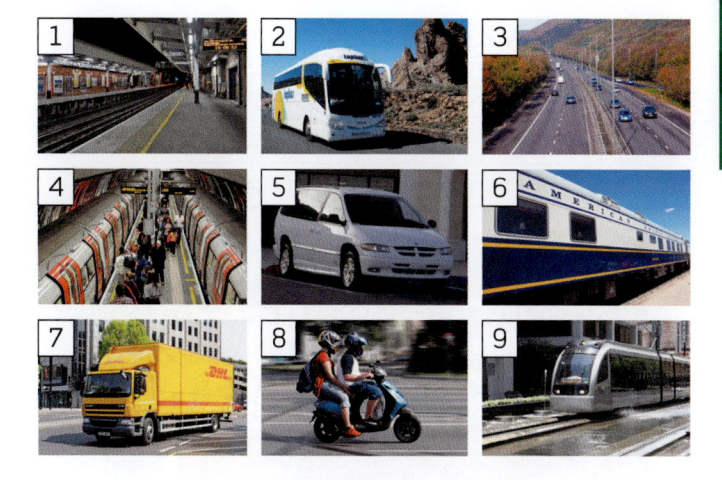

2 ON THE ROAD

> 🔍 **Compound nouns**
> Compound nouns are two nouns together where the first noun describes the second, e.g., *a child seat* = a seat for a child, *a bus stop* = a place for buses to stop, etc. In compound nouns, the first noun is stressed more strongly than the second. There are many compound nouns related to road travel.

a Complete the compound nouns.

belt /bɛlt/	camera /ˈkæmrə/	crash /kræʃ/	hour /ˈaʊər/	jam /dʒæm/
lane /leɪn/	light /laɪt/	limit /ˈlɪmət/	stand /stænd/	station /ˈsteɪʃn/
ticket /ˈtɪkət/	walk /wɔk/	work /wɜrk/	zone /zoʊn/	

1 bicycle lane
2 car _____ 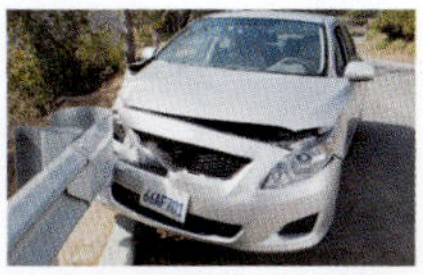
3 cross _____ 
4 gas _____ 
5 parking _____ 
6 pedestrian _____ 
7 road _____ 
8 rush _____ 
9 seat _____ 
10 speed _____ 
11 speed _____ 
12 taxi _____ 
13 traffic _____ 
14 traffic _____ 

b 🔊 2 3))) Listen and check. Then cover the compound nouns and look at the pictures. Remember the compound nouns.

3 HOW LONG DOES IT TAKE?

> 🔍 **How long does it take?**
> It **takes** about an hour to get from Princeton to New York City by train.
> It **took (me)** more than an hour to get to work yesterday.
> **How long does it take (you)** to get to school?
> Use *take* (+ person) + time (+ *to get to*) to talk about the duration of a trip, etc.

Read the information box above. Then ask and answer the questions with a partner.

1 How do you get to work / school? How long does it take?
2 How long does it take to get from your house to the center of town?

> 🔍 **Phrasal verbs**
> Learn these phrasal verbs connected with transportation and travel.
>
> *We **set off** at 7:00 in the morning to try to avoid the traffic.* (= leave on a trip)
>
> *I arrive at 8:15. Do you think you could **pick me up** at the station?* (= go somewhere in a car and get him/her, etc.)
>
> *I got on the wrong bus, and I **ended up** on the opposite side of town.* (= find yourself in a place / situation that you did not expect)
>
> *We're **running out of** gas. Let's stop at the next gas station.* (= finish your supply of something)
>
> ***Watch out!** / **Look out!** You're going to crash!* (= be careful or pay attention to something dangerous)

◀ p.24

Dependent prepositions

VOCABULARY BANK

1 AFTER VERBS

a Complete the **Preposition** column with a word from the list.

about   at   between   for   in   of   on   to   with

He apologized to the police officer for driving fast.

b 2 25))) Listen and check.

c Cover the **Preposition** column. Say the sentences with the correct preposition.

		Preposition
1	He apologized ___ the police officer ___ driving fast.	to , for
2	We're arriving ___ Miami on Sunday.	___
3	We're arriving ___ O'Hare Airport at 3:45.	___
4	Who does this book belong ___?	___
5	I never argue ___ my husband ___ money.	___ , ___
6	Could you ask the waiter ___ the check?	___
7	Do you believe ___ ghosts?	___
8	I can't choose ___ these two bags.	___
9	We might go out. It depends ___ the weather.	___
10	I dreamed ___ my childhood last night.	___
11	Don't laugh ___ me! I'm doing my best!	___
12	I'm really looking forward ___ the party.	___
13	If I pay ___ the gas, can you pay for the parking?	___
14	This music reminds me ___ our honeymoon in Italy.	___
15	I don't spend a lot of money ___ clothes.	___

2 AFTER ADJECTIVES

a Complete the **Preposition** column with a word from the list.

about   at   for   from   in   of   on   to   with

My brother is afraid of* bats.

*also *scared of* and *frightened of*

b 2 26))) Listen and check.

c Cover the **Preposition** column. Say the sentences with the correct preposition.

> 🔍 **Gerunds after prepositions**
> Remember that after a preposition we use a verb in the gerund (+ *-ing*).
> We're really excited **about going** to Brazil.
> I'm tired **of walking**.

◀ *p.31*

		Preposition
1	My brother is afraid* ___ bats.	of
2	She's really angry ___ her boyfriend ___ last night.	___
3	I've never been good ___ sports.	___
4	Eat your vegetables. They're good ___ you.	___
5	I'm very close ___ my older sister.	___
6	This exercise isn't very different ___ the last one.	___ (or *to*)
7	We're really excited ___ going to Brazil.	___
8	I'm fed up ___ listening to you complaining.	___
9	Krakow is famous ___ its main square.	___
10	My sister is very interested ___ astrology.	___
11	I'm very fond ___ my little nephew. He's adorable.	___
12	She's very passionate ___ riding her bike. She does about 30 miles every weekend.	___
13	I don't like people who aren't kind ___ animals.	___
14	She used to be married ___ a pop star.	___
15	I'm really happy ___ my new motorcycle.	___
16	My dad was very proud ___ learning to ski.	___
17	Why are you always rude ___ waiters and salespeople?	___
18	Rachel is worried ___ losing her job.	___
19	I'm tired ___ walking. Let's stop and rest.	___

Sports

VOCABULARY BANK

1 PEOPLE AND PLACES

a Match the words and pictures.

- ☐ captain /ˈkæptən/
- ☐ coach /koʊtʃ/
- 1 fans /fænz/
- ☐ players /ˈpleɪərz/
- ☐ referee /rɛfəˈri/
- ☐ umpire /ˈʌmpaɪər/
- ☐ spectators /ˈspɛkteɪtərz/
- ☐ the crowd /kraʊd/
- ☐ team /tim/
- ☐ stadium /ˈsteɪdiəm/
- ☐ sports arena /spɔrts əˈrinə/

b 🔊 3 2))) Listen and check. Cover the words and look at the pictures. Test yourself.

c Match the places and sports.

| course /kɔrs/ | ~~court~~ /kɔrt/ | field /fild/ |
| pool /pul/ | slope /sloʊp/ | track /træk/ |

1. tennis / basketball _court_
2. soccer / baseball _____
3. swimming / diving _____
4. running / horse racing _____
5. golf _____
6. ski _____

d 🔊 3 3))) Listen and check. Then test a partner.

A (book open) say a sport, e.g., *tennis*.
B (book closed) say where you play it, e.g., *tennis court*.

2 VERBS

🔍 **win** and **beat**
You **win** a game, competition, medal, or trophy.
You **beat** another team or person NOT ~~The Red Sox won the Yankees.~~

a Complete with the past tense and past participles.

beat	_beat_	_____
win	_____	_____
lose	_____	_____
tie	_____	_____

b Complete the **Verb** column with the past tense of a verb from **a**.

	Verb
1 Costa Rica ☐ the US 3–0.	_____
2 Costa Rica ☐ the game 3–0.	_____
3 The Chicago Bulls ☐ 78–91 to the Boston Celtics.	_____
4 Spain ☐ with Brazil 2–2.	_____

c 🔊 3 4))) Listen and check **a** and **b**.

d Complete the **Verb** column with a verb from the list.

do   get injured   get in shape   go   kick   score   throw   ~~train~~

	Verb
1 Professional sportspeople have to ☐ every day.	_train_
2 Don't play tennis on a wet court. You might ☐.	_____
3 A soccer player has to try to ☐ the ball into the goal.	_____
4 I've started going to the gym because I want to ☐.	_____
5 Our new striker is going to ☐ a lot of goals.	_____
6 Would you like to ☐ swimming this afternoon?	_____
7 My brothers ☐ yoga and tai-chi.	_____
8 In basketball, players ☐ the ball to each other.	_____

e 🔊 3 5))) Listen and check. Cover the **Verb** columns in **b** and **d**. Test yourself.

🔍 **Phrasal verbs**
It's important to **warm up** before you do any vigorous exercise. (= do light exercise to get ready, e.g., for a game)
My daughter **works out** every afternoon. (= exercises at a gym)
My team was **knocked out** in the semi-finals. (= eliminated)

◀ p.44

Relationships

VOCABULARY BANK

1 PEOPLE

a Match the words and definitions.

- classmate /ˈklæsmeɪt/
- close friend /kloʊs frɛnd/
- colleague /ˈkɑlig/
- ~~couple~~ /ˈkʌpl/
- ex /ɛks/
- fiancé /fianˈseɪ/ (*female* fiancée)
- partner /ˈpɑrtnər/
- roommate /ˈrummeɪt/

1. *couple* — two people who are married or in a romantic relationship
2. _____ — your husband, wife, boyfriend, or girlfriend
3. _____ — the person that you are engaged to be married to
4. _____ — a person that you share an apartment or house with
5. _____ — a person that you work with
6. _____ — (*colloquial*) a person that you used to have a relationship with
7. _____ — a very good friend that you can talk to about anything
8. _____ — a friend from school or college

b 🔊 3 19 Listen and check. Cover the definitions and look at the words. Remember the definitions.

2 VERBS AND VERB PHRASES

a Complete the sentences with a verb or verb phrase in the past tense.

be together   become friends   break up   get along   get in touch   get married
get to know   go out together   have something in common   lose touch   ~~meet~~
propose

1. I *met* Mark when I was studying at Boston University.
2. We _____ each other quickly because we went to the same classes.
3. We soon _____, and we discovered that we _____ a lot _____. For example, we both liked art and music.
4. We _____ in our second semester, and we fell in love.
5. We _____ for two years, but we argued a lot, and in our last semester of school, we _____.
6. After we graduated from college, we _____ because I moved to Chicago, and he stayed in Boston.
7. Five years later, we _____ again on Facebook. We were both still single, and Mark had moved to Chicago, too.
8. This time we _____ better than before, maybe because we were older.
9. After two months Mark _____ and I accepted.
10. We _____ last summer. A lot of our old college friends came to the wedding!

b 🔊 3 20 Listen and check.

c Look at the pictures. Try to remember the story.

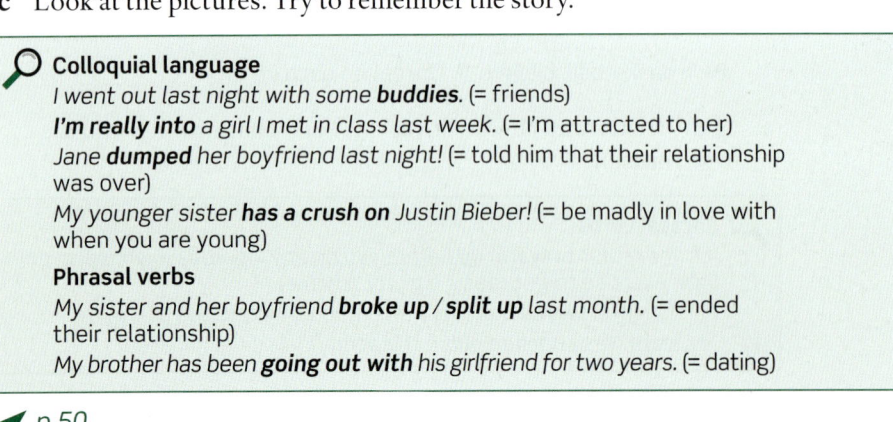

> 🔍 **Colloquial language**
> I went out last night with some **buddies**. (= friends)
> **I'm really into** a girl I met in class last week. (= I'm attracted to her)
> Jane **dumped** her boyfriend last night! (= told him that their relationship was over)
> My younger sister **has a crush on** Justin Bieber! (= be madly in love with when you are young)
>
> **Phrasal verbs**
> My sister and her boyfriend **broke up** / **split up** last month. (= ended their relationship)
> My brother has been **going out with** his girlfriend for two years. (= dating)

◀ *p.50*

Irregular verbs

🔊 5 45

Infinitive	Simple past	Past participle
be /bi/	was /wəz/ were /wər/	been /bɪn/
beat /bit/	beat	beaten /ˈbitn/
become /bɪˈkʌm/	became /bɪˈkeɪm/	become
begin /bɪˈgɪn/	began /bɪˈgæn/	begun /bɪˈgʌn/
bite /baɪt/	bit /bɪt/	bitten /ˈbɪtn/
break /breɪk/	broke /broʊk/	broken /ˈbroʊkən/
bring /brɪŋ/	brought /brɔt/	brought
build /bɪld/	built /bɪlt/	built
buy /baɪ/	bought /bɔt/	bought
can /kæn/	could /kʊd/	–
catch /kætʃ/	caught /kɔt/	caught
choose /tʃuz/	chose /tʃoʊz/	chosen /ˈtʃoʊzn/
come /kʌm/	came /keɪm/	come
cost /kɔst/	cost	cost
cut /kʌt/	cut	cut
do /du/	did /dɪd/	done /dʌn/
draw /drɔ/	drew /dru/	drawn /drɔn/
dream /drim/	dreamed /drimd/ (dreamt /drɛmt/)	dreamed (dreamt)
drink /drɪŋk/	drank /dræŋk/	drunk /drʌŋk/
drive /draɪv/	drove /droʊv/	driven /ˈdrɪvn/
eat /it/	ate /eɪt/	eaten /ˈitn/
fall /fɔl/	fell /fɛl/	fallen /ˈfɔlən/
feel /fil/	felt /fɛlt/	felt
find /faɪnd/	found /faʊnd/	found
fly /flaɪ/	flew /flu/	flown /floʊn/
forget /fərˈgɛt/	forgot /fərˈgɑt/	forgotten /fərˈgɑtn/
get /gɛt/	got /gɑt/	gotten /ˈgɑtn/
give /gɪv/	gave /geɪv/	given /ˈgɪvn/
go /goʊ/	went /wɛnt/	gone /gɑn/
grow /groʊ/	grew /gru/	grown /groʊn/
hang /hæŋ/	hung /hʌŋ/	hung
have /hæv/	had /hæd/	had
hear /hɪr/	heard /hərd/	heard
hit /hɪt/	hit	hit
hurt /hərt/	hurt	hurt
keep /kip/	kept /kɛpt/	kept
know /noʊ/	knew /nu/	known /noʊn/

Infinitive	Simple past	Past participle
learn /lərn/	learned /lərnd/	learned
leave /liv/	left /lɛft/	left
lend /lɛnd/	lent /lɛnt/	lent
let /lɛt/	let	let
lie /laɪ/	lay /leɪ/	lain /leɪn/
lose /luz/	lost /lɔst/	lost
make /meɪk/	made /meɪd/	made
mean /min/	meant /mɛnt/	meant
meet /mit/	met /mɛt/	met
pay /peɪ/	paid /peɪd/	paid
put /pʊt/	put	put
read /rid/	read /rɛd/	read /rɛd/
ride /raɪd/	rode /roʊd/	ridden /ˈrɪdn/
ring /rɪŋ/	rang /ræŋ/	rung /rʌŋ/
run /rʌn/	ran /ræn/	run
say /seɪ/	said /sɛd/	said
see /si/	saw /sɔ/	seen /sin/
sell /sɛl/	sold /soʊld/	sold
send /sɛnd/	sent /sɛnt/	sent
set /sɛt/	set	set
shine /ʃaɪn/	shone /ʃoʊn/	shone
shut /ʃʌt/	shut	shut
sing /sɪŋ/	sang /sæŋ/	sung /sʌŋ/
sit /sɪt/	sat /sæt/	sat
sleep /slip/	slept /slɛpt/	slept
speak /spik/	spoke /spoʊk/	spoken /ˈspoʊkən/
spend /spɛnd/	spent /spɛnt/	spent
stand /stænd/	stood /stʊd/	stood
steal /stil/	stole /stoʊl/	stolen /ˈstoʊlən/
swim /swɪm/	swam /swæm/	swum /swʌm/
take /teɪk/	took /tʊk/	taken /ˈteɪkən/
teach /titʃ/	taught /tɔt/	taught
tell /tɛl/	told /toʊld/	told
think /θɪŋk/	thought /θɔt/	thought
throw /θroʊ/	threw /θru/	thrown /θroʊn/
understand /ˌʌndərˈstænd/	understood /ˌʌndərˈstʊd/	understood
wake /weɪk/	woke /woʊk/	woken /ˈwoʊkən/
wear /wɛr/	wore /wɔr/	worn /wɔrn/
win /wɪn/	won /wʌn/	won
write /raɪt/	wrote /roʊt/	written /ˈrɪtn/

Vowel sounds

SOUND BANK

		usual spelling		! but also
tree		ee ea e	beef speed peach team refund medium	people magazine niece receipt
fish		i	dish bill pitch fit ticket since	pretty women busy decided village physics
ear		eer ere ear	cheers engineer here we're beard appearance	serious
cat		a	fan travel crash tax carry land	
egg		e	menu lend text spend plenty cent	friendly already healthy many said
chair		air are	airport upstairs fair hair rare careful	their there wear pear area
clock		o	shop comedy plot shot cottage on	watch want calm
saw		a aw al	bald wall draw saw walk talk	thought caught audience
horse		or ore	sports floor bore score	warm course board
boot		oo u*	pool moody true student	suitcase juice shoe move soup through

* especially before consonant + **e**

		usual spelling		! but also
bull		u oo	full cook book look good	could should would woman
tourist		A very unusual sound. sure plural		
up		u	public subject ugly duck cup	money someone enough country tough
computer		Many different spellings, /ə/ is always unstressed. about complain		
bird		er ir ur	person prefer learn dirty third curly turn	work world worse picture
owl		ou ow	hour around proud ground town brown	
phone		o* oa	broke stone frozen stove roast coat	owe slow although shoulders
car		ar	garden charge starter	heart
train		a* ai ay	save gate railroad plain may say gray	break steak great weight they
boy		oi oy	boiled noisy spoil coin enjoy employer	
bike		i* y igh	fine sign shy motorcycle flight frightened	buy eyes height

◯ vowels   ◯ vowels followed by /r/   ◯ diphthongs

Consonant sounds

SOUND BANK

		usual spelling	! but also
parrot	p pp	plate transport trip shopping apply	
bag	b bb	beans bill probably crab stubborn dubbed	
key	c k ck	court script kind kick track lucky	chemisty school stomach squid account
girl	g gg	golf grilled colleague forget aggressive luggage	
flower	f ph ff	food roof pharmacy nephew traffic affectionate	enough laugh
vase	v	van vegetables travel invest private believe	of
tie	t tt	taste tennis stadium strict attractive cottage	worked passed
dog	d dd	director afford comedy confident address middle	failed bored
snake	s ss c (before *e, i, y*)	steps likes boss assistant twice city cycle	science scene
zebra	z s	lazy freezing nose loves cousins	
shower	sh ti (+ vowel) ci (+ vowel)	short dishwasher selfish cash ambitious explanation spacious sociable	sugar sure machine chef
television		decision confusion usually	

		usual spelling	! but also
θ thumb	th	throw thriller healthy path math teeth	
ð mother	th	the that with farther together	
tʃ chess	ch tch t (+ ure)	change cheat watch match picture future	
dʒ jazz	j g dge	jealous just generous manager bridge judge	
l leg	l ll	limit salary until reliable sell rebellious	
r right	r rr	result referee elementary fried borrow married	written wrong
w witch	w wh	war waste western highway whistle which	one once
y yacht	y before **u**	yet year yogurt yourself university argue	
m monkey	m mm	mean arm romantic charming summer swimming	lamb
n nose	n nn	neck honest none chimney tennis thinner	knee knew
ŋ singer	ng before **g/k**	cooking going spring bring think tongue	
h house	h	handsome helmet behave inherit unhappy perhaps	who whose whole

○ voiced ○ unvoiced

This page has intentionally been left blank.

3A

American ENGLISH FILE

Workbook

Christina Latham-Koenig
Clive Oxenden
Jane Hudson

OXFORD
UNIVERSITY PRESS

Paul Seligson and Clive Oxenden are the original co-authors of
English File 1 and *English File 2*

Contents

1
- 4 **A** Mood food
- 7 **B** Family life
- 10 **PRACTICAL ENGLISH** Meeting the parents

2
- 11 **A** Spend or save?
- 14 **B** Changing lives

3
- 17 **A** Race across Florida
- 20 **B** Stereotypes – or are they?
- 23 **PRACTICAL ENGLISH** A difficult celebrity

4
- 24 **A** Failure and success
- 27 **B** Modern manners?

5
- 30 **A** Sports superstitions
- 33 **B** Love at Exit 19
- 36 **PRACTICAL ENGLISH** Old friends

- 69 **LISTENING**

STUDY LINK iChecker SELF-ASSESSMENT CD-ROM

Powerful listening and interactive assessment CD-ROM

Your iChecker disc on the inside back cover of this Workbook includes:

- **AUDIO** – Download ALL of the audio files for the Listening and Pronunciation activities in this Workbook for on-the-go listening practice.
- **FILE TESTS** – Check your progress by taking a self-assessment test after you complete each File.

Audio: When you see this symbol iChecker, go to the iChecker disc in the back of this Workbook. Load the disc in your computer.

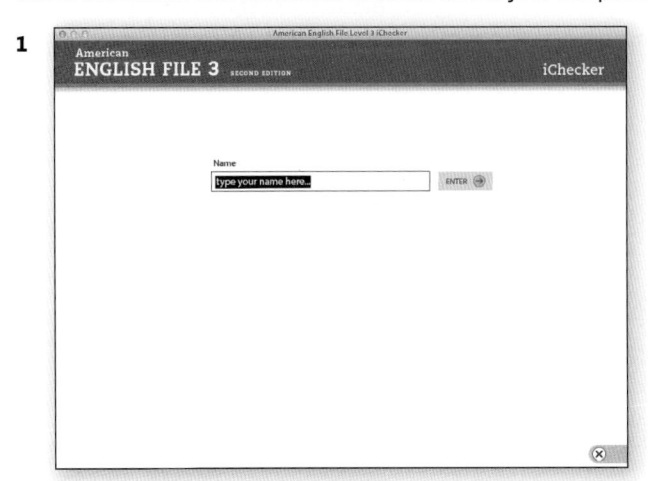

1 Type your name and press "ENTER."

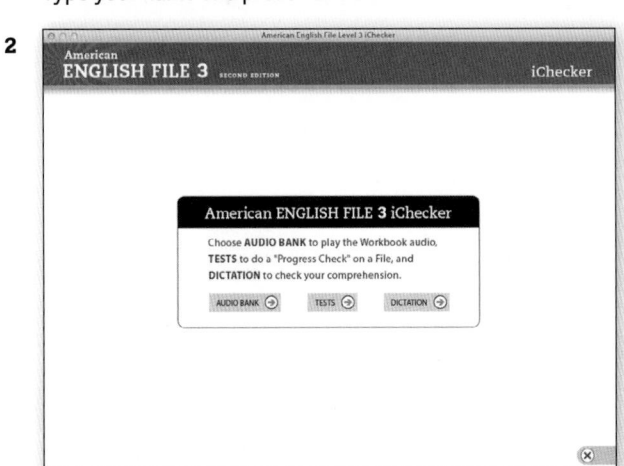

2 Choose "AUDIO BANK."

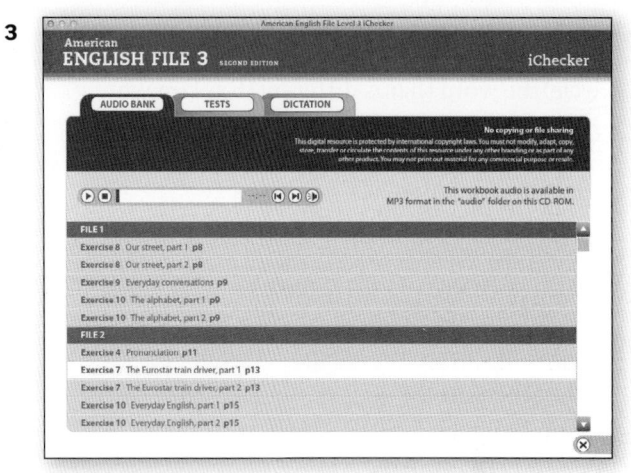

3 Click on the exercise for the File. Then use the media player to listen.

You can transfer the audio to a mobile device from the "audio" folder on the disc.

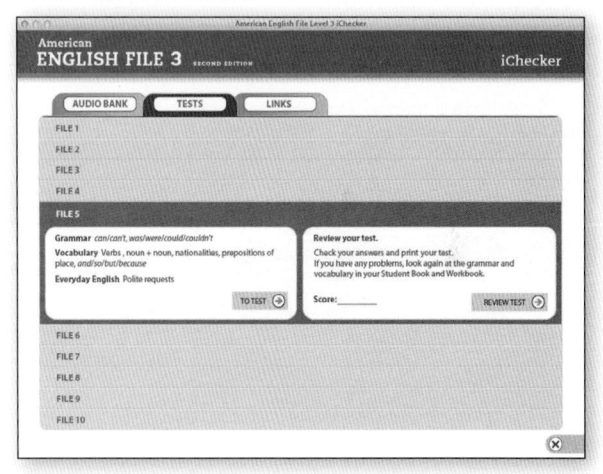

File test: At the end of every File, there is a test. To do the test, load the iChecker and select "Tests." Select the test for the File you have just finished.

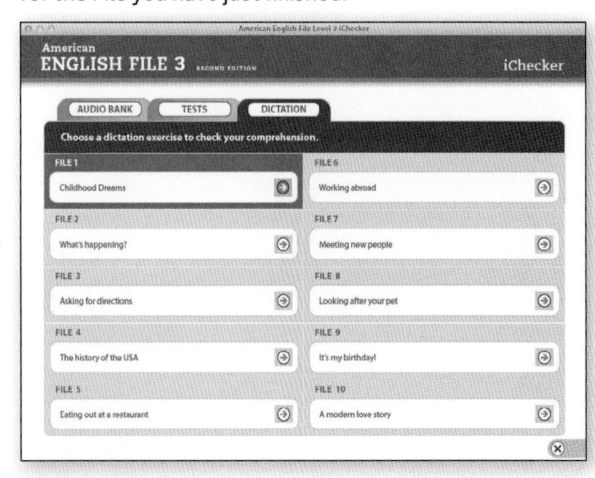

Dictation: At the end of every File, there is a dictation exercise. To do the dictation, select "Dictations" from the "File" menu.

The two biggest best-sellers in any bookstore are the cookbooks and the diet books. The cookbooks tell you how to prepare the food and the diet books tell you how not to eat any of it.

Andy Rooney, US humorist

1A Mood food

1 VOCABULARY food and cooking

a Circle the word that is different. Explain why.
1 **beans** grapes peach raspberry
   The others are all ___fruit___.
2 beef pork lamb salmon
   The others are all _____.
3 beet cabbage pear pepper
   The others are all _____.
4 eggplant lemon mango melon
   The others are all _____.
5 crab mussels beef shrimp
   The others are all _____.
6 cabbage cherry zucchini cucumber
   The others are all _____.

b Complete the crossword.

c Complete the sentences with the words in the box.

~~canned~~ fresh frozen low-fat raw spicy take-out

1 ___Canned___ tomatoes usually last for about two years.
2 I don't feel like cooking. Let's get _____ for dinner.
3 Are there any _____ peas in the freezer?
4 I'm don't really like _____ fish, so I never eat sushi.
5 Hannah's on a diet, so she bought some _____ yogurt to have for dessert.
6 They eat a lot of _____ food in Mexico.
7 We buy _____ bread from the bakery every morning.

Clues down ↓

Clues across →

1 G
  R
  I
  L
  L
  E
  D

2 PRONUNCIATION vowel sounds

a Write the words in the chart.

beef carton chicken chocolate cook crab
soup jar mango peach raw salt
sausage squid sugar tuna

1 fish	2 tree	3 cat	4 car
	beef		

5 clock	6 saw	7 bull	8 boot

b **ONLINE** Listen and check. Then listen again and repeat the words.

Pronouncing difficult words

c Write the words.
1. /bɔɪld/ — boiled
2. /ˈkæbɪdʒ/ —
3. /ˈspaɪsi/ —
4. /roʊstɪd/ —
5. /greɪps/ —
6. /frut/ —
7. /beɪkt/ —
8. /ˈmɛlən/ —
9. /zuˈkini/ —

d **ONLINE** Listen and check. Then listen again and repeat the words.

3 GRAMMAR simple present / continuous, action and nonaction verbs

a Are the highlighted phrases right (✓) or wrong (✗)? Correct the wrong phrases.

1. Does your girlfriend like seafood? ✓
2. Lucy's in the kitchen. She makes a cup of coffee. ✗
   She's making
3. Are you eating out every weekend? ☐
4. I don't know what to cook for dinner. ☐
5. Are you thinking the fish is cooked now? ☐
6. We're having lunch with my parents every Sunday. ☐
7. My mother's in the yard. She's mowing the lawn. ☐
8. I'm not wanting any potatoes with my fish, thanks. ☐
9. Do you prefer steamed rice to fried rice? ☐
10. Jack's on the phone. He orders some pizzas. ☐

b Complete the sentences with the simple present or continuous form of the verbs in parentheses.

1. Our neighbors _grow_ all of their own vegetables. (grow)
2. My mother _____ usually _____ on the weekend. (not cook)
3. Do you want to come for lunch on Sunday? We _____ roast chicken. (have)
4. We _____ tonight because there's a soccer game on TV. (not go out)
5. _____ you usually _____ your birthday with your family? (spend)
6. That restaurant _____ delicious mussels at lunchtime. (serve)
7. How often _____ you _____ in a typical week? (eat out)
8. I _____ an appetizer because I'm not hungry. (not have)
9. We _____ often _____ steak. (not buy)
10. My boyfriend's on a diet so he _____ on fried food. (cut down)

4 READING

a Read the article once and put the headings in the correct place.

A Can I eat apples?
B How can I prevent serious illnesses?
C How should I start the day?
D Do I really need to eat five a day?

The truth about healthy eating

Food experts are always telling us what we should and shouldn't eat, but they often give us different advice. Our food writer, Teresa Gold, has taken a look at all the information to figure out what is fact and what is fiction.

1 _C_
A typical American breakfast of fried eggs, bacon, toast, pancakes, and orange juice will certainly stop you from feeling hungry, but it's high in calories, which means that you'll gain weight if you eat it regularly. A healthier option is to have just an egg. Boil it instead of frying it, and eat it with a piece of toast made with whole-wheat bread. Breakfast cereals are very high in sugar, so if you feel like cereal, have granola – with no added sugar. You can also get your first vitamins of the day by drinking a glass of freshly squeezed orange juice.

2 _____
Fruits and vegetables contain the vitamins and minerals we need to stay healthy. But five is actually a fictional number thought up by an American nutritionist. She looked at what the average person ate and doubled it. According to more recent research, the right number is actually eight. The research shows that people who have eight pieces of fruit and vegetables a day are much less likely to suffer from heart disease than those who eat three.

3 _____
This particular fruit has had some bad publicity because dentists say it can harm our teeth. While it's true that apples do contain a little sugar, they are also a source of fiber. Nutritionists say that we need about 18 grams of fiber a day, and a medium apple – peel included – contains about 3 grams. Some varieties contain more fiber than others, so you should choose carefully.

4 _____
The key to good health is a balanced diet that contains fats and carbohydrates as well as proteins, vitamins, and minerals. Fats may be high in calories, but they also contain vitamins. According to the World Cancer Research Fund, you should only have about 500 grams of red meat per week – a steak is about 100 grams. One type of food on its own won't kill or cure you, but eating the right amount of the right food will stop you from getting sick.

b Read the article again. Mark the sentences T (true) or F (false).
1 A typical American breakfast every morning isn't good for you. _T_
2 The best breakfast is any type of cereal. __
3 An American nutritionist carefully calculated the amount of fruits and vegetables we should eat. __
4 We should eat more than five servings of fruits and vegetables per day. __
5 Apples contain a lot of sugar. __
6 All apples have the same amount of fiber. __
7 Fats can be good for us. __
8 You can eat as much red meat as you want to. __

c Look at the highlighted words and phrases. What do you think they mean? Use your dictionary to look up their meaning and pronunciation.

5 LISTENING

a ONLINE Listen to a radio call-in program about the article in exercise **4**. Check (✓) the caller(s) who completely agree with it.

A Kevin ☐   C Derek ☐
B Kate ☐   D Rosie ☐

b Listen again and answer the questions.
Which caller…?
1 thinks that some fruits and vegetables are unhealthy __
2 says that most children prefer fast food __
3 eats very little fruit __
4 is very healthy because he/she eats a lot of fruits and vegetables __

c Listen again with the audioscript on p. 69.

USEFUL WORDS AND PHRASES

Learn these words and phrases.

carbohydrates /kɑrboʊˈhaɪdreɪts/
protein /ˈproʊtin/
awake /əˈweɪk/
oily /ˈɔɪli/
powerful /ˈpaʊərfl/
relaxed /rɪˈlækst/
sleepy /ˈslipi/
stressful /ˈstrɛsfl/
beneficial /bɛnəˈfɪʃl/
ready-made food /rɛdi meɪd ˈfud/

Happy families are all alike; every unhappy family
is unhappy in its own way.
First line of **Anna Karenina** *by Leo Tolstoy, Russian writer*

1B Family life

1 GRAMMAR future forms

a Complete the sentences with the correct form of the verbs or phrases on the right.

1 My brother hates his job. *He's going to look for* a new one.   **he / look for** (an intention)
2 Don't worry about the drinks. _____ for them.   **I / pay** (an offer)
3 _____ some more coffee.   **I / make** (an offer)
4 Do you think _____ before you're 30?   **you / get married** (a prediction)
5 _____ to my cousin's wedding. We'll be on vacation.   **we / not go** (an arrangement)
6 **A** Are you ready to order?
   B Yes, _____ the steak.   **I / have** (an instant decision)
7 _____ 21 on my next birthday.   **I / be** (a fact)
8 _____ for dinner tonight. You paid last time.   **we / pay** (an offer)
9 I'm going to the mall. _____ long.   **I / not be** (a promise)
10 _____ a party for my grandmother's 80th birthday tomorrow.   **we / have** (an arrangement)

b Complete the dialogues with the correct future form of the verbs in parentheses.

1 **A** _Are_ you _going away_ this weekend? (go away)
   B No, we _____ here. Why? (stay)
   A We _____ a barbecue. Would you like to come? (have)

2 **A** I'm too tired to cook. I _____ some Chinese take-out food tonight. (order)
   B Good idea. I _____ the restaurant. What do you want for an appetizer? (call)
   A I _____ the spring rolls, please. (have)

3 **A** What time _____ you _____ in the morning? (leave)
   B I _____ the six o'clock train. (take)
   A I _____ you a ride to the train station. (give)

4 **A** What _____ you _____ tonight? (do)
   B I _____ the new James Bond movie. Do you want to come? (see)
   A No, thanks. I've already seen it. You _____ it! (love)

5 **A** I _____ you with the dishes. (help)
   B OK. I _____ and you can dry. But please be careful with the glasses. (wash)
   A Don't worry. I _____ anything! (not break)

2 each other

Rewrite the sentences with *each other*.

1. My brother's shouting at my sister and she's shouting at him.
   My brother and sister _are shouting at each other_.
2. Rob doesn't know Alex and Alex doesn't know Rob.
   Rob and Alex _____.
3. I'm not speaking to my sister and she isn't speaking to me.
   My sister and I _____.
4. I don't understand you and you don't understand me.
   We _____.
5. The coach respects the players and they respect him.
   The coach and the players _____.

3 PRONUNCIATION sentence stress

a **ONLINE** Listen and complete the sentences.
1. _When_ are you going to _book_ your _vacation_?
2. I'm _____ going to _____ the _____ yet.
3. I'm going to _____ _____.
4. _____ are you _____ _____?
5. I'm _____ some _____.
6. I'm _____ _____ my _____.
7. _____ will you _____ your test _____?
8. I _____ get them _____ _____.
9. I'll _____ them on _____.

b Listen again and repeat. Copy the rhythm.

4 VOCABULARY family, adjectives of personality

a Complete the sentences with a family word.
1. Your mother and father are your p_arents_.
2. Your grandfather's father is your gr_____-gr_____.
3. A child who has no brothers or sisters is an on_____ ch_____.
4. Your brother's daughter is your n_____.
5. Your father's sister is your a_____.
6. Your spouse, children, parents, and brothers and sisters are your im_____ f_____.
7. Your father's new wife is your s_____.
8. Your wife's or husband's father is your f_____-i_____-l_____.
9. Your aunts, uncles and cousins are your ex_____ f_____.
10. Your brother's or sister's son is your n_____.

b Match the comments with the personality adjectives in the box.

| aggressive ambitious independent |
| jealous reliable self-confident selfish |
| sensible ~~spoiled~~ stubborn |

1. "When I want something, my parents always give it to me."
   spoiled
2. "I don't like my boyfriend talking to other women."
   _____
3. "I'm always there when my friends need my help."
   _____
4. "Those are my pens and you can't borrow them."
   _____
5. "I'm going to go to bed early so I can sleep well before my test tomorrow."
   _____
6. "I'll hit you if you do that again!"
   _____
7. "I feel very comfortable when I'm speaking in public."
   _____
8. "I'd like to be the manager of a big multinational company."
   _____
9. "That's what I think and I'm not going to change my mind."
   _____
10. "I'd prefer to do this on my own, thanks."
    _____

c Write the opposite adjectives. Use a negative prefix if necessary.
1. generous   _cheap_
2. kind   _____
3. lazy   _____
4. mature   _____
5. organized   _____
6. sensitive   _____
7. talkative   _____
8. clean   _____

5 READING

a Read the article once. Why do the Bedouins prefer to live together in a big family group?

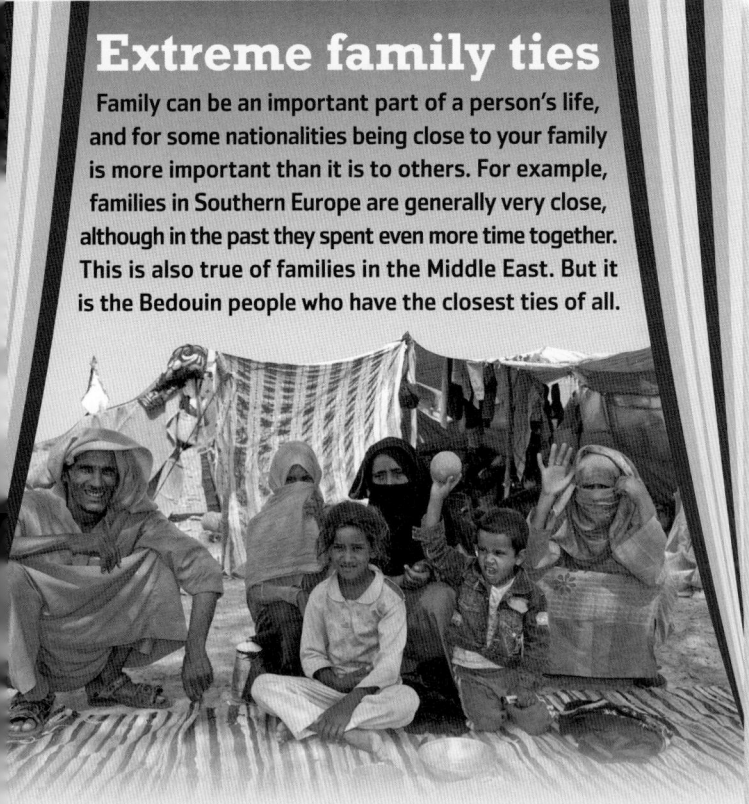

Extreme family ties

Family can be an important part of a person's life, and for some nationalities being close to your family is more important than it is to others. For example, families in Southern Europe are generally very close, although in the past they spent even more time together. This is also true of families in the Middle East. But it is the Bedouin people who have the closest ties of all.

Traditional Bedouin families live in large tents about half the size of a basketball court. The tents are divided into two sections: the first is for receiving guests in true Bedouin style – they have the reputation of being the world's most generous hosts. Visitors are always served a big meal as soon as they arrive. The second part of the tent is the family's shared kitchen, living room, dining room, and bedroom. They don't have tables and chairs, as the whole family sits on the floor to eat. And instead of beds, everybody sleeps on mattresses, which are piled into a corner of the room during the day.

Several generations usually share the tent. The head of the family is the mother, and she is the one who gives the orders. Her husband and her children live with her, even when the children are married and have their own children. The sons and sons-in-law look after the animals, while the daughters and daughters-in-law clean the tent, cook the meals, and take care of the younger grandchildren. The older ones are left to run around outside. There may often be as many as 30 people under the same roof.

The few young people who have left the family to live in the city visit their mothers nearly every day. It can be quite a surprise to see a shiny new Mercedes pull up outside one of the tents and watch a well-dressed man get out to greet his relatives.

Bedouin people do not like to be separated from their families and there is a very good reason why. If they are poor, sick, old, or unemployed, it is the family that supports them. Elderly people are never left alone, and problems are always shared. Children who work in the city are often responsible for their families financially. In this way, Bedouin families aren't just close; they are a lifeline.

b Read the article again. Choose the correct answers according to the information given.

1 In the past, most families in Southern Europe and the Middle East were…
   a smaller.   (b) closer.   c richer.
2 There isn't much … in a Bedouin tent.
   a furniture   b light   c space
3 Bedouin … spend most of the day inside.
   a men   b women   c children
4 Young Bedouins who live in the city…
   a hardly ever go home.
   b don't earn much money.
   c don't lose touch with their families.
5 Members of a Bedouin family help each other to…
   a survive.   b get a job.   c choose clothes.

c Look at the highlighted words and phrases. What do you think they mean? Use your dictionary to look up their meaning and pronunciation.

6 LISTENING

a **ONLINE** Listen to a couple, Terry and Jane, talking about going to live with the in-laws. What do they decide at the end of the conversation?

b Listen again and mark the sentences T (true) or F (false).

1 Terry and Jane are both very tired.   T
2 Terry is more optimistic about the future than Jane.   __
3 Terry's parents have suggested the family move in with them.   __
4 Terry says that if they all lived together, his parents would babysit.   __
5 Jane thinks that the new plan would mean less housework for her.   __
6 Jane worries that the grandparents would spoil the children.   __

c Listen again with the audioscript on p. 69.

USEFUL WORDS AND PHRASES

Learn these words and phrases.

boarding school /ˈbɔrdɪŋ skul/
childhood /ˈtʃaɪldhʊd/
gang /gæŋ/
gathering /ˈgæðərɪŋ/
rivalry /ˈraɪvəlri/
sick /sɪk/
value /ˈvælyu/
fight /faɪt/
aware of /əˈwɛr əv/
no wonder /noʊ ˈwʌndər/

ONLINE FILE 1

Practical English Meeting the parents

1 REACTING TO WHAT PEOPLE SAY

Complete the dialogues.

1	Ben	Oh, ¹ n_o_! I don't ² b_____ it!
	Charlotte	What's wrong!
	Ben	I didn't tell my mom that you don't eat meat.
	Charlotte	You're ³ k_____!
	Ben	No, I'm not. Never ⁴ m_____. I'll tell her now.
		Mom! Charlotte's a vegetarian.
	Mom	⁵ R_____?
	Charlotte	Yes, but it isn't a problem.
	Mom	What a ⁶ p_____! I made a meat lasagna. But there's plenty of salad.
	Charlotte	That's fine. Thanks, Mrs. Lord.
2	Steve	We have something to tell you. We found a house that we like.
	Jill	⁷ H_____ fantastic!
	Steve	And it isn't too expensive.
	Jill	That's great ⁸ n_____! Could I see it some time?
	Steve	⁹ W_____ a great idea! I'll call and make an appointment.

2 SOCIAL ENGLISH

Complete the dialogues with the phrases in the box.

~~a really nice guy~~   Go ahead   How do you see   I mean
How incredible   Not really   That's because   things like that

1 A What did you think of my dad?
  B He's _a really nice guy_ .
2 A _____ your future?
  B I think we'll be very happy together.
3 A I hear you speak Spanish. Are you bilingual?
  B _____. But I can speak it well.
4 A I'm sorry. I'm not very hungry.
  B _____ you ate too much for lunch!
5 A You know, I think we went to the same school.
  B _____!
6 A Can I have another piece of chicken, please?
  B _____. There's more in the kitchen.
7 A What kind of books do you read?
  B Biographies, history books, _____.
8 A You wouldn't want to go to the concert with us.
  B Yes, I would! _____, I love classical music.

3 READING

a Read the text and answer the questions.

In which place…?

1 can you see a celebrity	_Café Carlyle_
2 do musicians come to hear other musicians perform	_____
3 can you hear international styles of jazz	_____
4 can you see what's happening online	_____
5 should you buy a ticket before you go	_____
6 does the music finish very late	_____

Jazz in New York

New York is famous for its jazz, and for music fans no trip to the city is complete without a visit to one of the many jazz venues. Here are four of the many places you can go to hear jazz being performed.

Barbès
Barbès is a bar and performance venue in the Park Slope neighborhood of Brooklyn. Come here to listen to musical styles from all over the world, such as Mexican, Lebanese, Romanian, and Venezuelan along with traditional American styles. Usually $10 to get in.

55 Bar
Located in Greenwich Village, this small club, which started in 1919, has a very interesting history. Come to hear jazz guitarists play, and expect to see lots of serious jazz fans and music students from local colleges and music schools. Usually $10–20.

Smalls
This club was created in 1994, but has already become very famous in New York because well-known players such as Norah Jones began their careers here. The club closed in 2002, but opened again in 2004, with a more comfortable room and a website that features live streaming video of all performances. It opens from 4 p.m. to 4 a.m. $20 to get in.

Café Carlyle
Come to the first floor of the famous Carlyle Hotel to visit the Café Carlyle. It's particularly worth going on Monday nights – not only will you hear jazz from the Eddy Davis New Orleans Jazz Band, but you will also hear the famous movie director Woody Allen play with them. As well as being a director, Woody Allen is also a jazz musician. Sets at 8:45. The venue holds only 90 and is often sold out, so it's a good idea to book ahead. But it isn't cheap – tickets start at $100.

b Underline five words or phrases you don't know. Use your dictionary to look up their meaning and pronunciation.

2A Spend or save?

> When a man tells you he got rich through hard work, ask him: Whose?
> *Don Marquis, US Writer*

1 VOCABULARY money

a Complete the sentences with the correct verb in parentheses.

1. My sister _wastes_ a lot of money on clothes she never wears. (wastes / saves)
2. I can't _____ to buy a house of my own. (pay / afford)
3. You'll have to _____ a lot of money if you want to travel around the world next year. (cost / save)
4. Kevin _____ about $2,500 a month at his new job. (wins / earns)
5. That painting _____ a lot of money. (charges / is worth)
6. My uncle is doing a bike ride to _____ money for charity. (raise / save)
7. We still _____ the bank a lot of money. (owe / earn)
8. Mary _____ $5,000 from her grandfather when he died. (inherited / invested)
9. The plumber _____ me $250 to fix my shower. (cost / charged)
10. Can you _____ me $200 until I get paid? (borrow / lend)

b Complete the sentences with the correct preposition.

1. I'll pay _for_ the movie tickets if you get the snacks!
2. They charged us $5 _____ a bottle of water.
3. They got _____ debt when they bought their new house.
4. We borrowed some money _____ my parents.
5. My grandparents always pay _____ cash.
6. I don't mind lending money _____ family.
7. They spent a lot of money _____ their son's education.
8. Can I pay _____ credit card?
9. Phil invested all his money _____ his own company.

c Complete the advertisement with the words in the box.

ATM   ~~bank account~~   bills   coin   loan
mortgage   salary   taxes

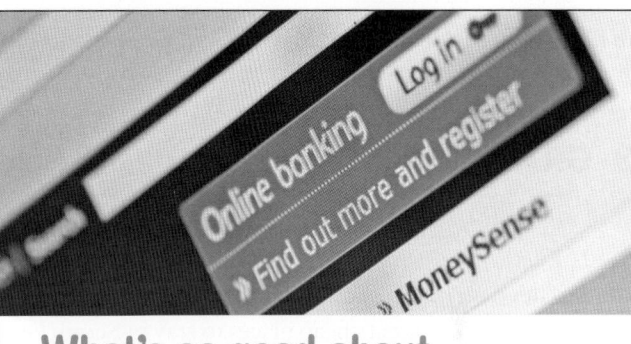

What's so good about CASH Internet Banking plc

OUR ACCOUNT SERVICES

Open a [1] _bank account_ with us and we'll give you a free gift – you'll get a tablet computer if you earn over $3,000 a month. Consult our online service 24/7 and use your card in the [2] _____ of any bank to take out as much or as little money as you want. Do you have a lot of change? Use our free [3] _____ counter and deposit the total directly into your savings account. Does your company pay your [4] _____ directly into the bank? Then we won't charge you anything for your card. We'll even pay all your [5] _____ for you, free of charge.

OUR FINANCING SERVICES

Do you need to borrow money for a car, a vacation, or a new laptop? We'll give you a [6] _____ of up to $10,000 for whatever you want to buy.

And how about a new house? We can give you a [7] _____ at one of the lowest interest rates on the market.

OUR EXTRA SERVICES

How much do you pay in [8] _____? Talk to our specialists to make sure you're paying the right amount – they can help you pay less.

Come to CASH Internet for the best accounts, the best services, and the best savings.

2 PRONUNCIATION the letter o

a Circle the word with a different sound.

1 up	2 clock	3 phone	4 horse	5 bird
money	honest	done	afford	work
nothing	shopping	owe	worse	world
~~sold~~	dollar	go	store	short
won	clothes	loan	mortgage	worth

b **ONLINE** Listen and check. Then listen again and repeat the words.

3 GRAMMAR present perfect and simple past

a Circle the correct answer.
1. I *have never owed* / *never owed* any money to the bank in my life.
2. They *have charged* / *charged* us too much for our meal last night.
3. I know some great cheap places to stay in Seoul. *I've been* / *I went* there a few times.
4. Paul *hasn't inherited* / *didn't inherit* anything from his grandmother when she died.
5. *You've lent* / *you lent* him money so many times, but he never pays you back!
6. How much *has your TV cost* / *did your TV cost*?
7. How many times *have you wasted* / *did you waste* money on clothes you never wear?
8. I *haven't had* / *didn't have* any coins, so I couldn't put any money in the parking meter.
9. *Have you ever invested* / *Did you ever invest* any money in a company?
10. My girlfriend has a high-paying job. She *has earned* / *earned* $85,000 last year.

b Complete the dialogues with the correct form of the verbs in parentheses.

1. **A** When ___did___ your son ___buy___ his car? (buy)
   B When he _____ his driving test last month. (pass)
2. **A** How much money _____ you _____ from your sister yesterday? (borrow)
   B About $100, but I already _____ it all. (spend)
3. **A** _____ you _____ a new house yet? (find)
   B Yes, and the bank _____ to give me a mortgage. (agree)
4. **A** _____ you ever _____ any money to a friend? (lend)
   B Only to my boyfriend when he _____ a new phone. (need)
5. **A** _____ your mother _____ an appointment with the doctor yet? (make)
   B Yes, she _____ him yesterday and she's seeing him tomorrow. (call)

4 READING

a Read the first chapter of a book about Daniel Suelo once. Where did he decide to live?
1. with friends ☐   3. in the country ☐
2. with family ☐   4. in a city ☐

The man who quit money

In the first year of the twenty-first century, a man standing by a busy road in the middle of the United States took his life savings out of his pocket – $30 – laid it inside a phone booth, and walked away. He was 39 years old, came from a good family, and had been to college. He was not mentally ill, nor did he have any problems with drugs or alcohol. The decision was made by a man who knew exactly what he was doing.

In the twelve years since then, as the stock market has risen and fallen, Daniel Suelo has not earned, received, or spent a single dollar. In an era when anyone who could sign his name could get a mortgage, Suelo did not apply for loans. As public debt rose to eight, ten, and finally thirteen trillion dollars, he did not pay taxes, or accept any type of help from the government.

Instead he went to live in a cave in Utah, where he picks fruit and wild onions, collects animals that have been killed on the road, takes old food that has gone past its sell-by date out of trash cans, and is often fed by friends and strangers. "My philosophy is to use only what is freely given or discarded," he writes. While the rest of us try to deal with taxes, mortgages, retirement plans, and bank accounts, Suelo no longer even has an ID card.

Daniel is not a typical tramp. He often works – but refuses to be paid. Although he lives in a cave, he is extremely social, remains close to friends and family, and has discussions with strangers on his website which he checks at the local library. He has ridden his bike long distances, traveled on freight trains, hitchhiked through nearly every state in the United States, worked on a fishing boat, collected mussels from Pacific beaches, caught salmon in streams in Alaska, and spent three months living in a tree after a storm.

"I know it's possible to live with zero money," Suelo declares. And he says you can live well.

b Read the chapter again and choose the correct answers.

1 What do we learn about the man in the first paragraph?
   a He had just left school.
   b He had thought about his actions carefully.
   c He had had a difficult childhood.
2 What has Daniel Suelo done since he changed his life?
   a He has gotten into debt.
   b He has bought a house.
   c He hasn't used any money.
3 How does he get enough to eat?
   a He finds food.
   b His family cooks for him.
   c He buys food.
4 What's Daniel Suelo like?
   a He's shy.
   b He's lazy.
   c He's outgoing.
5 How does he get from one place to another?
   a He rides his bike everywhere.
   b He uses different methods of transportation.
   c He always uses trains.

c Look at the highlighted words and phrases. What do you think they mean? Use your dictionary to look up their meaning and pronunciation.

d Complete the sentences with one of the highlighted words or phrases.

1 Clean fresh water often comes from mountain _streams_.
2 It's important to have a _____ _____ for when you get old.
3 The giant fish sculptures in Rio were made using _____ plastic bottles.
4 The early nineteenth century was an important _____ for opera.
5 He has shares in some companies, so he's interested in what happens on the _____ _____.
6 You might get sick if you eat food after its _____-_____.

5 LISTENING

a ONLINE Listen to four speakers talking about how they manage on their incomes. Match the speakers with their situation.

Speaker 1 _d_   a a single parent
Speaker 2 ___   b a family with children
Speaker 3 ___   c a single retired person on a pension
Speaker 4 ___   d a young person who lives with his / her parents

b Listen again and mark the sentences T (true) or F (false).

Speaker 1
1 He doesn't earn much money.   _F_
2 He saves most of his salary.   ___

Speaker 2
3 She doesn't own the house where she lives.   ___
4 She thinks money is more important than family. ___

Speaker 3
5 He can't live on his income.   ___
6 He isn't in debt.   ___

Speaker 4
7 She only works in a store on the weekends.   ___
8 She spends most of her money on her children. ___

c Listen again with the audioscript on p. 69.

USEFUL WORDS AND PHRASES

Learn these words and phrases.

backer /ˈbækər/
billionaire /ˈbɪlyənɛr/
brand /brænd/
customer /ˈkʌstəmər/
entrepreneurial /ɑntrəprəˈnəriəl/
low-paying /loʊ ˈpeɪyɪŋ/
rejection /rɪˈdʒɛkʃn/
salesman /ˈseɪlzmən/
self-made /sɛlfˈmeɪd/
wealthy /ˈwɛlθi/

> Only I can change my life. No one else can do it for me.
> *Carol Burnett, US actress & comedian*

2B Changing lives

1 GRAMMAR present perfect simple + *for* / *since*; present perfect continuous

a Write the words and phrases in the box in the correct column.

~~2005~~   a long time   a week   March   six months
I was little   the last two days   Tuesday
years and years   you last called

for	since
___	2005
___	___
___	___
___	___
___	___

b Complete the sentences with the present perfect form of the verb in parentheses and *for* or *since*.

1 I *'ve had* my car *for* about a month. (have)
2 My mom _____ sick _____ last Friday. (be)
3 We _____ each other _____ we were in school. (know)
4 He _____ for the same company _____ five years. (work)
5 They _____ in Miami _____ they got married. (live)
6 My parents _____ away _____ for three days. (be)
7 I _____ to go to Australia _____ a long time. (want)
8 She _____ to me _____ last year. (not speak)

c Complete the dialogues with the present perfect continuous form of the verbs.

1 A Have you heard Heather's new band?
   B No. *Have they been playing* together for a long time? (they / play)

2 A How long was your flight?
   B Twelve hours. _____ all day. (we / travel)

3 A My brother has a very good job in New York City.
   B Really? How long _____ _____ there? (he / work)

4 A Diana finally found a new apartment!
   B Oh good! _____ one for so long! (she / look for)

5 A Why does Eric's teacher want to see you?
   B _____ his homework lately. (he / not do)

6 A You're late.
   B Yes, I know. Sorry. _____ _____ long? (you / wait)

7 A You look exhausted.
   B _____ the kids all day! (I / take care of)

d Circle the correct form. If both forms are possible, check (✓) the sentence.

1 How long *have you lived* / *have you been living* abroad? ✓
2 I've studied / **I've been studying** Chinese for two years.
3 Hannah *has had* / *has been having* the same boyfriend since she was in school.
4 How long *has Mark played* / *has Mark been playing* the bass guitar?
5 *He's worked* / *He's been working* at this school since he started teaching.
6 *I've known* / *I've been knowing* you for years.
7 *We've gone* / *We've been going* to the same dentist since we were kids.
8 *You've worn* / *You've been wearing* that coat for years!

2 PRONUNCIATION sentence stress

a **ONLINE** Listen and complete the sentences.
1 I've been _traveling_ all _day_.
2 How _____ have they been going _____ together?
3 She's been _____ sick since _____.
4 They _____ been _____ here for long.
5 We've been _____ the house all _____.
6 I _____ been _____ well lately.

b Listen again and repeat the sentences. Copy the rhythm.

3 READING

a Read the article once and match photos 1–3 with paragraphs A–C.

b Read the article again. Answer the questions with the letters A, B, or C.

Which organization…?
1 takes people for two weeks or a month _B_
2 encourages sightseeing ___
3 offers accommodations in tents ___
4 says what volunteers should bring ___
5 gives volunteers free afternoons ___
6 lets volunteers stay with others in a hut ___
7 arranges accommodations with local people ___
8 only needs volunteers for part of the year ___

c Look at the highlighted words and phrases. What do you think they mean? Check with your dictionary.

d Complete the sentences with one of the highlighted words or phrases.
1 My little niece only wants to play on the _swing_ when we go to the park.
2 If you all _____ _____, we'll be able to buy our colleague a nice going-away present.
3 I'd rather see animals in _____ than in a zoo.
4 The school is organizing an after-school club for _____ children in the area.
5 The people waiting for the buses were standing underneath the _____ because it was raining.
6 We're moving to a new house this weekend. Can you come and _____ _____ _____ with the packing?

Do *you* want to be a volunteer?

A The Book Bus
Do you enjoy reading? Do you like children? Then why not volunteer for our mobile library service in Zambia? We work with underprivileged children in public elementary schools, and it's a lot of fun. We read stories, do art projects, and organize activities to help the children learn English. After breakfast at 7 a.m., we head to our first school in time for the beginning of the school day. Every morning we visit at least four schools, and we spend about an hour in each one. We get back to our campsite at around 2 p.m. for lunch, and after that you have the afternoon free to relax or prepare activities. The project takes place from May to September, and it's open to everyone. Volunteers have to pay for their own flight and make a contribution to the project.

B The Great Orangutan Project
Are you an animal lover? If you are, then you should come to Kubah National Park in Borneo. We need people to help us take care of our orangutans. Unfortunately, you won't be able to touch the animals because they are being prepared to be released into the wild, but you'll work very close to them. You'll spend your time in the Wildlife Center repairing the shelters where the orangutans live, or building new ones. You might have to make a swing, or install some ropes where the animals can play. You'll share a room in a wooden hut that looks out onto the rainforest. The program lasts for two or four weeks and it costs $1,935 or $2,820 respectively, excluding flights.

C Construction in Peru
Are you good at making things? If you are, and you'd like to take part in a construction project, how about coming to Peru to lend a hand? You'll be based in Cuzco in southeastern Peru, and you'll be involved in the construction of a small school, and a community center or an orphanage. You may have to paint and make repairs to existing buildings, or build new ones in and around the city. You'll live with a Peruvian family, and you'll eat all your meals together in their house. All of the houses have electricity and running water, but you'll have to go to an Internet cafe in Cuzco if you want to go online. You are expected to work from Monday to Friday, and on the weekends you can explore some of the fantastic sights in the region. Please bring your own work clothes.

4 VOCABULARY strong adjectives

a Complete the adjective for each picture.

1 She's absolutely fr*eezing*.
2 It's d_____! 
3 They're really e_____. 
4 He's h_____. 
5 It's absolutely en_____. 
6 They're f_____. 

b Complete the sentences with a strong adjective.

1 **A** Are you **sure** the meeting is today?
   B Yes, I'm absolutely _positive_.
2 **A** Is your boyfriend's apartment **small**?
   B Yes, it's really _____.
3 **A** Were your parents **angry** about your test scores?
   B Yes, they were _____.
4 **A** Is your sister **afraid** of insects?
   B Yes, she's absolutely _____ of them.
5 **A** Were you **surprised** when you passed your driving test?
   B Yes, I was really _____.
6 **A** Were the kids **hungry** when they arrived?
   B Yes, they were absolutely _____.

5 LISTENING

a ONLINE Listen to a news story about an American family who is traveling around the world doing volunteer work. Check (✓) the places they have already visited.

1 Australia ✓
2 Antarctica ☐
3 China ☐
4 Haiti ☐
5 India ☐
6 Kenya ☐
7 Paraguay ☐
8 Peru ☐
9 Russia ☐
10 Rwanda ☐
11 Thailand ☐
12 Zanzibar ☐

b Listen again and answer the questions.

1 What did J.D. Lewis use to do?
   He used to be an actor.
2 How old are the children?
   _____.
3 How much is the trip going to cost?
   _____.
4 What's the name of his organization?
   _____.
5 What did they do in Thailand?
   _____.
6 How did they help the children in Rwanda?
   _____.
7 Who did they help in Kenya?
   _____.
8 What does J. D. Lewis hope his organization will do in the future?
   _____.

c Listen again with the audioscript on p. 70.

USEFUL WORDS AND PHRASES

Learn these words and phrases.

blisters /ˈblɪstərz/
charity /ˈtʃærəti/
kayak /ˈkaɪæk/
ache /eɪk/
target /ˈtɑrgət/
melt /mɛlt/
paddle /ˈpædl/
risky /ˈrɪski/
go forward /goʊ ˈfɔrwərd/
sponsor projects /ˈspɑnsər ˈprɑdʒɛkts/

ONLINE FILE 2

A good traveler has no fixed plans.
Lao Tzu, Taoist Philosopher

3A Race across Florida

1 VOCABULARY transportation

a Complete the crossword.

Clues across →
1 It's a large vehicle that carries passengers and stops regularly to let them on and off.
3 It's where you wait for a train at a train station.
6 It's a fast road where traffic can travel long distances between large towns or cities.
8 It's bigger than a car but smaller than a truck.
9 It's a type of railway system that travels under the ground.

Clues down ↓
2 It's a like a motorcycle but less powerful.
4 It's a type of small train that moves by electricity along special rails.
5 It's very long and used for transporting people or things by rail.
7 It's used for transporting large quantities of things by road.

b Complete the compound nouns with one word.
1 Don't forget to put your _seat_ belt on.
2 You'll get a _____ ticket if you leave your car there.
3 Sorry we're late. We were stuck in a _____ jam downtown.
4 We got held up by the _____ work on the freeway.
5 I wish bike riders would use the _____ lane instead of the sidewalk.
6 We need to fill up at the _____ station before we leave.
7 Traffic is always worse during _____ hour.
8 There aren't any cabs waiting at the _____ stand.
9 Slow down! There are _____ cameras on this road.
10 We stopped at the _____ light and waited for it to turn green.

2 PRONUNCIATION /ʃ/, /dʒ/, and /tʃ/

a Circle the word with a different sound.

1 /dʒ/ jazz	2 /ʃ/ shower	3 /dʒ/ jazz	4 /tʃ/ chess
dangerous	crash	check-in	chemistry
bridge	seat belt	passenger	catch
(rush)	station	traffic jam	departure

b **ONLINE** Listen and check. Then listen again and repeat the words.

17

3 GRAMMAR comparatives and superlatives

a Complete the sentences with one word.

1 Gas isn't as expensive in the US __as__ it is in the UK.
2 My father drives more slowly _____ my mother.
3 They said that today was _____ hottest day of the year.
4 Let's go by train. It's _____ comfortable than the bus.
5 This is the _____ flight I've ever been on. I'll never fly with this airline again.
6 I think trains are _____ dangerous than cars. There are fewer accidents.
7 It's _____ to go by subway than by bus. Buses are much slower.
8 The 405 is the _____ crowded freeway in California.
9 You're at the Sheraton? We're staying at the same hotel _____ you.
10 Why don't we ride our bikes? It's the _____ expensive way to travel.

b Write sentences with the information from the survey. Use the comparative or the superlative.

Where to go?
We reveal the results from our reader survey of three popular vacation destinations.

	Cancun (Mexico)	Beijing (China)	Sydney (Australia)
It's cheap.	●●●	●●	●
It's crowded.	●	●●●	●●
It's easy to get to.	●●	●●●	●
It's exciting.	●●	●●	●●
It's hot.	●●●	●	●●●
It's relaxing.	●●	●	●●●

1 Cancun / cheap / Beijing
   __Cancun is cheaper than Beijing.__
2 Beijing / crowded / of the three destinations
   _____
3 Beijing / easy to get to / Sydney
   _____
4 Sydney / exciting / Cancun
   _____
5 Sydney / hot / Beijing
   _____
6 Sydney / relaxing / of the three destinations
   _____

c Rewrite the comparative sentences in **b** using (not) as ... as.

1 **expensive** (sentence 1)
   __Cancun isn't as expensive as Beijing.__
2 **difficult** (sentence 3)
   _____
   _____
3 **exciting** (sentence 4)
   _____
   _____
4 **cold** (sentence 5)
   _____
   _____

4 PRONUNCIATION linking

a ONLINE Listen and complete the sentences.

1 The __most__ __relaxing__ way to travel is by train.
2 The seven hours in the airport was the _____ _____ part of the vacation.
3 The _____ _____ place to visit is the museum.
4 Flying is a lot _____ _____ than going by bus.
5 They should have the party at their house. It's much bigger _____.
6 Scooters aren't _____ _____ motorcycles.

b Listen again and repeat the sentences. Listen carefully to the linked words. Copy the r<u>hy</u>thm.

5 READING

a Read the article once. Which is the oldest form of transportation?

Unusual ways of getting around

Bamboo trains
This is the best way to see rural Cambodia. A bamboo train, or *nori* as the locals call it, is a bamboo platform on wheels that travels along tracks. It's powered by an engine, and it can reach a speed of 25 miles per hour. Passengers sit on a grass mat on the nori. Noris may not be as comfortable as conventional trains, but they're certainly a lot cheaper. Pick up a nori from Battambang Station, but remember to agree on a price before you get on.

Totora reed boats 
These boats have been around for centuries. They are made from the reeds that grow on the banks of Lake Titicaca, one of the largest lakes in South America. As well as making boats from totora reeds, the local people use them to make their houses, which they build on floating islands. Totora reed boats are still used for hunting and fishing, but today some of the local people transport people across the lake in them. Traveling on a reed boat among the floating islands of the lake is a must for visitors to Peru.

Jeepney 
A jeepney is the most common form of public transportation in the Philippines. They are made out of the jeeps left on the islands by the American army at the end of World War II. People gave the jeeps a roof, put in two long seats on either side and painted them, turning them into small buses. Jeepneys have open windows instead of air conditioning. They're often packed with passengers and there are no bus stops – the driver just slows down to let the passengers jump on and off.

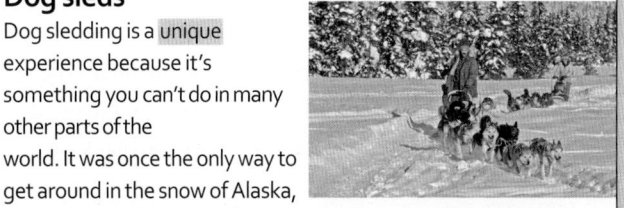

Dog sleds
Dog sledding is a unique experience because it's something you can't do in many other parts of the world. It was once the only way to get around in the snow of Alaska, but now its use is limited to winter sports and tourism. The best time to try it is from January to March – in the summer there isn't enough snow, so the dogs pull sleds on wheels. The ride can be a little bumpy because the sled sometimes goes over stones and the dogs bark a lot. All the same, it's an opportunity not to be missed.

b Read the article again. Mark the sentences T (true) or F (false).

1. Noris are a good way to see Cambodian cities. _F_
2. The train fare is not always the same. __
3. Totora reed boats are made from special plants. __
4. Today the boats are only used to carry tourists. __
5. Jeepneys are used by the military to transport soldiers. __
6. There are usually a lot of people in jeepneys. __
7. Most people in Alaska don't travel by dog sled anymore. __
8. Dog sleds are a very relaxing way to travel. __

c Look at the highlighted words and phrases. What do you think they mean? Use your dictionary to look up their meaning and pronunciation.

6 LISTENING

a ONLINE Listen to the experiences of five speakers who were doing dangerous things while they were driving. Match the speakers with the things they were doing.

Speaker 1 _E_   A Putting on makeup
Speaker 2 __   B Listening to his/her favorite music
Speaker 3 __   C Writing a text message
Speaker 4 __   D Setting or adjusting a GPS
Speaker 5 __   E Talking on a cell phone

b Listen again and answer the questions.

1. What did Speaker 1's car crash into? _A van_
2. How far had Speaker 2 driven past Denver before she realized her mistake? _____
3. Where did Speaker 3 end up? _____
4. Who did Speaker 4 almost hit? _____
5. What color was the traffic light when the accident happened to Speaker 5? _____

c Listen again with the audioscript on p. 70.

USEFUL WORDS AND PHRASES

Learn these words and phrases.

adjust (GPS) /əˈdʒʌst/
reach /ritʃ/
be ahead of /bi əˈhɛd əv/
crash (into) /kræʃ/
get stuck (in a traffic jam) /gɛt ˈstʌk/
get worse /gɛt ˈwɜrs/
turn red /tɜrn ˈrɛd/
turn around /tɜrn əˈraʊnd/
do your hair /du yər hɛr/
put on makeup /pʊt ɑn ˈmeɪkʌp/

Men want to be a woman's first love. Women like to be a man's last romance.
Oscar Wilde, Irish writer

3B Stereotypes – or are they?

1 GRAMMAR articles: *a / an, the*, no article

a Circle the correct answers.
1. I think *girls* / *the girls* are better at learning *languages* / *the languages* than *boys* / *the boys*.
2. Did you lock *door* / *the door* when you left *house* / *the house* this morning?
3. My sister works for *Japanese* / *a Japanese* company. She's *engineer* / *an engineer*.
4. I don't usually like *fish* / *the fish*, but *salmon* / *the salmon* we had last night was delicious.
5. We go to *movies* / *the movies* once *a week* / *the week*.
6. Don't worry! It's not *the end* / *end* of *the world* / *world*.
7. Do you think *women* / *the women* are more sensitive than *men* / *the men*?
8. What *beautiful* / *a beautiful* day! Let's have *lunch* / *a lunch* on the patio.

b Are the highlighted phrases right (✓) or wrong (✗)? Correct the wrong phrases.

1. That's pretty dress – the color suits you. ✗
   a pretty dress
2. He's hoping to visit his parents the next weekend. ☐
   _____
3. The money doesn't make people happy. ☐
   _____
4. My grandfather left school when he was 14. ☐
   _____
5. They go to the dentist about twice the year. ☐
   _____
6. Have you watched DVD that I lent you? ☐
   _____
7. That was one of the best meals I've ever had. ☐
   _____
8. What noisy child! Where are his parents? ☐
   _____
9. Alex is studying to become doctor. ☐
   _____
10. I love the cats, but my boyfriend doesn't like them. ☐
    _____
11. Her husband sits in front of the TV all day. ☐
    _____
12. She always gets to the work at five-thirty. ☐
    _____

2 PRONUNCIATION /ə/, sentence stress, /ðə/ or /ði/?

a ONLINE Listen and complete the sentences.
1. I'd like to _speak_ to the _manager_.
2. I put the _____ on the _____.
3. _____ are we going to _____ tonight?
4. Could you _____ the _____ for a minute?
5. She needs to see a _____ about her _____.
6. We want to _____ for a _____ tomorrow.

b Listen again and repeat. Copy the rhythm.

c ONLINE Listen and repeat the phrases. Pay attention to the pronunciation of *the*.
1. The conversation was about the woman next door.
2. The university invited a guest to speak at the meeting.
3. I sometimes go to the theater in the evening.
4. We took the elevator instead of walking up the stairs.
5. The office gave me all the information I needed.
6. The gray skirt is nice, but I prefer the black one.

3 READING

a Read the article once and put the headings in the correct place.

A Men are better navigators than women
B Women talk more than men
C Men don't see colors as well as women

Stereotypes supported by science

1 _____

Men have a reputation for wearing clothes that don't look good together – if men do look good, it's because their girlfriends or wives have helped them get dressed. Why's that?

Science says: Let's take a look at chromosomes – the parts of our DNA that control many things about us. The color red is carried only by the X chromosome. Women have two X chromosomes, and so they are more likely to be able to see red. Men only have one X chromosome. How we see color depends on the ability to see red, blue, and green, so women are more likely to see colors better. Being able to see colors well was important in prehistoric times when women looked for fruit for food. They had to be able to tell the difference between the types of fruit on the trees so that they didn't choose a type that was poisonous. For them, seeing different colors meant they could survive.

2 _____

Most men have a natural ability to read maps while women usually need to turn them around. How come?

Science says: Men are able to see the size and position of things much quicker than women. This ability is called "spatial awareness". Researchers discovered in a study of four-year-old children that only one girl has this ability for every four boys. Once again, the explanation can be found in the past. Do you remember those prehistoric women? Well, while they were looking for fruit, the men traveled long distances to hunt animals. When they had caught enough, they had to find their way home again. And this is where they learned "spatial awareness." The women didn't need it because they hardly ever went out of sight of their homes, but for the men, it was vital.

3 _____

Humans are social animals, so why is it that men don't like sharing their problems while women tell their best friends everything?

Science says: The answer is in the brain. The parts responsible for language are 17% larger in a woman's brain than in a man's brain. Also, women use both the left and the right side of the brain to use language, while men use only one side – their strongest side. And there's more. The part of the brain that connects the two parts together – the corpus callosum – is larger in women too, which means that they can move information from one part to the other part more quickly. Nobody is sure why these differences exist, but it's clear that women have a definite advantage over men when it comes to communication.

b Read the article again. Choose the right answers.

1 Men can find it difficult to perceive…
  a three colors.
  ⓑ one color.
  c any colors.
2 Seeing colors well helped prehistoric women…
  a find interesting things to eat.
  b cook food correctly.
  c choose the right fruit.
3 The results of the study showed that…
  a four-year-olds don't have spatial awareness.
  b boys learn spatial awareness before girls.
  c girls don't have spatial awareness.
4 Women didn't need spatial awareness in prehistoric times because…
  a the men were always with them.
  b they never left home.
  c they didn't travel far from home.
5 Men are worse at communicating because…
  a part of their brains is smaller.
  b their brains are 17% smaller.
  c their brains are larger.
6 The function of the corpus callosum in the brain is…
  a to communicate between both sides.
  b to store different languages.
  c to control the language process.

c Look at the highlighted words and phrases. What do you think they mean? Use your dictionary to look up their meaning and pronunciation.

d Complete the sentences with one of the highlighted words or phrases.

1 It's a _definite_ _advantage_ to have good test scores if you want to go to college.
2 Don't eat those mushrooms you found outside! They could be _____.
3 Who's _____ _____ making this mess?
4 She's _____ _____ to accept if you invite her husband as well.
5 Italian people _____ _____ _____ for being great cooks.
6 It's _____ that I finish the report before the end of the day.

4 VOCABULARY collocation: verbs / adjectives + prepositions

a Circle the correct prepositions.
1. They're arriving *at* / *on* / *in* Seoul on Friday.
2. That suitcase belongs *for* / *from* / *to* me.
3. We should ask someone *at* / *for* / *of* directions.
4. We might go camping, but it depends *in* / *of* / *on* the weather.
5. Everybody laughed *about* / *at* / *to* me when I fell off the chair.
6. Who's going to pay *for* / *of* / *with* the meal?
7. I dreamed *about* / *from* / *with* my old school friends last night.
8. That girl reminds me *about* / *of* / *to* my cousin.

b Complete the sentences with the correct prepositions.
1. Tony used to be married _to_ Teresa.
2. You can rely _____ me to help you with the party tomorrow.
3. They're worried _____ their teenage son.
4. We're not very interested _____ abstract art.
5. I'm very different _____ my sister.
6. Adam's very good _____ math.
7. I'm fed up _____ this weather.
8. He's famous _____ his role in *Sherlock Holmes*.

5 WHEN ARE PREPOSITIONS STRESSED?

a ONLINE Listen and complete the dialogues.

1. **A** Who did you _argue_ _with_?
   B I _____ with my _____.
2. **A** Who are you _____ _____?
   B I'm _____ at _____!
3. **A** What are you so _____ _____?
   B I'm _____ about my _____.
4. **A** What are you _____ _____?
   B I'm _____ to the _____.

b Listen again and repeat. Copy the rhythm.

6 LISTENING

a ONLINE Listen to a radio call-in program. Which speaker has the most traditional view about men doing the cooking?

1 Nick ☐   2 Eve ☐   3 Frank ☐   4 Martina ☐

b Listen again and mark the sentences T (true) or F (false).
1. Nick is unemployed. _T_
2. He wouldn't like to be a chef. ___
3. Eve cooks all the meals at her house. ___
4. She spends a lot of time cleaning the kitchen. ___
5. Frank thinks that girls work harder than they used to. ___
6. Frank thinks that girls nowadays can cook. ___
7. Martina's partner does all the cooking. ___
8. Martina respects men who can cook. ___

c Listen again with the audioscript on p. 71.

USEFUL WORDS AND PHRASES

Learn these words and phrases.

claim (vb) /kleɪm/
reduce /rɪˈdus/
almost /ˈɔlmoʊst/
slightly /ˈslaɪtli/
whereas /wɛrˈæz/
according to /əˈkɔrdɪŋ tu/
in fact /ɪn ˈfækt/
range from /ˈreɪndʒ frəm/
tend to /ˈtɛnd tə/
be skeptical of /bi ˈskɛptɪkl əv/

ONLINE FILE 3

Practical English A difficult celebrity

1 GIVING OPINIONS

Complete the dialogue.

John I love this song. Can you turn it up?
Anna Do I have to? It's really old.
John It may be old, but it's one of my favorites. ¹ _Personally_, I think pop music was better in the past than it is now. What do you ² th_____?
Anna No, I don't think that's ³ r_____. In my ⁴ op_____, there is some great music around. And some of today's singers have amazing voices.
John I ⁵ ag_____. But very few of them write their own music. If you ⁶ as_____ me, the real musicians are the ones who write the songs and then perform them live on stage. Don't you ⁷ ag_____?
Anna To be ⁸ h_____, I don't know a lot about it. I just turn the radio on and listen to what they're playing!

2 SOCIAL ENGLISH

Complete the dialogues. Use a phrase containing the word in parentheses.

1 **A** Hello! _I'm   back_! (back)
   B Hi! Did you have a good day?
2 **A** I'm going out for a walk now. Do you want to come?
   B _____.
   I'll get my coat. (minute)
3 **A** I brought you some flowers.
   B Thank you. That's _____. (kind)
4 **A** _____ what you said about moving to California? (mean)
   B Yes. I think it'll be a great opportunity for us.
5 **A** You look upset. What's the matter?
   B Nothing really. _____ my boyfriend's away and I really miss him. (just)

3 READING

a Read the text. Mark the sentences T (true) or F (false).

1 New York taxis are all the same model of car.   _F_
2 A medallion number has four numbers and one letter.   ___
3 An off-duty cab won't pick you up.   ___
4 You should stand in the street until a taxi stops for you.   ___
5 When you get in a taxi, the price starts at 50 cents.   ___
6 You pay per minute if you are not moving.   ___
7 Taxi drivers like to be paid in cash.   ___

NEW YORK TAXIS

New York taxis provide an essential service to New Yorkers and tourists for getting around the city. There are over 12,000 yellow medallion taxicabs so it doesn't take long to see one.

What does a New York taxi look like?
New York taxis come in many different shapes and sizes, but to be official taxis they must be yellow. They must also have a special code called a medallion number: one number, then one letter, and two more numbers. A bronze badge with the same code should also be displayed on the hood.
Only taxis with the above are legally licensed to pick you up!

How will I know when a New York taxi is available?
It's all in the lights! When just the center light illuminates the medallion number, the taxi is available to be hailed. When the center light is off and both sidelights are on (illuminating the words "Off Duty"), the taxi is off duty. When no lights are illuminated, the taxi is already in use.

How to hail a New York taxi.
First, try to hail a taxi in the direction you are already going; it saves time and money. When you see an available taxi, make sure it's safe and step off the sidewalk while holding your hand up high. If for any reason you don't get the driver's attention, step back onto the sidewalk and wait for the next available taxi and repeat the process. It's as simple as that.

New York taxi fares.
Once you step into the cab the meter will be turned on. This is called the "flag-drop fare" and is $2.50. After that it will cost you 50 cents for every one-fifth of a mile, or 50 cents per minute if you are stuck in traffic. There is a flat-rate charge of $52 from Manhattan to JFK Airport.
If you're happy with the trip, you should tip your driver between 15% and 20% of the total fare. Paying by cash is preferred, however all taxis now accept credit cards.

b Underline five words or phrases you don't know. Use your dictionary to look up their meaning and pronunciation.

> Failure is not falling down. Failure is falling down and not getting up again.
>
> Richard Nixon, former US President

4A Failure and success

1 GRAMMAR can, could, be able to

a Circle the correct form. Check (✓) if both are correct.

1 She *can* / *is able to* swim really well because she used to live by the ocean. ✓
2 You don't need to *can* / *be able to* drive to live in the city.
3 Luke *could* / *was able to* read when he was only three years old.
4 If it doesn't rain tomorrow, *we can* / *we'll be able to* go for a long walk.
5 Sorry, I've been so busy that I *haven't could* / *haven't been able to* call until now.
6 If Maria had a less demanding job, she *could* / *would be able to* enjoy life more.
7 I've never *could* / *been able to* dance well, but I'd love to learn.
8 We're really sorry we *couldn't* / *weren't able to* come to your wedding.
9 I *used to can* / *used to be able to* speak a little Portuguese, but I've forgotten most of it now.
10 *Can you* / *Will you be able to* make it to dinner tonight?
11 To work for this company, you *must can* / *must be able to* speak at least three languages.
12 I hate *can't* / *not being able to* communicate with the local people when I'm traveling.

b Read Tyler Ruiz's résumé. Then complete the sentences with the correct form of *can*, *could*, or *be able to*.

1 Tyler ___can___ sail.
2 He _____ speak a little Chinese when he started working in Hong Kong.
3 He _____ speak German.
4 He _____ design websites since 1999.
5 He'd like _____ speak Russian.
6 He _____ finish his Ph.D. before he left the US.
7 He _____ speak a little Russian soon.

Name: Tyler Ruiz
Date of Birth: 09/22/1980

Education
Degree in French with Marketing (2003)
Master's in Business Administration (2006)
Started Ph.D. in Business (2009) – incomplete

Work Experience
1998–2000: Trainer and Operator with Texas Instruments, London
2003–2009: Assistant then Marketing Manager, Texas Instruments, Dallas, USA
2009–present: Managing Director, AHH Marketing Services Ltd., Hong Kong

Other Skills
IT skills – advanced.
Course in web design 1999.

Languages
French (fluent) Chinese (basic) certificate 2008
I hope to start Russian classes next January.

Hobbies and Interests
Watersports, especially sailing and windsurfing

---

2 PRONUNCIATION sentence stress

ONLINE Listen and repeat the sentences. Copy the rhythm.

1 She can **sing very well**.
2 I've **never** been **able** to **ski**.
3 Can you **read** a **map**?
4 You **won't** be **able** to **go out tomorrow**.
5 He **hasn't** been **able** to **walk very fast** since he **hurt** his **leg**.
6 They **aren't able** to **come tonight**.

3 READING

a Read the article once and match paragraphs A–D with photos 1–4.

Steven Spielberg 1
Isaac Newton 2
Bill Gates 3
Thomas Edison 4

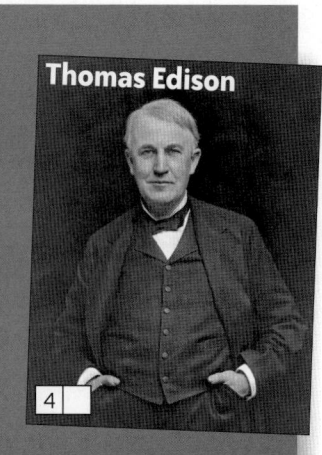

Failure: the first step toward success

Many people who have found success started out by failing. Below are four of the most famous.

A Some people consider this man to be the greatest scientist who has ever lived. However, his early life was nothing special. He was very small as a child and he was a very bad student. When he was twelve, his mother took him out of school so that he could learn how to run the family farm. Unfortunately, he wasn't very good at that either, so in the end he was sent back to school. After eventually passing his exams, he went to Cambridge University where he became a brilliant scholar. Later, he developed his law of gravity.

B This man is one of the most famous inventors of all time, which is incredible when you think he only went to school for three months. After his teacher lost patience with him, his mother taught him at home and he learned many important lessons from reading books. His working life started as badly as his schooling had, and he was fired from his first two jobs. However, this gave him more time to experiment – by the end of his life he had invented over a thousand devices. His most famous invention was a certain type of lightbulb.

C Ask anyone to name the most famous movie director in Hollywood and many of them will say this man's name. However, his movie career started badly, as he was rejected three times from film school. He eventually started his studies at a different school, but he dropped out to become a director before he had finished. Since then he has won the Oscar for best director twice, and three of his movies have broken box office records. He went back to school in 2002 to finish his studies and earn his BA degree.

D Although he is one of the most successful businessmen and computer programmers of all time, this man didn't actually finish college. He was very bright at school and went to Harvard University, but he spent most of his time using the college's computers for his own projects and didn't do much studying. After dropping out, he decided to start his own company with a friend. This company failed, but he persisted and won a contract with IBM which eventually resulted in his company becoming one of the most powerful and recognized brands in the world today.

b Read the article again. Mark the sentences T (true) or F (false).

1. Isaac Newton almost became a farmer. *T*
2. He was never a very good student. ___
3. Thomas Edison missed three months of school when he was a child. ___
4. He didn't make a good impression on his bosses at the start of his working life. ___
5. Steven Spielberg couldn't go to the film school he wanted to. ___
6. He has never finished his degree. ___
7. Bill Gates failed out of college. ___
8. His first company wasn't successful. ___

c Look at the highlighted words and phrases. What do you think they mean? Use your dictionary to look up their meaning and pronunciation.

d Complete the sentences with one of the highlighted words or phrases.

1. The child's parents *lost patience* with her and sent her to her room.
2. He wasn't enjoying college, so he _____ _____ after the first year.
3. After several months, she _____ managed to persuade her boyfriend to see an opera.
4. My colleague _____ _____ for sending personal emails from work.
5. My husband refuses to buy expensive _____ of clothing.
6. There was a huge line at the _____ _____ because it was the opening night of the movie.

4 VOCABULARY -ed / -ing adjectives

a Right (✓) or wrong (✗)? Correct the wrong adjectives.

1 Turn the channel! This is a bored TV show. ✗
    boring
2 Taking care of small children can be very tired. ☐
    _____
3 His test scores were very disappointing. ☐
    _____
4 I was very embarrassed when my phone rang in the meeting. ☐
    _____
5 Junko was very surprising because she didn't know they were coming. ☐
    _____
6 We took a lot of pictures because the view was so amazing. ☐
    _____
7 Are you interested in car racing? ☐
    _____
8 She felt frustrating because she couldn't get on the surfboard. ☐
    _____

b Complete the sentences with the correct form of the adjectives in parentheses.

1 I enjoyed the book, but the movie was a little _boring_. (bored / boring)
2 I felt very _____ when I realized my mistake. (embarrassed / embarrassing)
3 He's _____ because the printer isn't working. (frustrated / frustrating)
4 The final quarter of the game was really _____. (excited / exciting)
5 We haven't heard from her since she arrived in Bangkok – it's very _____. (worried / worrying)
6 Your trip sounds really _____ – tell me more! (interested / interesting)
7 I'm tired of this terrible weather – it's so _____. (depressed / depressing)
8 Max was very _____ when he wasn't chosen for the job. (disappointed / disappointing)

c Circle the -ed adjectives in exercise b where -ed is pronounced /ɪd/.

Reflexive pronouns

d Complete the sentences with the correct word.

1 The best way to get healthy is to make _yourself_ exercise every day.
2 Jon and Danny help _____ to food whenever they come to my house.
3 Jenna painted the bathroom _____.
4 The computer turns _____ off if nobody uses it for a while.
5 I always sing to _____ when I'm in the shower.
6 We found the apartment _____, without any help from a real estate agent.

5 LISTENING

a **ONLINE** You are going to hear five speakers talking about mistakes they have made in a foreign language. Listen and complete the sentences.

Speaker 1 was speaking _French_ to _____.
Speaker 2 was speaking _____ to _____.
Speaker 3 was speaking _____ to _____.
Speaker 4 was speaking _____ to _____.
Speaker 5 was speaking _____ to _____.

b Listen again and complete the table.

	What they wanted to say	What they actually said
Speaker 1	_inhaler_	
Speaker 2		
Speaker 3		
Speaker 4		
Speaker 5		

c Listen again with the audioscript on p. 71.

USEFUL WORDS AND PHRASES

Learn these words and phrases.

link /lɪŋk/
scuba dive /ˈskubə daɪv/
skills /skɪlz/
(dance) steps /stɛps/
multilingual /mʌltiˈlɪŋɡwəl/
fluently /ˈfluəntli/
basic phrases /beɪsɪk ˈfreɪzɪz/
language barrier /ˈlæŋɡwɪdʒ bæriər/
teach yourself books /titʃ yərˈsɛlf bʊks/
more exceptions than rules /mɔr ɪkˈsɛpʃnz ðən rulz/

4B Modern manners?

> When a man opens the car door for his wife it's either a new car or a new wife.
>
> *Duke of Edinburgh, husband of Queen Elizabeth II*

1 VOCABULARY phone language

Complete the sentences.

1. You must not use your phone in a qu*iet* z*one*.
2. When you finish a phone call, you h_____ u_____.
3. If someone doesn't answer their phone, you can leave a m_____ on their v_____.
4. If you're in a meeting, you can put your phone on s_____ or v_____ mode.
5. If someone's phone is off, you can c_____ b_____ later.
6. The sound your cell phone makes when someone calls you is a r_____.
7. If you want to text your friends more cheaply, you can use in_____ m_____.
8. When you call someone, you have to d_____ their number by pressing some keys.
9. If someone is already talking on their cell phone when you call, the line is b_____.
10. You can protect the display of your cell phone or computer with a sc_____.

2 GRAMMAR modals of obligation: *must, have to, should*

a Circle the correct form. Check (✓) if both are possible.

b Correct any mistakes in use or form in the highlighted phrases. Check (✓) the correct sentences.

1. People must not use their cell phones when they're talking to you.
   People shouldn't use
2. I must go to work by bus yesterday. My car was being repaired.
   _____
3. Do you have to wear a suit and tie at work?
   _____
4. You don't have to play soccer here. It says "no ball games."
   _____
5. My father is a taxi driver and he should work nights.
   _____
6. I didn't have to cook last night because we went out for dinner.
   _____
7. In the future, maybe everyone must speak English and Chinese.
   _____
8. You don't look well. You should to go home.
   _____

What you need to know before you visit the US

1. You *have to / must* have a visa to enter the country. ✓
2. You *must not / don't have to* drive on the left! Here we drive on the right!
3. You *must not / don't have to* pay to visit most museums and art galleries. Entrance is usually free.
4. You *have to / should* go on a ferry to visit the Statue of Liberty. You can't go by bus.
5. You *have to / must* wear a seat belt at all times in a car.
6. You *must / should* always try to arrive on time for an appointment or meeting. Americans are very punctual!
7. If you are sightseeing in New York, you *must / should* buy a MetroCard that gives you cheaper travel on the subway and buses.
8. You *must not / don't have to* smoke in any public building. It is prohibited by law.
9. When talking to Americans, you *shouldn't / don't have to* ask them about their salary. Some people might think this is rude.
10. You *must / have to* answer some questions when you go through immigration.

3 PRONUNCIATION silent consonants, linking

a Cross out the silent consonant in the words.

1 write
2 receipt
3 hour
4 shouldn't
5 exhausted
6 walk
7 could
8 debt

b **ONLINE** Listen and check. Then listen again and repeat the words.

c Listen and repeat the sentences. Try to link the words.

1 You shouldn't talk on the phone when you're driving.
2 You must always wear your seat belt in the car.
3 You don't have to wear a uniform.
4 You shouldn't ask a friend for money.
5 You have to watch out for pickpocketers.
6 You should take a present for them.

d **ONLINE** Listen and check. Then listen again and repeat the sentences.

4 READING

a Read the article once and check (✓) the best summary.

1 How men should behave toward women in the 21st century. ☐
2 How men behaved toward women in the past. ☐
3 The difference between men's and women's manners. ☐

Ladies first?

Nobody knows how long people have been using the words "Ladies First," nor is anyone sure where the concept came from. However, neither of these facts matters today. The important question is whether the tradition is still relevant, and if men should continue respecting it.

In the past, there was a strict set of rules concerning men's behavior toward women – or rather "ladies" as they were called then. Men wearing hats used to take them off in the presence of women. They used to stand up whenever a woman entered or left a room, and they did the same at a dining table. Men used to hold a door for a woman to allow her to go through first. They always used to pay for meals – but we'll come back to that one later. All of these customs were considered good manners, and people looked down on men who did not conform.

In fact, this set of rules actually made things easier for men. If they broke a rule, they knew perfectly well that they were going to offend somebody. Today, it is much easier to cause offense without meaning to. For example, if a man opens a door to let a woman through first, and she does so without saying thank you, the man may feel offended. And if a man invites a woman to a restaurant of his choice on their first date, and then asks her to pay her half of the check, it may be the woman who gets upset. Women no longer want to be treated as the weaker sex, which leaves men in a dilemma. On one hand, men are conscious of the "Ladies First" tradition, but on the other, they do not want to offend. Often, they don't know what to do.

The best advice is this: if in doubt, men should follow the rules of "Ladies First." Even if the woman considers the behavior inappropriate, she will still realize that the man has good manners. This is particularly relevant on that first date we were talking about. If the man has invited the woman out, then he should pay the check. Actually, it's the invitation to dinner itself that is important here, not the amount of money spent. In general, women appreciate a picnic or a home-made dinner just as much as an expensive meal.

So the answer to our original question is: yes. "Ladies First" is still relevant today, but not in the same way as it was in the past. Most women appreciate a kind gesture made by a man, but he should never accompany it with the words "Ladies First" – it spoils the effect completely!

b Read the article again and choose the right answer.
1 According to the article…
   a the idea of "Ladies first" started in the Middle Ages.
   b the idea of "Ladies first" is a new idea.
   ⓒ it's not known when the idea of "Ladies first" started.
2 In the past…
   a men didn't know how to behave toward women.
   b "Ladies first" was very polite.
   c it didn't matter if men broke the rules.
3 Nowadays, men…
   a aren't sure how to behave toward women.
   b behave in the same way toward women.
   c have new rules to follow.
4 According to the article, men should…
   a not think about what women want.
   b follow the rules of "Ladies first."
   c not follow the rules of "Ladies first."
5 According to the article, women…
   a always want expensive things.
   b don't like it when men cook.
   c like a meal at home or in a restaurant.

c Look at the highlighted words and phrases. What do you think they mean? Use your dictionary to look up their meaning and pronunciation.

d Find the highlighted words or phrases in the text to match the definitions.
1 not right for a particular situation
   inappropriate
2 an action that shows other people how you feel
   _____
3 understand the value of something
   _____
4 an idea
   _____
5 upset somebody
   _____
6 thought they were better than
   _____

5 LISTENING

a ONLINE Listen to a radio program about good manners in different countries. What kind of advice do the four people ask about? Check (✓) the correct answers. There is one piece of advice you do not need to use.
1 Advice about how to behave in business situations. ☐
2 Advice about body language. ☐
3 Advice about meeting new people. ✓
4 Advice about forming a line. ☐
5 Advice about visiting someone's house. ☐

b Listen again and choose the right answers.
1 According to the expert, in Thailand you should not give a "wai" to…
   a people who are older than you.
   b anyone.
   ⓒ people who are younger than you.
2 When is it polite to say thank you in Brazil?
   a when a friend offers you a drink
   b when a stranger opens a door
   c both a and b are correct
3 Which gesture, often made by police officers, is an insult in Greece?
   a "Come here."
   b "Stop."
   c "Go away."
4 A foreign person in Korea…
   a must not bow to anyone.
   b must bow to everyone.
   c can bow to show politeness.
5 According to the expert, if a Korean person is happy, they bow very…
   a quickly.
   b slowly.
   c deeply.

c Listen again with the audioscript on p. 71.

USEFUL WORDS AND PHRASES

Learn these words and phrases.

etiquette /ˈɛtəkət/
manners /ˈmænərz/
host / hostess /hoʊst/ /ˈhoʊstəs/
behave /bɪˈheɪv/
deserve /dɪˈzɜrv/
disturb /dɪˈstɜrb/
inappropriate /ɪnəˈproʊpriət/
insulting /ɪnˈsʌltɪŋ/
allergic to /əˈlərdʒɪk tə/
should have (written) /ʃʊd əv/

ONLINE **FILE 4**

> It's not whether you win or lose that matters, but whether I win or lose.
>
> Sandy Lyle, Scottish golfer

5A Sports superstitions

1 GRAMMAR past tenses

Complete the sentences with the correct form of the verbs in parentheses. Use the simple past, past continuous, or past perfect.

1 We were late. When we __arrived__ (arrive), everyone else __had finished__ (finish) their lunch and they __were sitting__ (sit) on the patio having coffee.
2 They _____ (drive) to the airport when they suddenly _____ (remember) that they _____ (not turn off) the lights.
3 The game _____ (already / start) when we _____ (turn on) the TV. The Red Sox _____ (lose) and they _____ (play) very badly.
4 I _____ (not recognize) many people at my old school reunion because everyone _____ (change) a lot in twenty years.
5 My sister _____ (wait) to go out for dinner yesterday when her boyfriend _____ (call) her to say that he _____ (not can) come because his car _____ (break down).
6 Real Madrid _____ (beat) Barcelona yesterday. Barcelona _____ (win) 1–0 in the first half, but Madrid _____ (score) two goals in the second half.
7 He _____ (run) to the station, but the nine o'clock train _____ (already / leave). The station was empty except for two people who _____ (wait) for the next train.
8 It _____ (start) raining when I _____ (walk) to work. I _____ (call) a car service because I _____ (not wear) a coat and I _____ (not have) an umbrella.

2 PRONUNCIATION /ɔr/, /ər/

a (Circle) the word with a different sound.

1 /ɔr/ horse	2 /ər/ bird	3 /ɔr/ horse	4 /ər/ bird
four	first	course	court
shorts	hurt	floor	serve
warm up	sports	score	shirt
(work out)	world	worst	worse

b **ONLINE** Listen and check. Then listen again and repeat the words.

3 READING

a Read the article on p. 31 once. Complete the sentences.

1 The boy was playing _____.
2 He cheated by taking _____.

b Read the article again. Mark the sentences T (true) or F (false).

1 According to the article, people usually learn not to cheat when they are young children. __F__
2 Blank tiles can be used when players don't have the right letter. ___
3 The boy was one of the best players in the tournament. ___
4 The previous day, the boy had beaten Arthur Moore. ___
5 Moore caught the boy while he was making a word. ___
6 He saw the boy take a blank tile out of his pocket. ___
7 The boy answered the tournament director's questions truthfully. ___
8 He wasn't allowed to continue playing. ___

c Look at the highlighted words and phrases. What do you think they mean? Use your dictionary to look up their meaning and pronunciation.

d Complete the sentences with one of the highlighted words or phrases.

1 James __discretely__ bought the present when his wife wasn't looking.
2 Sam _____ telling lies about her colleagues.
3 The athlete was _____ after he made three false starts.
4 My computer is broken, so I'm going to _____ it with a new one.
5 She became _____ when she found the train tickets in his pocket.
6 He couldn't _____ the man of lying because there was no proof he had done anything bad.
7 Jack beat his _____ 6–1, 6–3.
8 They _____ to stealing after they lost their jobs.

It's normal for young children to cheat when they're playing board games. As they grow older, they realize that the fun is actually in taking part in the game, not necessarily in winning it. By the time they reach their teens, they have usually learned not to cheat. Sadly, this was not the case for a player in a national board game championship held annually in the US. The player wanted to win so much that he resorted to cheating.

The board game was Scrabble. This is a word game that was created in 1938 by an American architect named Alfred Mosher Butts. In the game, players have to make words from individual letters on small squares called "tiles," and then put the words on a board. Two of the most useful tiles in the game are the blanks, which are tiles without any letters on them. A blank isn't worth any points, but a player can use it to replace any letter of the alphabet.

The cheater in this particular tournament was a 15-year-old boy from Orlando, Florida. He had surprised organizers in the early stages of the competition by beating some of the best players, despite the fact that he had never played in competitions before. This made some of the other players suspicious, including the man who caught him, 43-year-old Arthur Moore. Moore had already played the boy the day before, and Moore had won the game, although the boy had had both of the blank tiles. In Scrabble, before a new game starts, the players put the tiles from the previous game back into a small bag. This time, Moore had a good look at the tiles on the table before he and his opponent put them in the bag to start the game. He was not surprised to see that the two blanks were together on the table in front of the boy. As the two players were putting the tiles into the bag, Moore discretely watched the boy's left hand. He saw the boy pick up the two blanks, and put his hand under the table. This was the signal for Moore to call one of the organizers and accuse the boy of cheating.

When the boy was taken away for questioning, he admitted to taking the two blanks during the game and hiding them under the table. As a result of his cheating, the tournament director disqualified him and banned him from playing in the competition again.

4 VOCABULARY sports

a Read the definitions and write the words.

1 an area of water that swimmers use
 sw_imming_ p_ool_
2 the person who controls a soccer game
 r_____
3 an area where skiing is done
 s_____
4 to hit something with your foot
 k_____
5 somebody who is very enthusiastic about sports
 f_____
6 an area where golf is played
 c_____
7 exercise to become healthy and strong
 g_____ in s_____
8 an area of ground where people play soccer
 f_____
9 a person who trains people to compete in certain sports
 c_____
10 a large structure, usually with no roof, where people can sit and watch sports
 st_____

b Complete the sentences with the simple past of the verbs in the box.

| beat | get injured | lose | play | score |
| throw | tie | train | warm up | win |

1 The US _played_ Russia last night for the championship.
2 The team _____ hard every day before the tournament.
3 The Canadian runner _____ the race. He got the gold medal.
4 The players _____ _____ by jogging and doing easy exercises just before the game started.
5 Joe _____ the score when he hit a home run!
6 I didn't play well in the semifinal round. I _____ 2–6, 1–6.
7 Marc _____ the ball to his brother, but his brother dropped it.
8 Brazil _____ Sweden. They had a much better team.
9 The Argentinian striker _____ four goals in the last game.
10 Our best player _____ _____ in the second half, and was taken off the field to see the team's doctor.

5 LISTENING

a **ONLINE** Listen to a radio program about a sports scandal. Which country won the competition in the end?
 _____

b Listen again and mark the sentences T (true) or F (false).

1 The scandal happened during the tennis tournament of the 2012 Olympics. _F_
2 South Korea and India were involved in the scandal. ___
3 It happened during the first stage. ___
4 One way they cheated was by hitting the shuttlecock into the net. ___
5 The same thing happened in another match. ___
6 The teams cheated because they had been offered money. ___
7 The crowd didn't enjoy the matches. ___
8 South Korea won the silver medal. ___

c Listen again with the audioscript on p. 72.

USEFUL WORDS AND PHRASES

Learn these words and phrases.

fate /feɪt/
rituals /ˈrɪtʃuəlz/
superstition /supərˈstɪʃn/
bounce /baʊns/
cheat /tʃit/
reveal /rɪˈvil/
sweat /swɛt/
a lucky charm /ə ˈlʌki tʃɑrm/
result in /rɪˈzʌlt ɪn/
tie your shoelaces /taɪ yər ˈʃuleɪsɪz/

5B Love at Exit 19

> Love is like war: easy to begin but very hard to stop.
> HL Mencken, US journalist

1 GRAMMAR usually and used to

a Correct any mistakes in the highlighted phrases. Check (✓) the correct sentences.

1 Where did you used to live before you moved here?
   did you use to live?
2 Jerry used to have a beard, but he shaved it off last week.
   ✓
3 I usually go to the gym when I leave work.
   _____
4 My wife doesn't use to wear makeup. She doesn't like it.
   _____
5 Did you use to have long hair?
   _____
6 I use to walk to work. My office is only ten minutes from my house.
   _____
7 Carol didn't used to talk to me, but now she always says hello.
   _____
8 Do you use to get up late on Sundays?
   _____
9 Did you used to watch cartoons when you were little?
   _____
10 We don't usually stay in expensive hotels, but this weekend is special.
   _____

b Complete the sentences with *usually* or the correct form of *used to*, and the verbs in parentheses.

1 She _used to wear_ glasses, but now she has contact lenses. (wear)
2 He _____ animals, but now he has a dog. (not like)
3 I _____ my parents on Sunday. It's good to talk to them. (call)
4 I _____ French classes, but I stopped because I don't have time now. (take)
5 We never _____, but now we go to restaurants twice a week. (eat out)
6 I _____ late, but today I have a lot to do. (not work)
7 My sister _____ very shy, but now she's confident. (be)
8 They _____ me a present on my birthday, but this year they forgot! (give)

2 PRONUNCIATION sentence stress; the letter s

a ONLINE Listen and repeat. Copy the rhythm.

1 **Where** did you **use** to **live**?
2 Did you **use** to **wear glasses**?
3 They **used** to **have** a lot of **money**.
4 He **used** to **go** to my **school**.
5 We **used** to **work together**.
6 You **used** to **have long hair**.
7 We **didn't use** to **get along**.
8 I **didn't use** to **like** it.

b Circle the word with a different sound.

1 snake	2 zebra	3 shower	4 television
see	eyes	tissue	usually
(friends)	easy	please	pleasure
most	especially	sure	decision
social	nowadays	sugar	music

c ONLINE Listen and check. Then listen again and repeat the words.

3 VOCABULARY relationships

a Complete the sentences with the people in the box.

classmates   close friend   colleague   couple
ex   fiancé   roommate   ~~wife~~

1 We're married. — She's my _wife_.
2 I share an apartment with her. — She's my _____.
3 I work with him. — He's my _____.
4 We used to go to school together. — We were _____.
5 I'm going to marry him. — He's my _____.
6 I used to go out with her. — She's my _____.
7 We've known each other for a long time. I tell her everything. — She's a _____.
8 We've been going out together for three years. — We're a _____.

33

b Complete the text with the simple past of the verbs in the box.

> be together   become friends   break up
> get along   get to know   get in touch   get married
> go out together   have (sth) in common
> lose touch   ~~meet~~   propose

Anna [1] _met_ Luke when she started work. They [2] _____ each other quickly because they sat next to each other in the office. They soon [3] _____ and they discovered that they [4] _____ a lot _____ because they were both sports fans. They [5] _____ a few times after work and they fell in love. They [6] _____ for a year, but they argued a lot, and in the end they [7] _____. After that, Anna got a new job in a different town and so they [8] _____. Ten years later, they [9] _____ again on Facebook. They were both still single and Mark had changed jobs, too. They decided to try again, and this time they [10] _____ better than before, maybe because they weren't working together. After six months, Luke [11] _____ and Anna accepted. They [12] _____ last spring. A lot of their old colleagues from work came to the wedding!

4 READING

a Read the article once. How many friends does the average American have?

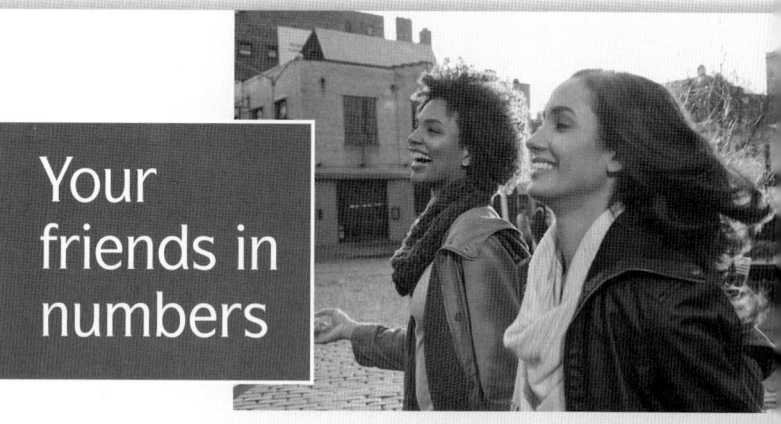

_____.

Your friends in numbers

How many friends does the average person have? A researcher at Cornell University recently did a study to learn the number of friends a typical American has. He interviewed more than 2,000 adults aged 18 and over in his study. He asked them to list the names of the people they had discussed serious matters with in the last six months. About 48% of the people taking part gave the researcher one name, 18% gave him two, and about 29% gave him more than two.

These results contrast dramatically with the news published by the social networking site Facebook recently. They said that the average user on the site has 130 friends. The Cornell University study found the average number of friends to be a lot lower – 2.03 to be exact. The researcher from Cornell has explained that the difference lies in the definition of the word *friend*. A friend on Facebook may be a person who the user has met by chance or someone that they will never meet in real life. However, the friends in the researcher's study are close friends, who participants feel comfortable discussing their problems with.

In a similar study conducted 25 years ago, participants had a higher number of close friends. Then, the average number was three. Despite the lower number, the researcher does not believe that people are getting more isolated. Instead he thinks it's a sign that they are becoming better at choosing who they can trust with their secrets.

This is supported by the number of people in the study who could not think of any names of close friends they would discuss their personal problems with. The percentage of these participants is the same this time as it was 25 years ago. In both studies, just over 4% of the participants gave researchers no names. Apparently, the people who fall into this category are more likely to be men, or people with less education.

In general, the researcher from Cornell regards these findings as positive. In his opinion, they suggest that, at least in the case of Americans, people are not becoming less sociable.

b Read the article again and choose the best answer.

1. Most people in the Cornell University study had spoken about something important with…
   - ⓐ one person.
   - b two people.
   - c more than two people.
2. The news published by Facebook is different from the results in the Cornell study because…
   - a the people are different ages.
   - b the studies are from different years.
   - c the relationships aren't the same.
3. According to a previous study, people had _____ close friends in the past.
   - a more
   - b the same number of
   - c fewer
4. The number of people with no close friends is _____ it was in the past.
   - a higher than
   - b the same as
   - c lower than
5. The results of the Cornell study show that Americans today are _____ they used to be.
   - a more sociable than
   - b as sociable as
   - c less sociable than

c Look at the highlighted words and phrases. What do you think they mean? Use your dictionary to look up their meaning and pronunciation.

d Complete the sentences with one of the highlighted words or phrases.

1. I found an old painting _by_ _chance_ while I was cleaning the attic.
2. I wouldn't _____ my son with my phone. He'd probably break it.
3. How much money does _____ _____ _____ earn per year?
4. They talked about _____ _____ first, and then moved on to the less important things.
5. The richer parts of town _____ _____ with the poorer outskirts.
6. Some teenagers are _____ _____ _____ because they spend so much time on their computers.

5 LISTENING

a ONLINE You are going to hear a radio program about research on love and attraction. Number the topics in the order you hear them.

a How to use your eyes at a first meeting. __
b Body language at a first meeting. __
c How to use your voice at a first meeting. _1_
d How much to smile at a first meeting. __

b Listen again and mark the sentences T (true) or F (false).

1. It's very important to say the right thing the first time you talk to someone you like. _F_
2. A person's body language can make them more attractive. __
3. Looking into someone's eyes can make them feel more attracted to you. __
4. There were two weddings after an experiment in New York. __
5. Standing up straight is a good way to keep someone's attention. __
6. A person will copy your body language if they think you are interesting. __
7. It is impossible to know if someone is smiling when you're talking to them on the phone. __
8. Often when one person smiles, other people smile too. __

c Listen again with the audioscript on p. 72.

USEFUL WORDS AND PHRASES

Learn these words and phrases.

candle /ˈkændl/
commuter /kəˈmyutər/
cute /kyut/
likely /ˈlaɪkli/
raise the barrier /reɪz ðə ˈbæriər/
addicted to (sth) /əˈdɪktəd tə/
night shifts /ˈnaɪt ʃɪfts/
turn out (to be) /tərn ˈaʊt/
exchange a few words /ɪksˈtʃeɪndʒ ə fyu wərdz/
find the courage (to do sth) /faɪnd ðə ˈkərɪdʒ/

ONLINE FILE 5

Practical English Old friends

1 PERMISSION AND REQUESTS

a Complete the requests with the correct form of the verbs in the box.

do join pass meet take visit

1 Could you _do_ me a big favor? [d]
2 Do you mind if I _____ you? ☐
3 Would you mind _____ me at the airport? ☐
4 Is it OK if we _____ my parents this weekend? ☐
5 Can you _____ the salt? ☐
6 Do you think you could _____ me to the train station? ☐

b Match the requests from **a** with the responses a–f.

a Of course not. Take a seat.
b Sure. Here it is.
c Yes, of course. What time's your train?
d It depends what it is!
e Not at all. When do you land?
f Sure. Which day would be best?

2 SOCIAL ENGLISH

Complete the dialogue.

Jay	Dan! It's great to ¹s_ee_ you.
Dan	You too, Jay. It's been years.
Jay	How ²c_____ you're so late?
Dan	My flight was delayed, and then I had to wait forever for a taxi.
Jay	Well, you're here now. Do you want something to eat?
Dan	No ³w_____, man! I want to go out and see the city!
Jay	Don't you want to unpack first?
Dan	No, I can do that later. But I'll take a shower, if you don't ⁴m_____.
Jay	Sure. Go ahead.
Dan	This is great. You and me getting ready to go out.
Jay	Yeah. It's just like the old ⁵d_____.
Dan	OK, I'm ready. Let's go. We have a lot to ⁶t_____ about.

3 READING

Getting around the US

The US is huge, so flying is the quickest way to get around the country. It can be expensive though, so here are some other ways of getting around.

If you aren't in a hurry, the best alternative is to go by car. You have to be at least 25 years old to rent a car in the States, and you need a valid driver's license and a major credit card to do so. There are a lot of rental car companies, and their prices vary a lot. Compare companies before you decide which one to use, and remember it can be cheaper to book for a week than for a day.

If you prefer to be driven rather than driving yourself, the next best way to travel is by bus. Greyhound is the major long-distance bus company, and it has routes through the US and Canada. Tickets are much cheaper if you buy them seven days in advance, and there are often other offers. If you're traveling with a friend, your companion gets 50% off if you buy the tickets three days before you travel, and children between the ages of two and eleven get a 40% discount.

An alternative to using the bus is to take the train. Amtrak is the American rail company, and it has long-distance lines connecting all of the biggest cities. It also runs buses from major stations to smaller towns and national parks. Fares vary depending on the type of train and the seat, but you need to reserve at least three days ahead to get a discount. Students with an international student card get 15% off the regular fare. Bring your own food because the dining car is expensive.

a Read the text and answer the questions.

1 What do you need to rent a car in the US?
   You need a valid driver's license and a major credit card.
2 What is the difference between all the car rental companies?
   _____
3 Where does the Greyhound bus company operate?
   _____
4 How can you save money if you're traveling alone by bus?
   _____
5 How much do students pay on Amtrak trains?
   _____
6 What should long-distance rail passengers take with them?
   _____

b <u>Underline</u> five words or phrases you don't know. Use your dictionary to look up their meaning and pronunciation.

Listening

1 A 🔊

Host Welcome back to the show. Today, we've been discussing Teresa Gold's article *The Truth About Healthy Eating*. And now it's time for you, the listeners, to tell us what you think. The lines are open, so all you have to do is call 1-800-555-5792 and talk to one of our operators. That's 1-800-555-5792. And it looks like we have our first caller. Kevin from Miami, tell us what you think about the article.

Kevin Well, I'd like to say that I don't agree with the article at all. I don't eat many fruits or vegetables, and I'm perfectly healthy. I haven't called in sick to work for years – I can't remember the last time I had to stay in bed. This five-a-day thing is garbage, isn't it?

Host Um … thank you, Kevin. I think we have another caller on line two. Kate from Chicago, are you there?

Kate Yes, I am. Well, I'm sure the writer knows what she's talking about, but it isn't that easy. I mean, it's hard enough to get kids to eat vegetables at the best of times, but with all these burger and pizza places around, it's almost impossible. Once they get the taste for junk food, you can forget the five-a-day, that's for sure!

Host Thanks, Kate. And who's our next caller?

Derek Um, my name's Derek and I'm from Washington, D.C.

Host And what do you think, Derek?

Derek Well, I'd like to say that I think that the article is right. I mean, the writer talks about eating a lot of fruits and vegetables, which is something that we've always done in my family. My mom's a great cook. She always uses completely natural ingredients in her cooking, and we're almost never sick….

Host Thank you, Derek. Let's go back to line two again, where we have Rosie from Boston. Rosie, what's your opinion?

Rosie Well, the writer seems to think that ALL fruits and vegetables are good for you, and I don't think that's true. I mean, what about potatoes? They contain a lot of carbohydrates, which can make you gain weight if you aren't careful – it's even worse if you fry them. And then some fruits, like melon for example, have a lot of sugar. Personally, I think you should eat a little of everything and not too much of one thing.

Host Thanks, Rosie. And that's all we have time for today. We'll be speaking to the writer of the article after the break.

1 B 🔊

Terry I'm exhausted!
Jane Me too. I haven't stopped all day.
Terry Neither have I.
Jane Oh, well. I guess it'll get easier when the kids grow up.
Terry Do you think so?
Jane Of course. When they're older, they'll be more independent. We won't have to do everything for them anymore.
Terry And how long will that take? Five, six years? Or maybe never!
Jane Look, what's the problem, Terry?
Terry Nothing. It's just that we never have time for each other these days. We're always with the kids!
Jane But that's what happens when you have kids. It'll get better!
Terry I don't know… My parents were talking about us going to live with them. Do you think it would be easier for us if we lived with my parents?
Jane Well, I guess it'd have its advantages.
Terry Yeah, I mean for one thing there'd always be someone to take care of the kids.
Jane That sounds good.
Terry And we could go out in the evening without the kids. Just imagine that!
Jane Hmm. That doesn't really matter to me.
Terry And there would be more people to share the housework, too. It wouldn't always be the same person who does the shopping, cleans the house, and cooks the meals.
Jane Yes, but there would be more people in the house, so there would be more work to do. Shopping and cooking for six isn't the same as doing it for four.
Terry I guess so.
Jane And another disadvantage is that we wouldn't have any privacy.
Terry True.
Jane And you know what your parents are like. They let the kids do everything they want to do.
Terry Hmm. I guess you don't want to move in with my parents, then.
Jane Not really, no. Would you like to move in with mine?
Terry No, definitely not … Actually, things aren't so bad right now.
Jane I agree.
Terry And the kids will be older soon.
Jane Yes, they will.
Terry That's settled then. We're staying here.
Jane Fine.

2 A 🔊

Speaker 1: Can I live on my salary? Well, I don't really have many problems, because I'm still living with my mom and dad. Don't get me wrong, I give my mom some money for rent, but it's definitely much cheaper than living on your own. I actually have a pretty good salary – I'm a graphic designer. I don't really spend much – I buy some new clothes every now and then, and I have to put gas in my car, of course, but apart from that, it's really just going out on the weekends. Most of my money goes into a savings account so that I can buy my own house one day.

Speaker 2: I find it really hard to live on my income because I only have a part-time job. Being on my own with my daughter means that my mom has to take care of her when I'm at work. At least I don't have to pay for childcare! The house we live in is rented, so that's where most of the money goes. I don't think I'll ever be able to afford our own place because the bank won't give me a mortgage. Apart from the rent, my money goes to food and clothes for my daughter. Still, I shouldn't complain. I have an amazing daughter, and that's all that really matters.

Speaker 3: I think I'm really lucky. I'm pretty healthy for my age, I have enough money to live on, and I have my children and grandchildren! When I say I have enough money, I don't go on any fancy vacations or anything like that. But I'm comfortable. I've paid the mortgage, so that's one less expense, and I don't have any loans to pay either. My one little luxury is going out for lunch a few times a week with some friends. I guess that's where most of my money goes – on food!

Speaker 4: Can we live on our salaries? Well, I'm not so sure, actually! My husband is a teacher, so he doesn't earn that much – definitely not enough to raise two children! That means I have to work, too – I have a full-time job at the local supermarket. And really, that's our biggest problem, because we need someone to take care of the children. Our babysitter costs a fortune – we spend more on child care than we do on our mortgage! Then there's food and new clothes for the children, too. Honestly, it isn't cheap having kids these days!

2 B))

Host And now to end the show with an inspirational story, we have John to tell us about an incredible trip.

John Yes, thank you, Nora. Have you ever thought about traveling around the world and trying to help people as you go? Well that's what an American father and his two adopted sons are currently doing. J.D. Lewis is a single parent and a former actor. He's taken his sons, Jackson, age 14 and Buck, age 9, out of school for a year to make the trip with him. And their plan is to help people along the way by doing volunteer charity work.

Host That sounds wonderful, but it must be an expensive trip. How much will it all cost?

John It's going to cost them $300,000 dollars in total.

Host That's a lot of money. How did they afford it?

John Well, J.D Lewis didn't have all the money, so he set up an organization called Twelve in Twelve to help raise money, and with the help of individuals and some companies, they managed to raise the money.

Host Twelve in Twelve – that's an unusual name. Why did he call it that?

John For a very good reason. Not only is their trip going to last twelve months, but their plan is to visit twelve countries. This month, they're in Australia, where they're working with the most important ethnic group in the region – the Aborigines. J.D and his family are helping to get medical supplies to these people, who often live a long way from the major cities.

Host And is that the first place they've visited?

John Oh, no. So far they've visited seven countries. Their first stop was Russia, where they took care of babies in an orphanage in the city of Tomsk. From there, they traveled to China, where they worked with children with physical disabilities in Beijing. Then, they flew to Thailand where they helped take care of the animals at the Elephant Nature Park.

Host What a variety of places. Where did they go next?

John Their next stop was India, where they worked with children in the poorest district of the city of Hubli. Then they left Asia and flew to Africa. In Rwanda, they taught English to children who had lost their parents in the civil war. From there, they went to Zanzibar, an island off the coast of Tanzania.

Host That sounds very exotic! What did they do there?

John They helped families prepare an art fair, where they could sell things that they had made. Next, they went to Kenya, where they wrote and acted in a play with children who have HIV.

Host Wow, I bet that was very rewarding. Did they go anywhere else in Africa?

John No, that was the end of Africa. From Kenya, they flew to Australia, which is where they are right now.

Host All that sounds amazing, but their trip isn't over, is it?

John No, J.D. and his family still have four places to go: Antarctica, Paraguay, Peru, and Haiti. Not only are they trying to do things to help other people, but they are hoping to learn a lot of new things themselves. And J.D. Lewis hopes that the Twelve in Twelve organization will encourage other families to do what he has done with his sons.

Host Well, good luck to J.D. Lewis and his family on the rest of their incredible trip. And that's all we have time for tonight. Join us again tomorrow when we'll be bringing you more real-life stories.

3 A))

Speaker 1: One morning last winter, I was driving to work late when my cell phone rang. I knew it was my boss, so I answered it. Suddenly, the van in front of me stopped because there was someone crossing the road. I was talking to my boss, so I reacted too late, and my car went into the back of the van. Luckily, I was driving really slowly at the time, so I didn't do much damage to the van, but the front of my car was a real mess. Since then, I never use my phone when I'm driving.

Speaker 2: I was driving to Colorado one summer to visit my parents, who live in Denver. It's a long trip, so I had taken my MP3 player with me to connect to the car radio. Surprisingly, there wasn't much traffic on the freeway, so I arrived in Denver pretty quickly. However, I was having such a good time listening to my music, that I completely missed the exits for Denver. I didn't realize until I had gone another 20 miles, so I had to turn around and drive all the way back again! It just goes to show what can happen when you aren't concentrating.

Speaker 3: We were on vacation last year, when we had a little accident. We were going somewhere we'd never been before, so we were following the instructions on my GPS. We heard on the radio that there'd been a big accident on one of the roads we needed to travel on, so I started adjusting my GPS to find a different road to take. I took my eyes off the road and suddenly we came to a sharp turn in the road. I saw the turn too late, so I went straight ahead and drove into the middle of a field. We were really lucky, though, because no one was hurt.

Speaker 4: I don't usually get up early enough to put my makeup on, so I usually put it on in my car. Well, I used to put it on in the car – now I wait until I get to my office. That's because I had kind of a shock the other week, when I almost didn't stop at a crosswalk. I was looking in the mirror instead of at the road, so I didn't see this little boy run out—to tell you the truth, I hadn't even seen that there was a crosswalk there. I just had time to step on the brakes and I missed the little boy by about an inch. I was really shocked afterward, though.

Speaker 5: I was driving into town to meet my girlfriend for dinner when she sent me a text message. I decided to read it, in case it was important. Anyway, the message said that my girlfriend was already at the restaurant, and I wanted her to know that I was going to be a little late, so when I stopped at a red light, I started to write a reply. But I didn't notice when the traffic light turned green, and the car behind crashed into the back of me.

The driver of the car said he thought I was going to start driving, so he moved forward and hit me. Of course I didn't tell him I was texting.

3 B

Host Traditionally in the US, women have cooked more than men, but it looks as though things might be changing. According to a recent survey by a frozen foods company, almost half of all men in this country now prepare the family meals. And they aren't just doing it because they have to – it's because they enjoy it. The survey showed that 44 percent of men who were questioned do all of the cooking, and surprisingly, 15 percent of women questioned said that they didn't know *how* to cook. So it seems as if men are moving into the kitchen, and maybe women are moving out. Is this good news? What do you think? Call us at 1-800-555-3364 and tell us your opinion. I'll give you that number again – that's 1-800-555-3364.

And here's our first caller, Nick from San Deigo, California. Nick, what do you think about this new trend?

Nick I'm pretty excited to see more men in the kitchen. In fact, I'm one of them! I lost my job a few months ago, and now I do all the cooking at home. I make a different dish every day, and sometimes I meet up with my friends to exchange recipes. My girlfriend says she really likes my food, and she even thinks that I should train to be a professional chef. I'm seriously thinking about doing that.

Host Well, good luck to you, Nick. Who's our next caller? Ah, yes … It's Eve from Seattle, Washington. Do you cook, Eve?

Eve No, I don't. But my husband does. He's a much better cook than I am, so we decided from the beginning that he would do all the cooking. And he makes some great meals – mostly curries. But there's one problem.

Host What's that, Eve?

Eve He makes a terrible mess in the kitchen, and I have to clean up after him. I don't know what's worse, actually, cooking myself or cleaning the kitchen!

Host Oh, come on Eve – it can't be that bad! Now I think we have someone on line 2. Yes, it's Frank from Hartford. What do you think about men taking over the kitchen, Frank?

Frank Well, I'm not surprised, to be honest with you. It seems to me that girls are getting lazier and lazier these days – it's only the older moms and grandmothers who know how to cook. I mean, how can a woman get married if she can't cook?! I think it's a disgrace!

Host Thank you, Frank. So, not all of our listeners think it's a good thing. How about our next caller, Martina, calling from South Florida? Is it good news or bad news for you, Martina?

Martina Good news. Definitely. In my house, I do all the cooking. My boyfriend doesn't cook at all – he can't even fry an egg! I mean, we both work full time, so why can't we share the cooking? I'm really fed up with it, I really am. But I'm really happy for all those women out there who have found a real man. I know how you feel when you have to do everything yourself.

Host Let's hope Martina's boyfriend is listening, so that he knows how she feels. We'll take some more calls after the break.

4 A

Speaker 1: I suffer from asthma and I usually carry an inhaler around with me just in case I get an attack. Anyway, I was on a work trip – I was in Paris – I had forgotten my inhaler, and I was having problems breathing. So I went to a pharmacy and asked for "un aspirateur," which I thought was the French word for inhaler. I realized it wasn't when the girls behind the counter looked very confused. It turned out that I had asked for a vacuum cleaner, "aspirateur," instead of an inhaler, "inhalateur."

Speaker 2: I was in Istanbul with a Turkish friend of mine, and we decided that we wanted to buy some bread. I wanted to try out the Turkish I knew, so I said that I would ask for it. So we found this tiny little store and we went in. I said to the salesperson in my best voice "taze erkek" which I thought meant "fresh bread." Unfortunately, I got the word for bread "ekmek" confused with the word for man "erkek," so what I had actually asked for was "a fresh young man." Luckily, my friend came to my rescue and asked for the bread correctly, but I felt a little embarrassed!

Speaker 3: I was 14, and I was on an exchange visit with my school in Madrid. It was the first night, and I was at home with my Spanish host family, the Garcías, having dinner. We'd finished the main course and it was time for dessert, so the wife, Maria, asked me if I'd like some fruit. I saw some bananas in the fruit bowl, so I asked for a "platón," at which point the whole family looked at me strangely. They then explained to me that I'd actually asked for a large plate. "Platón" means "large plate" whereas "banana" is "plátano."

Speaker 4: I was in Rio De Janeiro in Brazil with my husband, and it was a very hot day, so we decided to take a break from our sightseeing. We found a street vendor selling cold drinks and snacks near the beach. I was so hot and tired that I quickly ordered what I thought was ice cream. I said "uma cosquinha por favor." As soon as I'd finished speaking, the street vendor burst out laughing. He quickly apologized and explained in English that I'd asked him for a tickle and not ice cream. Tickle in Portuguese is "cosquinha" and ice cream is "casquinha."

Speaker 5: I'm an American living in Korea. Usually, I can communicate pretty well in Korean. I speak Korean with my wife every day, and I have a tutor that I meet with every week to practice my conversation skills. So, one day I went to the store to buy a few things. I usually take my young son with me, but he wasn't with me this particular day. When the salesperson asked me about my son, my answer confused her because I accidentally said "eh-jeh uhb-suh-yo," which means "he's dead." What I meant to say was "Yuh-gi uhb-suh-yo" which means "he's not here."

4 B

Host Hello and welcome to *The Traveler's Guide*. Now, last week we asked our listeners who are going to travel abroad to send us their questions about good manners in other countries, and we've invited our resident expert Ruth Dempsey to the show to answer them. Welcome to the program, Ruth.

Ruth Thank you.

Host So the first question, Ruth. This comes from Katy in Denver, who is going to travel around Thailand next summer. Katy wants to know what she should do when she first meets people in Thailand.

Ruth Well, Katy, most of the time, a simple handshake will be fine. But if someone gives you a "wai", that is a small bow with the hands held together close to the body, you must do the same. But, if the person is of lower social status than you, so if they are younger than you, or they are a waiter, for example, you shouldn't return the "wai."

Host Very useful advice, Ruth. The next question is from Mark in Dallas, who is going to Brazil with his girlfriend, to meet her family for the first time. He asks: "Is there anything I should or shouldn't do?"

Ruth Like Americans, Brazilians are very warm, friendly, and open. However, there are a few differences to remember. Always say thank you when someone opens a door for you, offers you something to eat or drink, or even when your girlfriend's mother clears the plates from the table. It's very important to be polite. Also, don't speak when you have food in your mouth. Brazilians find this incredibly rude.

Host That sounds like good advice for you, Mark. OK, our next question is from Julie in Oklahoma City. She's going to Greece on vacation, but doesn't speak the language. She asks: "Since I don't speak any Greek, I'll be communicating mostly with my hands. Are there any gestures I shouldn't use?"

Ruth Absolutely, Julie. The most important one to remember is the "thumbs up," which in the US means "good" or "OK." But it is very insulting to a Greek person. Another one is the US hand gesture for "stop," where you show someone your hand with your fingers straight together, like a police officer. But again this is an insult in Greece.

Host Good luck, Julie. And we have time for one more, and this question is from Kendra in Chicago. She's going to South Korea for work, and she would like some tips on business behavior over there.

Ruth The most important thing to remember is that South Koreans like to bow a lot. As a foreigner, you won't be expected to, but it is a good way of showing respect, and the deeper you bow, the happier you are.

Host Very interesting. Ruth Dempsey, thank you for joining us.

Ruth My pleasure.

Host And we'll be right back after a check of the headlines.

5 A

Host Welcome back to the show. We've been talking about famous sports cheaters on today's program, and now we're going to hear about another scandal. The sport was badminton, and the venue was the 2012 Olympic Games in London. Tom is here to tell us about it. Hi, Tom.

Tom Hello, everybody.

Host So who was involved in the scandal, Tom?

Tom Well, the scandal involved four of the teams in the women's doubles competition. In total, eight players were disqualified for cheating: two pairs from South Korea, a pair from China, and a pair from Indonesia.

Host And what exactly happened?

Tom Well, basically the teams played badly on purpose to make sure they lost their matches.

Host Why would they do that?

Tom Well, to explain that I'll very quickly tell you about how the competition works. The matches are divided into different stages. Teams play against other teams in their group in the first stage, and if they win, they play in the next stage. So sometimes, a team might get a good opponent very early in the competition, which means it might not get through to the next stage.

Host Got it. So when did the cheating happen?

Tom Well, the problem started on the last day of the first stage. In the morning, the first Chinese team won its match, finishing second in its group. The second Chinese team was going to play against a South Korean team that evening, and whichever team won that match would most likely play against the first Chinese team in the next stage.

Host Why was this a problem?

Tom Neither team wanted to play against the first Chinese team because the South Korean team was sure it would lose, and the second Chinese team didn't want to play against a team from the same country yet, because that would mean that only one Chinese team was left to try to win a medal. So both teams tried to lose against each other instead.

Host How did they do that?

Tom Well, both the South Koreans and the second Chinese team started missing shots. When they served, they either hit the shuttlecock into the net or they hit it so hard that it went outside the lines on the court. In the end, they looked like amateurs, when in fact, they were some of the best players in the world.

Host So who lost the match?

Tom The second Chinese team. South Korea beat them in both sets.

Host What about the other two teams?

Tom Well, they tried to do exactly the same thing in the next match.

Host Which teams were these again?

Tom Indonesia and another South Korean pair.

Host So in both matches, the teams tried to lose instead of trying to win so they'd have a better chance of winning a medal. Is that right?

Tom Yes. That's exactly what happened. And it was really obvious, too – all the spectators started booing, it was so bad. After the second match, there was an investigation and all eight players were disqualified.

Host And what about the competition? Did it stop there?

Tom No, it continued without the disqualified players.

Host And who won the gold medal in the end?

Tom The first Chinese team. They beat the Japanese team in both sets. Actually, it was a very good match!

Host Tom, thanks for joining us.

Tom My pleasure.

5 B

Host Hello, and welcome to the show. Now, a lot of research has been done recently about love, what causes it, and what we do to attract someone. Mary is in the studio with us today, and she's going to explain the results of some of these studies to us. Mary, welcome to the show.

Mary Hello.

Host Let's start with how to meet new people. Some people like to start a conversation with a person they like by saying something funny. But how useful is this?

Mary Not very useful at all I'm afraid, Jeremy. Research shows that only 7% of attraction has anything to do with what you say. It's the tone and the speed of your voice that make a difference. This makes up 38% of the attraction.

But the most important thing of all is body language. This contributes to a massive 55% of the attraction.

Host So what can we do to improve our body language?

Mary Well, it seems that the best way to make the person you're talking to feel attracted to you is to look into their eyes. An American psychologist did an experiment about this in New York. He got complete strangers to stare into each other's eyes for two minutes without talking. Afterward, many of the couples said that they had strong feelings of attraction to each other, and one of the couples even got married!

Host Really? Then staring must be the thing to do! Is there any more advice on body language?

Mary Well, it's important to have a relaxed body position. You need to show the other person that you're comfortable being with them. Also, try not to be far away from them. Of course, there is a comfortable distance, but try leaning a little closer to them than usual, it will show you're interested, and hold their attention better. Don't forget to watch their body language, too. If they position their body in a similar way to you, it means they find you interesting, too. This is called mirroring.

Host Is there anything that seems to work well when you're talking to someone you're attracted to?

Mary Not surprisingly, it seems that you'll have a better chance if you smile. Anyone who's ever spoken to someone on the phone will tell you that it's easy to tell when the other person is smiling, because you can hear it in their voice. When talking to a potential partner, a smile will not only affect your tone of voice, keeping it light and fun, but it will also show the other person that you are happy to be with them. And don't forget that a smile is extremely contagious, and before long the other person will be smiling back at you. This will make them feel happier, a feeling that they will quickly connect with you.

Host How interesting, and very true! Unfortunately, that's all we have time for now, Mary, but thank you so much for joining us.

Mary You're welcome.

OXFORD
UNIVERSITY PRESS

198 Madison Avenue
New York, NY 10016 USA

Great Clarendon Street, Oxford, OX2 6DP,
United Kingdom

Oxford University Press is a department of the University of Oxford. It furthers the University's objective of excellence in research, scholarship, and education by publishing worldwide. Oxford is a registered trade mark of Oxford University Press in the UK and in certain other countries.

© Oxford University Press 2014

The moral rights of the author have been asserted.

First published in 2014
2023 2022 2021 2020 2019
16 15 14 13 12 11 10

No unauthorized photocopying

All rights reserved. No part of this publication may be reproduced, stored in a retrieval system, or transmitted, in any form or by any means, without the prior permission in writing of Oxford University Press, or as expressly permitted by law, by license or under terms agreed with the appropriate reprographics rights organization. Enquiries concerning reproduction outside the scope of the above should be sent to the ELT Rights Department, Oxford University Press, at the address above.

You must not circulate this work in any other form and you must impose this same condition on any acquirer.

Links to third party websites are provided by Oxford in good faith and for information only. Oxford disclaims any responsibility for the materials contained in any third party website referenced in this work.

General Manager: Laura Pearson
Executive Publishing Manager: Erik Gundersen
Senior Managing Editor: Louisa van Houten
Associate Editor: Yasuko Morisaki
Associate Editor: James Power
Design Director: Susan Sanguily
Executive Design Manager: Maj-Britt Hagsted
Associate Design Manager: Michael Steinhofer
Senior Designer: Yin Ling Wong
Electronic Production Manager: Julie Armstrong
Production Artists: Elissa Santos, Julie Sussman-Perez
Image Manager: Trisha Masterson
Image Editors: Liaht Pashayan
Production Coordinator: Brad Tucker

ISBN: 978 0 19 479633 0 MULTI-PACK A (PACK)
ISBN: 978 0 19 477590 8 STUDENT BOOK/WORKBOOK A (PACK COMPONENT)
ISBN: 978 0 19 436059 3 ONLINE PRACTICE (PACK COMPONENT)

Printed in China

This book is printed on paper from certified and well-managed sources.

STUDENT BOOK ACKNOWLEDGEMENTS

The authors and publisher are grateful to those who have given permission to reproduce the following extracts and adaptations of copyright material:

p.8 Extract from "He claims we used to play Cowboys and Indians. I recall him trying to suffocate me" by Tim Lott, The Times, November 20, 2010. Reproduced by permission of NI Syndication. p.8 Extract from "The seven ages of an only child" by Joanna Moorhead, The Guardian, March 4, 2006. Copyright Guardian News & Media Ltd 2006. Reproduced by permission. p.3–4 Extract from "The millionaire who couldn't write his name" by Karen Bartlett, The Times, February 4, 2011. Reproduced by permission of NI Syndication. p.7 Extract from "Blue Peter presenter Helen Skelton begins epic Amazon kayaking adventure" by Cassandra Jardine, Telegraph Online, January 23, 2010. © Telegraph Media Group Limited 2010. Reproduced by permission. p.7 Extract from "Blue Peter presenter Helen Skelton's Amazon diaries: week one", Telegraph Online, January 31, 2010. © Telegraph Media Group Limited 2010. Reproduced by permission. p.7 Extract from "Blue Peter presenter Helen Skelton's Amazon diaries: week two", Telegraph Online, February 8, 2010. © Telegraph Media Group Limited 2010. Reproduced by permission. p.5 Extract from "Gossip with the girls but men only have four subjects" by Peter Markham, The Daily Mail, October 18, 2001. Reproduced by permission of Solo Syndication. p.8 Extract from "New baby? No problem for Commando Dad" by Neil Sinclair, The Times, May 7, 2012. Reproduced by permission of NI Syndication. p.3–4 Extract from "Alex Rawlings most multi-lingual student in UK" by Hannah White-Steele, Cherwell.org, February 24, 2012. Reproduced by permission. p.6–7 Extract from "Debrett's guide to mobile phone etiquette", Telegraph Online, August 5, 2011. © Telegraph Media Group Limited 2011. Reproduced by permission. p.8 Extract from "Mother-in-law from hell sends harsh lesson in manners to 'uncouth' bride-to-be in email that becomes worldwide sensation", The Daily Mail, June 29, 2011. Reproduced by permission of Solo Syndication. p.2 Extract from "Very superstitious: Andy Murray, Wimbledon and sport stars everywhere" by Matthew Syed, The Times, July 1, 2009. Reproduced by permission of NI Syndication. p.5 Extract from "Sealed with a kiss and 35¢: how a singer and a toll booth operator set out on the road to love" by Will Pavia, The Times, February 14, 2012. Reproduced by permission of NI Syndication. p.5–6 Extract from "What does your profile picture say about you?" by Una Mullally, The Irish Times, October 29, 2011. Article Courtesy of the Irish Times. p.7–8 Extract from "Yes, Looks do Matter" by Pam Belluck, The New York Times, April 26, 2009 © 2009 The New York Times. All rights reserved. Used by permission and protected by the Copyright Laws of the United States. The printing, copying, redistribution, or retransmission of this Content without express written permission is prohibited. p.3–4 Extract from "The Chinese way of bringing up children" by Alexandra Frean, The Times, January, 10 2011. Reproduced by permission of NI Syndication. p.3–4 Extract from "Don't shout. Don't swear. And use pink envelopes drenched in aftershave: How to complain successfully by the King of the complainers" by Julia Lawrence, The Daily Mail, October 15, 2011. Reproduced by permission of Solo Syndication. p.9 Extract from "A real Good Samaritan" from BBC News at bbc.co.uk/news, December 24, 2010. Reproduced by permission. p.9 Extract from "Your Good Samaritan stories" from BBC News at bbc.co.uk/ news, January 7, 2011. Reproduced by permission. p.3 Extract from "Not exactly life-changing, is it…" by Matt Rudd, The Sunday Times, October 9, 2011. Reproduced by permission of NI Syndication. p.7 Extract from "A Maestro Sets the Tone" by David Masello, The New York Times, January 18, 2012 © 2012 The New York Times. All rights reserved. Used by permission and protected by the Copyright Laws of the United States. The printing, copying, redistribution, or retransmission of this Content without express written permission is prohibited. p.15 Extract from "The Importance of Doing What You Love" by Stephanie Lewis, www.workawesome.com, March 31, 2012. Reproduced by permission. p.19 Extract from "How Bob Dylan changed my life" by Bob Dylan, The Times, June 24, 2011. Reproduced by permission of NI Syndication. p.14 "Girls & Boys" Words and Music by Benji Madden and Joel Madden © 2002, Reproduced by permission of EMI Music Publishing Ltd, London W8 5. Source: p.3–4 The Times

We would also like to thank the following for permission to reproduce the following photographs: Cover: Gemenacom/shutterstock.com, Andrey_Popov/shutterstock.com, Wavebreakmedia/shutterstock.com, Image Source/Getty Images, Lane Oatey/Blue Jean Images/Getty Images, BJI/Blue Jean Images/Getty Images, Image Source/Corbis, Yuri Arcurs/Tetra Images/Corbis, Wavebreak Media Ltd./Corbis; pg.6 (market) Alessandro Della Valle/Keystone/Corbis, (Steve) Steve Anderson; pg.7 (escargot) Miscellaneoustock/Alamy, (shrimp) Yiap Creative/Alamy, (dessert) Davide Piras/Alamy, (chicken) Iain Bagwell/Getty Images, (mussels) Steve Anderson; pg.8 Gerard Fritz/Getty Images; pg.9 (bike) PhotoAlto/Superstock, (grandma) Rena Latham-Koenig; pg.10 Tim Lott; pg.11 (Sarah Lee) Loop Images Ltd/Alamy, (girl) ableimages/Alamy, (siblings) Inti St. Clair, Inc./SuperStock/Corbis; pg.14 (man) Judith Haeusler/cultura/Corbis, (car) Car Culture/Corbis, (woman) Alexey Tkachenko/Getty Images, (bkgd) Lostandtaken.com; pg.15 Steve Stock/Alamy; pg.17 Ringo Chiu/ZUMAPRESS/Newscom; pg.18 Jane Cadwallader; pg.20 (lizard) Martin Harvey/Alamy, (woman) BBC, (bird) John Cancalosi/Getty Images, (butterfly) Stockbyte/Getty Images; pg.21 (mosquito) Redmond Durrell/Alamy, (kayak) BBC, (dolphin) Kevin Schafer/Corbis, (fish) boryak/istockphoto; pg.23 (Goodwill) Goodwill Industries International; pg.24 (Miami) Murat Taner/Getty Images, (bkgd) Maciej Noskowski/Getty Images; pg.25 (Lotus) Nick Greening/Alamy, (Foust) Bo Bridges/Corbis, (seaplane) Jad Davenport/National Geographic Society/Corbis, (Wood) Frederick M. Brown/Getty Images, (Ferrera) Andres Otero/WENN/Newscom, (boat) OUP/Amana Images Inc.; pg.26 Don Mason/Blend Images/Corbis; pg.27 Belinda Images/SuperStock; pg.29 (men) Tim Klein/Getty Images, (women) Westend61/Superstock; pg.30 (camo) CollinsChin/istockphoto.com; pg.36 Michael Cogliantry/Getty Images; pg.37 (1) Carlo A/Getty Images, (2) Lilly Roadstones/Getty Images, (3) miya227/shutterstock, (4) Brüderchen & Schwesterchen GmbH/Corbis, (5) Tara Moore/Getty Images, (6) Radius Images/Getty Images, (Alex) OUP; pg.38 (old phone) Ninette Maumus/Alamy; pg.39 John Lund/Paula Zacharias/Blend Images/Corbis; pg.40 (left) Murray Sanders/SWNS.com, (right) James Dadzitis/SWNS.com; pg.43 (conductor) Charles Eshelman/FilmMagic/Getty Images, (bikes) Steven Greaves/Corbis; pg.44 (1) Richard Drury/Getty Images, (2) Carlos Caetano/shutterstock, (3) David Madison/Getty Images, (4) Kathy Quirk-Syvertsen/Getty Images, (5) Moe Kafer Cutouts/Alamy, (6) Urban Zone/Alamy, (7) Ray Moller /Getty Images, (8) Corbis Flint/Alamy, (9) Sami Sarkis/Getty Images, (10) Richard Watkins/Alamy; pg.45 (Crosby) Peter Diana/ZUMA Press/Corbis, (Terry) Albert Pena/Icon SMI/Corbis, (Toure) Adrian Dennis/AFP/Getty Images, (Wurz) Rick Dole/getty Images, (player) Simon Bruty/Sports Illustrated/Getty Images, (lines) Marc Debnam/Getty Images, (ball) OUP/Photodisc; pg.46 (referee) Graham Chadwick/Allsport/Getty Images, (marathon) David Madison/Getty Images, (soccer) Bob Thomas/Getty Images; pg.48 (toll) Shannon DeCelle, (couple) Stephen Lance Dennee; pg.54 (castle) Dov Makabaw/Alamy, (alley) Oleg Korshakov/Getty Images; pg.55 (Highclere Castle) Jeff Gilbert /Alamy, (Casa Lomo) Angelo Cavalli/SuperStock; pg.56 (War Horse) Dreamworks SKG/The Kobal Collection, (Indian Jones) Lucasfilm Ltd/Paramount/The Kobal Collection, (ET) Universal/The Kobal Collection, (Minority Report) 20th Century Fox/Dreamworks/The Kobal Collection, (Catch Me If You Can) Dreamworks/The Kobal Collection/Cooper, Andrew; pg.57 Courtesy of Dagmara Walkowicz; pg.58 (Martin) PhotoAlto/Alamy, (Phone) Cyberstock/Alamy, (Annabel) Mark Roberts/Getty Images, (Sean) Paper Boat Creative/Getty Images, (Sarah) Guido Mieth/Getty Images; pg.60 (Brand) V Labissiere/Splash News/Corbis, (1) Rex Features, (2) Suzanne Kreiter/The Boston Globe via Getty Images, (3) Allen J. Schaben/AFP/Getty Images; pg.61 (before) Charlie Gray/Contour by Getty Images, (after) Ken McKay/Rex; pg.63 (theater) Bob O'Connor/Getty Images, (Kong) AF archive/Alamy; pg.65 Shed-Media; pg.66 (envelope) Mark Bassett/Alamy, (music) Erin Patrice O'Brien; pg.68 (kitchen) Carolyn Barber/Getty Images; pg.69 (Vivienne) Tetra Images/Corbis, (Mauro) Tim Kitchen/Getty Images, (Andrea) Echo/Getty Images, (Carlos) Burke/Triolo Productions/Getty Images, (living room) David Papazian/Getty Images, (kitchen) Kim Sayer/Getty Images, (bedroom) Ryan McVay/Getty Images; pg.70 RIA Novosti/Alamy; pg.71 Radius Images/Corbis; pg.74 Devon Anne/Shutterstock; pg.75 (dress) Ivor Toms/Alamy; pg.79 (blood pressure) Ragnar Schmuck/Corbis, (bugs) Michael Freeman/Corbis, (meeting) OUP/zefa RF, (microscope) OUP/Deco; pg.80 (Corcoran) AP Photo/Jeff Christensen, (burger) CBS Foods, (John) Frederick M. Brown/Getty Images, (Cuban) Richard DuCree/USA Network/NBCU Photo Bank via Getty Images, (sharks) abrakadabra/shutterstock, (Perry) Perry's Music, LLC 2012; pg.81 Jorg Greuel/Getty Images; pg.84 Ekaterina Nosenko/Getty Images; pg.85 (street) Sven Hagolani/fstop/Corbis, (bike) Smith Collection/Getty Images, (bike bkgd) Stephen Smith/Getty Images; pg.86 (Beatles) Popperfoto/Getty Images, (Gates) Joe McNally/Getty Images; pg.87 Stefan Sollfors/Alamy; pg.94 (Jobs) Diana Walker/SJ/Contour by Getty Images, (1) oliver leedham/Alamy, (2) Tony Avelar/Bloomberg via Getty Images, (3) Jay L. Clendenin/Los Angeles Times/Contour by Getty Images, (4) Visions of America/UIG via Getty Images, (5) Laurent Fievet/AFP/Getty Images; pg.96 (Barbie) Teenage doll/Alamy, (Love) Charlotte Marie Marshall/Alamy, (sneakers) Peter Kramer/Bravo/NBCU Photo Bank via Getty Images, (Chrysler Building) Jorg Hackemann/Shutterstock.com; pg.97 (soccer) ALLSTAR Picture Library/Alamy, (Ikea) david pearson/Alamy, (toaster) Niall McDiarmid/Alamy, (rolex) John Henshall/Alamy, (building) Chris Ryan/Getty Images, (stopwatch) artpartner-images/Getty Images, (Vertigo) Paramount/The Kobal Collection/Bass, Saul, (Breakfast at Tiffanys) Courtesy Everett Collection/Rex; pg.98 (Wood) Steve Schapiro/Corbis, (Splendour) Silver Screen Collection/Getty Images; pg.99 (Walken) Trinity Mirror/Mirrorpix/Alamy, (Wagner) Phil Roach/Globe Photos/ZUMAPRESS/Newscom, (Davern) Paul Harris, PacificCoastNews/Newscom; pg.100 (Green) Popperfoto/Getty Images, (reader) David Paul Morris/Bloomberg via Getty Images; pg.103 (Dylan) Popperfoto/Getty Images; pg.104 Steve Stock/Alamy; pg.105 Craig Hibert/SWNS.com; pg.106 (Crosby) Peter Diana/ZUMA Press/Corbis, (Sorvino) Suzanne Kreiter/The Boston Globe via Getty Images, (Rutterschmidt) Allen J. Schaben/AFP/Getty Images, (Toure) Adrian Dennis/AFP/Getty Images, (McVey) Rex Features; pg.110 (Terry) Albert Pena/Icon SMI/Corbis, (feet) Mark Thompson/Allsport/Getty Images; pg.113 (Sofia) Westend61/Corbis, (Angela) OUP/Blend Images; pg.114 KidStock/Getty Images; pg.115 (subway) Juan Antonio/AGE fotostock, (metrocard) Bora/Alamy, (bike) Stan Honda/AFP/Getty Images, (bus) wdstock/istockphoto, (taxi bottom) hanusst/istockphoto, (taxi top) Songquan Deng/Shutterstock.com; pg.117 Paramount/The Kobal Collection; pg.118 (Thailand) Viacheslav Khmelnytskyi/Alamy, (Mexico) John Edward Linden/Arcaid/Corbis; pg.119 Creative Crop/Getty Images; pg.121 (car) CandyBox Photography/Alamy, (facebook) Erkan Mehmet/Alamy, (bus) Anna Peisl/Corbis; pg.152 (1) Dave King/Getty Images, (2) Gastromedia/Alamy, (3) jon whitaker/Getty Images, (4) studiomode/Alamy, (5) Food and Drink Photos/Alamy, (6) Annabelle Breakey/Getty Images; pg.155 (1 top) David Cole/Alamy, (2 top) Peter Titmuss/Alamy, (3 top) MkStock/Alamy, (4 top) Greg Balfour Evans/Alamy, (5 top) Dick Reed/Corbis, (6 top) Robert Harding Picture Library Ltd/Alamy, (7 top) Justin Kase ztwoz/Alamy, (8 top) imagebroker/Alamy, (9 top) Bill Cobb/SuperStock, (1 bottom) Tom And Steve/Getty Images, (2 bottom) Chris Ryan/Getty Images, (3 bottom) Stellar Stock/Masterfile, (4 bottom) Ian Dagnall/Alamy, (5 bottom) kickstand/Getty Images, (6 bottom) Michael Runkel/Alamy, (7 bottom) John Nordell/Getty Images, (8 bottom) Peter Ptschelinzew/Getty Images, (9 bottom) Tetra Images/Alamy, (10 bottom) AKP Photos/Alamy, (11 bottom) StacieStauffSmith Photos/shutterstock, (12 bottom) Bo Zaunders/Corbis, (13 bottom) Alan Schein/Corbis, (14 bottom) JTB Media Creation, Inc./Alamy; pg.157 (1) Caro/Alamy, (2 left) imagebroker/Alamy, (2 right) VisitBritain/Andrew Orchard/Getty Images, (3) Matthew Ashton/AMA/Corbis, (4) Corbis Super RF/Alamy, (5) Jonathan Larsen/Diadem Images/Alamy, (6) Mark Davidson/Alamy, (7) Dmitry Korotayev/Epsilon/Getty Images, (8) Stadium Bank/Alamy, (9) Scott W. Grau/Icon SMI/Corbis; pg.159 (1) New Line/The Kobal Collection/Bridges, James, (2) 20th Century Fox/The Kobal Collection, (3, The Help) Dreamworks LLC/The Kobal Collection, (4) Zoetrope/United Artists/The Kobal Collection, (5) Warner Bros./The Kobal Collection/Buitendijk, Jaap, (6) Hammer/The Kobal Collection, (7, 10) Touchstone Pictures/The Kobal Collection, (8) Warner Bros/The Kobal Collection, (9) Lucasfilm/20th Century Fox/The Kobal Collection, (11) Universal/Studio Canal/Working Title/The Kobal Collection/Sparham, Laurie, (12) Morgan Creek International/The Kobal Collection/Farmer, J; pg.160 (1) PBWPIX/Alamy, (2) Fancy Collection/SuperStock , (3) Jenna Woodward Photography/Getty Images, (4) Ocean/Corbis, (5) D. Hurst/Alamy, (6) Somos/Superstock, (7) altrendo images/Getty Images, (8) Philipp Nemenz/Getty Images, (9) OUP/Masterfile, (10) Win Initiative/Getty Images, (11, 18) OUP/BananaStock, (12) Karen Spencer/Alamy, (13) Silas Manhood/Alamy, (14) Lusoimages-Abstract/Alamy, (15) William Radcliffe/Science Faction/Corbis, (16) PhotoAlto/Alamy, (17) Aflo Foto Agency/Alamy, (19) Kris Timken/Getty Images, (20) Juan Silva/Getty Images; pg.161 (UK) keith morris/Alamy, (US) Will & Deni McIntyre/Corbis; pg.162 (modern) Fotosearch/Getty Images, (rustic) Southern Stock/Getty Images; pg.163 (crowd) Tomas Abad/Alamy, (beach) John Short/Design Pics/Corbis.

Commissioned photography by: Gareth Boden pp.26, 27, 30 (two dads in park), 38 (mobile phone) 68, 75 (Macbook pro, Tiffany heart necklace). Ryder Haske: pp.12, 13, 32, 33, 52, 53, 72, 73, 92, 93. MM studios pp.96 (Beatles album, Penguin books), p.152 (meat, fish and vegetable groups).

Pronunciation chart artwork by: Ellis Nadler

Illustrations by: Peter Bull: pp.20–21, 25, 116; Mark Duffin: 81; Alex Green/Folio Art: p.100–101; Olivier Latyk/Good Illustration Ltd: pp.34, 35, 90, 138, 162; Lyndon Hayes/Dutch Uncle: pp.16, 19, 30, 59, 76–77, 80; Astushi Hara/Dutch Uncle: pp.49, 79, 120, 133, 134, 135, 137, 138, 142, 143,144, 145, 148, 149, 150, 151, 156, 158, 161, 164; Sophie Joyce: p.47; Jonathan Krause: p.64; Tim Marrs: pp.50–51, 88–89; Joe McLaren: pp.4–5, 41; Matt Smith: pp.30/31.

WORKBOOK ACKNOWLEDGEMENTS

The authors and publisher are grateful to those who have given permission to reproduce the following extracts and adaptations of copyright material:

p.19 Extract from http://www.roughguides.com/article/10-unusual-types-oftransport/. Copyright © 2013 ROUGH GUIDES LTD. Reproduced by permission of Rough Guides Ltd.; p.47 Extract from 'Why houses with history will sell' by Christopher Middleton, The Telegraph, 20 June 2011. © Telegraph Media Group Limited 2011. Reproduced by permission; p.51 Extract from 'Ten tips for safe shopping online this Christmas' by Stephen Ellis, The Telegraph, 8 December 2008. © Telegraph Media Group Limited 2008. Reproduced by permission; p.57 Extract from 'Lucky it wasn't raining! Moment driver was catapulted through sunroof of flipping car…and walked away unharmed' by Emma Reynolds, The Daily Mail, 10 July 2012. Reproduced by permission of Solo Syndication; p.61 Extract from 'What to do when you spill a drink on your laptop' by Jack Schofield, The Guardian, 5 July 2012. Copyright Guardian News & Media Ltd 2012. Reproduced by permission; p.64 Extract from 'This much I know: Usain Bolt' by Mark Bailey, The Guardian, 17 June 2012. Copyright Guardian News & Media Ltd 2012. Reproduced by permission; p.67 Extract from 'Oxford Bookworms Library: The Thirty-Nine Steps' by John Buchan, retold by Nick Bullard, Series Editor Jennifer Bassett. © Oxford University Press 2007. Reprinted by permission; p.23 Extract from www.newyorktaxis.org. Reproduced by permission; p.62 Extract from Slate, © 12 November 2008 Issue, The Slate Group All rights reserved. Used by permission and protected by the Copyright Laws of the United States. The printing, copying, redistribution, or retransmission of the Material without express written permission is prohibited; p.36 Extract from 'USA Getting there & around', www.lonelyplanet.com. Reproduced with permission from the Lonely Planet website www.lonelyplanet.com © 2012 Lonely Planet.

Illustrations by: Satoshi Hashimoto/Dutch Uncle: pp.14, 57; Anna Hymas/New Division: p.20; Tim Marrs: p.13; Jerome Mireault/Colagene: pp.28, 40; Ellis Nadler: pronunciation symbols; Roger Penwill: p.59; Ron Tiner: pp.67, 68; Kath Walker: p.41.

We would also like to thank the following for permission to reproduce the following photographs: Cover: Gemenacom/shutterstock.com, Andrey_Popov/shutterstock.com, Wavebreakmedia/shutterstock.com, Image Source/Getty Images, Lane Oatey/Blue Jean Images/Getty Images, BJI/Blue Jean Images/Getty Images, Image Source/Corbis, Yuri Arcurs/Tetra Images/Corbis, Wavebreak Media Ltd./Corbis; pg.4 (2 across) studiomode/Alamy, (3 across) Gastromedia/Alamy, (5 across) Food and Drink Photos/Alamy, (1 down) Annabelle Breakey/Getty Images, (2 down) Dave King/Getty Images, (4 down) jon whitaker/Getty Images; pg.6 Mike Kemp/Tetra Images/Corbis; pg.7 (1) Sean Justice/Getty Images, (2) Image Source/Corbis, (3) JGI/Getty Images, (4) PhotoAlto/Eric Audras/Getty Images, (5) Jose Luis Pelaez Inc/Getty Images; pg.9 Stefano Ravera/Alamy; pg.10 Brian Hamill/Getty Images; pg.11 2020WEB/Alamy; pg.15 (bus) Thomas Cockrem/Alamy, (construction) Ryan Smith/Somos Images/Corbis, (orangutan) Andrew Watson/Getty Images; pg.16 (1) Lobke Peers/shutterstock, (2) LJSphotography/Alamy, (3) Rich Legg/Getty Images, (4) John Rowley/Getty Images, (5) Denis Scott/Corbis, (6) Everynight Images/Alamy; pg.18 (China) Ma Hailin/Xinhua Press/Corbis, (Mexico) Danny Lehman/Corbis, (Australia) John Gollings/Arcaid/Corbis; pg.19 (boat) Julia Rogers/Alamy, (sled) Accent Alaska.com/Alamy, (train) STRINGER/CAMBODIA/X80007/Reuters/Corbis, (jeep) Christian Kober/Robert Harding World Imagery/Corbis; pg.22 (man) Ann Summa/Corbis, (woman) Flashon Studio/shutterstock; pg.23 Bufflerump/shutterstock.com; pg.24 Erik Isakson/Blend Images/Corbis; pg.25 (Speilberg) Luc Roux/Sygma/Corbis, (Newton) The Gallery Collection/Corbis, (Gates) Peer Grimm/dpa/Corbis, (Edison) CORBIS; pg.27 (Liberty) Rubens Alarcon/shutterstock, (Times Square) Kobby Dagan/shutterstock.com; pg.32 Michael Regan/Getty Images; pg.34 (friends) Dreampictures/Image Source/Corbis, (couple) Monkey Business Images/shutterstock; pg.36 Car Culture/Getty Images; pg.38 (Knebworth House) Steven Vidler/Eurasia Press/Corbis, (Anna Karenina) 2012/Moviestore/Rex; pg.39 (carousel) Ambient Images Inc./Alamy, (table) Anna Clopet/CORBIS, (rink) Kiet Thai/Getty Images, (bridge) Andrew C Mace/Getty Images; pg.42 Dimitri Otis/Getty Images; pg.44 Ken Seet/Corbis; pg.45 epa european pressphoto agency b.v./Alamy; pg.47 (Graceland) Jon Arnold Images Ltd/Alamy, (cabin) jpbcpa/istock, (apartment) cdrin/shutterstock.com; pg.48 Jeff Morgan 12/Alamy; pg.51 auremar/shutterstock; pg.52 Mira Oberman/AFP/Getty Images; pg.53 Blend Images/shutterstock; pg.54 C. Devan/Corbis; pg.55 (dentist) Julian Abram Wainwright/epa/Corbis, (golf) Andrew Geiger/Getty Images; pg.57 Top-Pics TBK/Alamy; pg.58 Mathew Crowcoot/Newsteam/SWNS Group; pg.59 Tokyo Space Club/Corbis; pg.60 (keyboard) S.E.A. Photo/Alamy, (plug) Carsten Reisinger/Alamy, (outlet) Joe Belanger/shutterstock, (switch) Olivier Le Queinec/shutterstock, (headphones) Bryan Solomon/shutterstock, (USB) cristi180884/shutterstock, (speaker) arigato/shutterstock, (mouse) vasabii/shutterstock, (screen) yanugkelid/shutterstock, (remote) MNI/shutterstock, (flashdrive) bogdan ionescu/shutterstock, (adaptor) Freer/shutterstock; pg.61 R and R Images/Getty Images; pg.63 (Selena) AP Photo/Blanca Charolet, Premier Postage via Hispanic PR Wire, HO, (Jay Z) Ben Rowland/The Hell Gate/Corbis, (bridge) Imaginechina/Corbis, (Kyi) Anindito Mukherjee/epa/Corbis, (Craig) EON/DANJAQ/SONY/The Kobal Collection/Maidment, Jay, (Mesa Verde) MarclSchauer/shutterstock, (Louvre) Migel/shutterstock.com, (Everest) Pal Teravagimov/shutterstock; pg.64 (1) NetPhotos/Alamy, (2) leolintang/shutterstock, (3) Alexander Demyanenko/shutterstock, (4) Erkan Mehmet/Alamy, (5) Asianet-Pakistan/shutterstock.com, (6) Bernd Kohlhas/Corbis, (7) Ferenc Szelepcsenyi/shutterstock, (8) claudiodivizia/istock, (Bolt) Christopher Morris/Corbis; pg.65 (1) pockygallery/shutterstock, (2) Burdika/shutterstock, (3) Graphic design/shutterstock, (4) anaken2012/shutterstock, (5) Anton Prado PHOTO/shutterstock, (6) maniacpixel/shutterstock; pg.66 Arthur Turner/Alamy.